LEVIATHAN ON A LEASH

For David — I'm thrilled to
have you as a colleague.

Sean
4 October 2022

Leviathan on a Leash

A THEORY OF STATE RESPONSIBILITY

SEAN FLEMING

PRINCETON UNIVERSITY PRESS

PRINCETON & OXFORD

Published by Princeton University Press
41 William Street, Princeton, New Jersey 08540
6 Oxford Street, Woodstock, Oxfordshire OX20 1TR

press.princeton.edu

All Rights Reserved
Library of Congress Control Number: 2020943833
ISBN 9780691206462
ISBN (e-book) 9780691211282

British Library Cataloging-in-Publication Data is available

Editorial: Ben Tate and Josh Drake
Production Editorial: Nathan Carr
Jacket/Cover Design: Pamela L. Schnitter
Production: Danielle Amatucci
Publicity: Alyssa Sanford and Amy Stewart
Copyeditor: Tash Siddiqui

Jacket/Cover Credit: Shutterstock

This book has been composed in Arno

Printed on acid-free paper. ∞

Printed in the United States of America

10 9 8 7 6 5 4 3 2 1

For Newfoundland and Labrador

CONTENTS

PREFACE

WHAT DOES it mean to hold a state responsible? The question that motivates this book harks back to 2011, when I was an undergraduate at Memorial University of Newfoundland. In a course on International Political Economy, I was struck by all of the responsibility-talk about states: Greece is in debt; developing states are bound by bilateral investment treaties; rich states have duties to help poor states. Surely, I thought, this responsibility-talk must be metaphorical, because the burdens of states' debts and obligations ultimately fall on flesh-and-blood human beings. Then, as now, I was sceptical of the idea that states are 'agents' or 'actors' that can have responsibilities in the same way that human beings do. However, for reasons that I explain in the Introduction, I had to admit that this responsibility-talk about states could not be eliminated in favour of responsibility-talk about individuals. The debts of a state are not equal to the sum of the debts of its members, and treaty obligations are not equivalent to the obligations of individual leaders, officials, or citizens.

In this book, I develop a theory of state responsibility that assuages my own scepticism of collective responsibility. I provide a way of making sense of the practice of holding states responsible, without the metaphysical baggage of corporate agents, wills, or intentions. The theory of state responsibility that I develop is 'political' in three senses: it is metaphysically thin; it is built from the political vocabulary of authorization and representation; and it is sensitive to the facts of contemporary politics. My aim is not to provide a philosophical theory of state responsibility from on high, but to develop a theory that helps us to grapple with the many practical problems posed by sovereign debts, treaties, reparations, and sanctions.

This book began life as a PhD thesis at Cambridge in 2015. The greatest thanks are due to Duncan Bell, who was my supervisor. It is difficult to think of the right adjective for him, but 'superhuman' is hardly an exaggeration. He believed in this project from the beginning, and his mentorship and encouragement were invaluable at every stage. David Runciman was my secondary supervisor. His work has had a deep influence on mine, as will become obvious in what follows, and I am grateful to have had his guidance along the way. Christopher Brooke's comments on the earliest outlines and drafts helped to keep the project on track. Duncan Kelly and Anthony Lang examined my PhD thesis and provided many valuable suggestions for turning it into a book. Along with Toni Erskine's work, Lang's work inspired me to pursue this topic in the first place. Harry Gould and Paul Sagar went over the manuscript with a fine-toothed comb and often seemed to understand my arguments better than I did. Their suggestions and criticisms made this a better book. Finally, thanks are due to the many people with whom I have had lively discussions over the past four years, including Greg Conti, Michael Foran, Léonie de Jonge, Adam Lerner, Tobias Müller, Alice Musabende, Joshua Smeltzer, Benjamin Studebaker, Daniel Williams, and Sam Zeitlin.

My longtime mentors, Luke Ashworth, Antonio Franceschet, and Alex Marland, introduced me to the study of politics and opened many doors for me along the way. They saw some potential in my twenty-year-old self and did whatever they could to cultivate it. I will forever be grateful for that.

My family taught me most of what I know, including what matters in life. In no particular order, I thank Rhonda Fleming, Pat Janes, Hank and Sandy Janes, Kevin and Eileen Fleming, Kevin Fleming Jr., Steve and Josephine Janes, Bud Janes, Mike Fleming, and the Dunphy clan from the west coast of Newfoundland. These folks provided inspiration, moral support, great company, places to stay, rides, food, poems, songs, knitted hats, maple sap, campfires, pick poles, wreaths, berry-picking spots, and many good laughs. I also thank Andrew Breen, Jordan Hattar, Shaun McCabe, Luke Power, and Anton Stefansson for helping me unwind and enjoy the moment.

Special thanks are due to the Rothermere Foundation, which funded my PhD through a Rothermere Fellowship. I am grateful to the Harmsworth family for establishing the Fellowship and for generously supporting Memorial University from the beginning. I also thank the Government of Newfoundland and Labrador, the Social Sciences and Humanities Research Council of Canada, and Trinity Hall, Cambridge for additional funding. A Junior Research Fellowship at Christ's College, Cambridge has given me the time to turn this project into a book in short order.

I am grateful to the many people at Princeton University Press who made this process so smooth. In particular, Ben Tate shepherded this book through peer review and made sure it ended up in print as soon as possible.

Finally, I thank Cambridge University Press and SAGE Publishing for allowing me to reuse parts of two earlier articles: 'Moral Agents and Legal Persons: The Ethics and the Law of State Responsibility' (Fleming 2017b) and 'The Two Faces of Personhood: Hobbes, Corporate Agency and the Personality of the State' (Fleming forthcoming b).

ABBREVIATIONS OF HOBBES' WORKS

AB   2011 [1682]. 'An Answer to a Book Published by Dr. Bramhall, late Bishop of Derry; called "The Catching of Leviathan."' In *Leviathan Parts I and II*, revised edition, eds. A. P. Martinich and Brian Battiste. Peterborough, ON: Broadview, 386–403.

AW   1976 [1642–43]. *Thomas White's* De Mundo *Examined*, trans. Harold W. Jones. London: Bradford University Press.

B   1990 [1681]. *Behemoth, or The Long Parliament*. Chicago: University of Chicago Press.

D   1839 [1655]. *De corpore*. In *The English Works of Thomas Hobbes of Malmesbury Volume I*, ed. William Molesworth. London: John Bohn.

DC   1998 [1642/1647]. *On the Citizen* [*De cive*], trans. Richard Tuck and Michael Silverthorne. New York: Cambridge University Press.

DH   1991 [1658]. *On Man* [*De homine*], trans. Charles T. Wood, T.S.K. Scott-Craig, and Bernard Gert. In *Man and Citizen*, ed. Bernard Gert. Indianapolis: Hackett, 34–85.

EL   1994 [1640]. *Human Nature and De Corpore Politico* [*The Elements of Law, Natural and Politic*]. Oxford: Oxford University Press.

L   2012 [1651]. *Leviathan: The English and Latin Texts* [English *Leviathan*], ed. Noel Malcolm. Oxford: Clarendon Press.

LL   2012 [1668]. *Leviathan: The English and Latin Texts* [Latin *Leviathan*], ed. Noel Malcolm. Oxford: Clarendon Press.

LEVIATHAN ON A LEASH

Introduction

State Responsibility and Corporate Personality

THE PRACTICE OF HOLDING states responsible is central to modern politics and international relations. States are commonly blamed, praised, punished, obligated, and held liable. On an almost daily basis, one hears about the latest round of sanctions against the latest rogue state; the latest treaty that states have signed or repudiated; the latest heavily indebted state to reach the brink of bankruptcy; or the latest call for reparations from former colonial states. The assumption in each case is that the state—as distinct from its individual leaders, officials, or citizens—is the entity that bears the responsibility in question. This book examines the theoretical and normative underpinnings of this so-called 'state responsibility'. Why, and under which conditions, should we assign responsibilities to whole states rather than to particular individuals?

There are two contemporary theories of state responsibility. According to the *agential theory*, states can be held responsible because they are 'moral agents' like human beings, with similar capacities for deliberation and intentional action. The model for state responsibility is an ordinary case of individual responsibility, such as a criminal trial. According to the *functional theory*, states can be held responsible because they are legal persons that act vicariously through their officials. States are 'principals' rather than agents, and the model for state responsibility is a case of vicarious liability, such as when an employer is held financially liable for the actions of her employee. While the agential theory is dominant in International Relations, Political Theory, and Philosophy, the functional theory is dominant in International Law.[1] There are also some critics in every discipline who see the practice of holding states responsible as 'guilt by association' on a grand scale.

1. I use upper case (e.g., International Relations) to refer to the academic disciplines and lower case (international relations) to refer to the subject matter.

1

The purpose of this book is to reconstruct and develop a forgotten under-standing of state responsibility from Thomas Hobbes' political thought. Like proponents of the agential and functional theories, Hobbes considers states to be 'persons', meaning that actions, rights, and responsibilities can be at-tributed to them. States can be said to wage war, possess sovereignty, and owe money. What makes Hobbes unique is that he does not consider states to be agents or principals. Unlike an agent, the state cannot will or act on its own; it needs representatives to will and act on its behalf. Unlike a principal, the state cannot authorize its own representatives. States are like 'Children, Fooles, and Mad-men that have no use of Reason', who are 'Personated by Guardians, or Curators; but can be no Authors' (*L* XVI. 248).[2] Although the state is inca-pable of acting on its own, it can nevertheless exercise rights and incur respon-sibilities through the representatives who act in its name. Hobbes' 'Artificiall Man' is conceptually more like an artificial child or 'Foole'.

I argue that Hobbes' idea of state personality provides a richer understand-ing of state responsibility than the agential theory or the functional theory. According to what I call the *Hobbesian theory*, state responsibility is structur-ally different from ordinary individual responsibility and from vicarious indi-vidual responsibility. Instead, it involves a complex triad of relations between the state, its government, and its subjects.[3] Subjects are the principals who authorize the government; the government is the collection of agents who represent the state; the state is the 'person' that is responsible for the conse-quent debts and obligations; and subjects, in turn, share the costs and burdens of their state's responsibilities. As I argue throughout the book, no individual-level analogue can fully capture the logic of state responsibility, and analogiz-ing between states and individuals often leads us astray.

The Hobbesian theory has both theoretical and practical advantages. First, it avoids the two traps into which critics and proponents of state responsibility tend to fall: reductionism, or treating corporate entities as aggregates of human beings; and anthropomorphism, or treating corporate entities as human be-ings writ large. Despite what Hobbes' description of the state as an 'Artificiall Man' suggests, he drew a sharp distinction between human persons and cor-porate persons. Because the Hobbesian theory captures the unique conceptual structure of corporate forms of personhood, it illuminates many features of state responsibility that the agential and functional theories obscure.

---

2. I cite Hobbes' *Leviathan* (*L*) according to the chapter number and the page number from the 2012 Clarendon edition.

3. For reasons that I explain in the next section, I follow Hobbes in using 'subject' rather than 'citizen'.

Second, the Hobbesian theory is conceptually and ontologically thinner than the agential and functional theories. Since it is built entirely from the basic concepts of authorization and representation, it eliminates the need for the metaphysics of corporate agency and for organic conceptions of the state. The Hobbesian theory explains how state responsibility can be understood and justified from the perspective of ontological and normative individualism. It therefore provides a powerful rebuttal against individualist critics who see corporate personality and responsibility as collectivist dogmas.

Third, the Hobbesian theory translates readily into a set of practical guidelines and policy prescriptions. While the concept of corporate agency is difficult to operationalize, the concepts of authorization and representation provide a familiar and intuitive guide for our normative judgments. The Hobbesian theory is also versatile enough to help us grapple with technological developments, such as autonomous weapons, that challenge both our concept of the state and our concept of responsibility. As the state becomes mechanized, Hobbes' mechanistic conception of the state becomes increasingly apt.

This book can be read as a work of 'realist' political theory.[4] I start from the position that politics constitutes a distinct normative domain, and I develop a theory of responsibility that is appropriate for the political domain. Although the Hobbesian theory of state responsibility is abstract and general, it is not in any sense an 'ideal' theory. Nor is it an attempt to apply an ideal theory of corporate or collective responsibility to the non-ideal case of the state. An ideal theory of state responsibility would be nonsensical, because the practice of holding states responsible is inherently unjust, tragic, and lamentable. State responsibility would have no place in a just world, or even a 'reasonably' just world. Instead, political leaders would be held personally responsible for their wrongs, debts, and agreements, and ordinary citizens would never have to bear the costs of decisions that they did not personally make. But here we are, in a world full of sovereign debts, treaties, reparations, and economic sanctions, with no way out. This book provides a theory of state responsibility for the real world.

§1 The Idea of State Responsibility

Many of our basic political and economic practices presuppose that the responsibilities of states are distinct from the responsibilities of individuals. Sovereign debt is one salient example. The debts of Greece cannot be

---

4. E.g., Galston (2010), Hall (2015, 2017), Rossi and Sleat (2014), Sagar (2016), and Waldron (2016).

identified with the debts of individual Greeks. The members of government who borrowed the money are not expected to repay it from their own bank accounts, and they do not take the debt with them when they leave office. As Skinner (2015) points out, 'sovereign debt' is 'a stupid thing to call it—it's state debt. . . . Who is the debtor? Well you can hardly answer, "the government". Governments come and go, but that debt doesn't come and go.' Nor are Greek subjects the debtors. Although journalists sometimes write as though each subject of a state owes a fraction of its debt, this cannot be literally true, since Greece does not owe less money whenever one of its subjects dies. As Maitland (2003: 70–71) argues, the only way to make sense of sovereign debt is to suppose that the state is a 'corporation' with its own moral and legal personality (see also Runciman, 2000a: 95–97). *Greece* owes the money; *Greeks* do not.

State responsibility is a uniquely modern phenomenon. What makes possible the distinction between the responsibilities of states and the responsibilities of individuals is the 'modern idea of the State as a form of public power separate from both the ruler and the ruled' (Skinner, 1978: 353). If the state were simply the rulers, then the responsibilities of states would be nothing more than the personal responsibilities of government officials. If the state were simply the ruled, then the responsibilities of states would be nothing more than the personal responsibilities of subjects. The idea that the state is a 'corporate' entity that is distinct from both ruler and ruled was not fully developed until the mid-seventeenth century (Skinner, 2002: 394–404). Only then did it become possible to speak of the responsibilities of states as distinct from those of rulers and subjects.

Although state responsibility is a type of corporate responsibility, an adequate theory of state responsibility cannot be deduced from a general theory of corporate responsibility. Jacob Levy (2015: 57) has argued that it is mistake to treat groups as 'big individuals or small states'. Similarly, I argue that it is a mistake to treat states as big individuals or big groups.

States have three features that distinguish them from most other corporate entities. First, states are involuntary associations. People typically choose to join universities and companies, but most people do not choose their states and cannot easily leave. Holding states responsible therefore carries a much greater risk of 'misdirected harm' (Erskine, 2010; Stilz, 2011: 191). Second, states are non-participatory. Even in democratic states, most people rarely participate in making laws and policies, and many people—children, incapacitated people, and often prisoners and resident foreigners—are entirely excluded from the decision-making process. We might hold a committee or a team responsible for a discriminatory policy because each member participated in making that policy (Gilbert, 2000, 2006; Tuomela, 2007: Chapter 10), but participatory accounts of collective responsibility do not apply to the state (see §23 below). Third, states are not subject to the principle of limited liability. While the personal assets of shareholders cannot be seized to satisfy the obligations of a corporation, the personal assets of subjects can be seized (as in the 2013 'haircut' of personal bank accounts in Cyprus) to satisfy the obligations of a state (Pasternak, 2013: 364). State responsibility is an ethically distinct and especially complicated kind of corporate responsibility.

State responsibility should not be confused with national responsibility. Although the two concepts are superficially similar, they involve different types of collective responsibility (Feinberg, 1968). National responsibility concerns the responsibilities that individuals have because of their national identities (Abdel-Nour, 2003; Butt, 2006; Miller, 2007). For example, as Jaspers (1961) famously asked, are the German people guilty of the Holocaust? National responsibilities are 'distributive': the responsibility of a nation implies the responsibility of each of its members. State responsibilities are 'non-distributive': the responsibility of a state is conceptually independent from the responsibilities of its members (Erskine, 2003; Lang, 2007). One could consistently say that Germany is guilty but that the German people are not, and vice versa. Whereas national responsibilities attach to each member of the nation, state responsibilities attach to the state *as distinct from* its members.

I construe 'responsibility' broadly to cover both prospective responsibility (duties and obligations) and retrospective responsibility (wrongdoing and punishment).[5] Prospective responsibilities prescribe what a state ought to do in the future; retrospective responsibilities relate to a state's past actions (Erskine, 2003: 8; Gilbert, 2006: 94–95). Whereas issues of prospective responsibility include treaty obligations and the responsibility to protect, issues of retrospective responsibility include economic sanctions and reprisals. Some responsibilities are simultaneously prospective and retrospective; reparations are prospective responsibilities to make amends for past wrongs. Claims about responsibility are essentially claims about what someone ought (not) to do or what someone ought (not) to have done. This book aims to explain why it makes sense to address some ought-claims to states rather than to individuals.

Throughout the book, I refer to individuals as 'subjects' rather than 'citizens', as Hobbes does in *Leviathan*. Citizens are the people whom the state legally recognizes as such, whereas subjects are the people who are subject to the

---

5. The distinction between prospective and retrospective responsibility corresponds roughly to the distinction in International Law between obligation and responsibility. I use 'state responsibility' more broadly than it is used in International Law, where it refers exclusively to retrospective responsibility for wrongful actions (ILC, 2001).

coercive power of the state. Citizenship is a legal category; 'subjecthood' is a political category. Although there is a large overlap between the two categories, they are not coextensive, and the distinction is important. Some citizens, such as expatriates, are not subjects.[6] Some subjects, such as resident foreigners, are not citizens. In a few states, such as Qatar and Kuwait, *most* subjects are not citizens. In other states, such as Ireland, a significant proportion of citizens are not subjects. Subjecthood is the important category for state responsibility, because the people who are subject to the state's coercive power bear the burdens of its debts, treaty obligations, and reparative obligations.

The passive connotation of 'subject', as opposed to the active connotation of 'citizen', is apt for a book about state responsibility. The members of the state can play an active role in determining what their state does, such as by voting, campaigning, or protesting. Yet each member of the state is 'subjected' to the consequences of the state's actions regardless of whether he or she is personally responsible for them. Most Iraqis had nothing to do with the 1990 invasion of Kuwait, but many suffered and even died because of the resulting sanctions and reparations against Iraq.[7] Many young Greeks in the aftermath of the 2007–2008 financial crisis were seriously disadvantaged by debts that previous governments incurred before they were even born. The people who bear the burdens of debts, reparations, treaty obligations, and sanctions are often just unlucky that they were born in a particular state at a particular time. Idealized notions of active citizenship serve to maintain the illusion that the members of the state bring these burdens on themselves. I call the members of the state 'subjects' in recognition of the grim reality that they are 'subjected' to many burdens that they have done nothing to morally deserve.

§2 The Three Fundamental Questions

Any cogent and complete theory of responsibility must answer three 'Fundamental Questions' about the entity in question.

1. *The Question of Ownership*: How can actions be attributed to the entity?
2. *The Question of Identity*: How can the entity be identified over time?
3. *The Question of Fulfilment*: How can the entity discharge its responsibilities?

---

6. Most expatriates are no longer subjects of their states of origin, but there are exceptions. The Internal Revenue Service taxes American citizens who live abroad, which makes them, to a limited degree, subjects of the United States.

7. I return to the case of Iraq in §6.3 and §24.1.

Every judgment of responsibility depends on judgments of ownership, identity, and fulfilment. For example, the judgment that a person is guilty of theft depends on three auxiliary judgments: (1) that the person who took the object intended to do so, such that the act of theft was his; (2) that the accused and the thief are the same person; and (3) that the accused is fit to be held responsible for the theft. It is both unjust and nonsensical to hold the accused responsible if any of these auxiliary judgments fail. We would not find the accused guilty of theft if he took the object by mistake (lack of ownership). Much less would we punish his identical twin for theft (lack of identity) or try to punish the thief if he were deceased (impossibility of fulfilment). Whether we judge the accused to be responsible depends in large part on our judgments of ownership, identity, and fulfilment.

The Fundamental Questions are perennial questions in ethics and law, although they are rarely posed alongside each other. The Question of Ownership involves issues of intent and representation, such as whether agents are responsible for the unintended consequences of their actions and whether following orders mitigates responsibility (Estlund, 2007; Finkelstein, 2005). The accused might not be guilty of theft, even if he did take the object intentionally, if he were commanded to do so under the threat of force. The person who commanded him might instead be the 'owner' of the theft. The Question of Identity concerns the transmission of responsibility through time (Glannon, 1998; Shoemaker, 2012; Weiss, 1939). For instance, Parfit's (1984) 'non-identity problem' implies that the 'victim' of the theft would have no claim to compensation if the theft had somehow caused him to exist in the first place. If, through some series of events, the 'victim' were conceived because his family's fortune was stolen, then he would have no claim to compensation. The Question of Fulfilment covers the old issue of whether 'ought implies can', as well as more recent issues of whether a lack of motivation or feasibility precludes responsibility (Estlund, 2011; Gilabert and Lawford-Smith, 2012). The accused might not be guilty of theft, or might instead be excused, if he had a medical condition that impaired his impulse control. We might say that his obligation not to steal was unfulfillable under the circumstances. A great deal of thought about responsibility concerns issues of ownership, identity, and fulfilment.

The Fundamental Questions apply to any theory of responsibility, whether the entities in question are humans, non-human animals, groups, or machines. For example, there is increasing interest in the question of whether it makes sense to assign responsibilities to artificial intelligences (AIs), such as robots and computer systems (e.g., Bostrom and Yudkowsky, 2014; European Parliament, 2017; Floridi and Sanders, 2004). One issue is whether AIs can 'own' actions or whether ownership resides with the people who program them.

Does it make sense to 'blame' a self-driving vehicle for running over a pedestrian in anything but a metaphorical sense? Another issue is how it is possible to identify AIs over time. If the vehicle's navigation software is replaced, is it still the same vehicle? Yet another issue is how AIs can be *held* responsible. If a self-driving vehicle can act wrongly, then can it be punished? The Fundamental Questions apply no less to AIs than to human beings, although the answers will certainly be different.

A theory of state responsibility must answer the very same questions. I examine how the agential and functional theories of state responsibility answer the Fundamental Questions in Chapter 1, and I develop Hobbesian answers to the Fundamental Questions in Chapters 3–5. For now, I simply pose the questions.

First, how can actions be attributed to a state? It is necessary to determine what counts as an 'act of state' in order to determine what states are responsible for. For example, was the 2014 missile attack on Malaysian Airlines Flight MH17 an act of Russia or simply an act of particular pro-Russian rebels? Russia cannot be responsible for the attack unless the attack can be attributed to Russia. A theory of state responsibility must explain how actions of states can be distinguished from actions of individuals, despite the fact that states act only through individuals.

Second, as Aristotle (1992: III.3, 175) asked, 'how are we to tell whether a state is still the same state or a different one?' Unless states retain their identities despite changes in their populations, territories, and governments, they cannot be responsible for what their antecedents have done. Britain cannot owe reparations to former British colonies, for example, unless it is the same state as the one that colonized them in the first place. A theory of state responsibility must explain how states can be identified over time as their constituents change.

Third, how can a state fulfil its responsibilities? Corporate entities cannot act on their own, so their responsibilities must be distributed to individuals in order to be fulfilled. The debts of states must be paid by their taxpayers, the treaties of states must be implemented by their legislators, state apologies must come from their leaders, and punishing states inevitably harms their subjects. The question, then, is what makes the distribution of responsibility legitimate. For example, why should Greeks bear the burden of their state's debt? Many did not vote for the governments that borrowed the money, and some young Greeks had not yet been born when the money was borrowed. A theory of state responsibility must provide a justification for distributing states' responsibilities to their subjects.

The Fundamental Questions provide a structured way to interpret and evaluate theories of state responsibility. The agential, functional, and

Hobbesian theories answer each question differently, which makes the questions useful points of comparison.

§3 Back to Hobbes

Returning to Hobbes for a theory of state responsibility may seem antiquarian or anachronistic. Much has been written about state responsibility since the mid-seventeenth century, and Hobbes could never have foreseen contemporary issues of sovereign debt, economic sanctions, or reparations. Hobbes obviously does not provide all of the answers. However, he does provide some crucial but forgotten insights that help us to understand state responsibility in the present. His theory of state personality lays the groundwork for a theory of state responsibility.

One reason to return to Hobbes is that his theory of the state helped to make state responsibility possible. He provides one of the first unambiguously modern theories of the state, as well as the first systematic exposition of the idea that the state is a person. Skinner (2002: 404) points out that Hobbes, 'more clearly than any previous writer on public power . . . enunciates the doctrine that the legal person lying at the heart of politics is neither the *persona* of the people nor the official person of the sovereign, but rather the artificial person of the state'. Given that Hobbes' theory of the state paved the way for the idea of state responsibility, we would do well to understand it.

Another reason to return to Hobbes is that his idea of state personality has no counterpart in the current scholarship on state responsibility. What makes Hobbes unique, as I explained above, is that he considers the state to be a person but neither an agent nor a principal. Hobbes' state is represented 'by fiction' (Runciman, 2000b; Skinner, 2007), much like a child or a 'Foole', which (unlike an agent) wills and acts only through its representatives but (unlike a principal) cannot authorize its own representatives. For example, an incapacitated defendant in a trial can neither represent herself nor authorize a lawyer to represent her. However, if the judge authorizes a lawyer to represent her, then she is nevertheless a person as far as the court is concerned. The defendant can act vicariously through a court-appointed lawyer. The personality of the state is conceptually similar. Although the state 'can do nothing but by the Person that Represents it' (*L* XVI. 388), it can nevertheless be said to make laws, borrow money, sign treaties, and wage wars. The actions of the sovereign are attributable to the state, much as the actions of the lawyer are attributable to the incapacitated defendant. The subjects are the 'principals'; the sovereign is the 'agent'; but the state is the person that owns the actions that the sovereign performs.

Hobbes' idea of the state may seem like nothing more than the 'fiction theory' of corporate personality applied to the state. The fiction theory dates back at least to Pope Innocent IV, who declared in 1245 that a corporate entity, such as a guild or a church, is only a *persona ficta* and therefore cannot be excommunicated (Dewey, 1926: 665–66; Kantorowicz, 1957: 305–6; Koessler, 1949: 436–39). The idea that corporate personality is a fiction is now ubiquitous in politics and law.

Although Hobbes might be considered a proponent of the fiction theory in a broad sense, he differs from other proponents of the fiction theory in several important ways. First, whereas proponents of the fiction theory consider corporations to be creations of law, Hobbes considers the state to be a precondition for law.[8] Hobbes' state is a fiction, but it is not a *legal* fiction.

Second, whereas the fiction theory carries the connotation that corporate personality is *just* a fiction, and hence that it should not be taken too seriously, Hobbes reifies the fiction. He refers to the state as both an 'Artificiall Man' and a 'Mortall God' (*L* Intro. 16, XVII. 260). Only in his earliest political work, *The Elements of Law,* and then only once, does Hobbes explicitly say that 'a body politic . . . is a fictitious body' (*EL* XXI.4).[9] Even here, the 'body politic' that he refers to is an assembly, not a state (see §10 below). Not once in *Leviathan* does he say that the personality of the state is fictitious, even though his theory of personhood clearly implies it (Runciman, 2003: 30). He downplays this implication because he wants to emphasize that the personality of the state has very real and important consequences. Having a separate personality from the sovereign gives the state an 'Artificiall Eternity of life', or continuity over time, despite the deaths of individual sovereigns and members of sovereign assemblies (*L* XIX. 298). For Hobbes, the fiction of state personality was the only thing that prevented subjects from falling back into the state of nature after each generation.

Third, and most importantly for my purposes, Hobbes' theory of the state is much more sophisticated than the present-day fiction theory. Hobbes does not simply maintain that corporate entities are fictions in order to avoid ontological commitments. He also provides a well-developed account of attribution that explains how real actions and responsibilities can be attributed to fictional entities (see Fleming, 2017a). There are more and less plausible ways of representing the state, just as there are more and less plausible ways of representing a fictional character, such as Robin Hood or Harry Potter (see §14.1). The fiction of state personality cannot be used in any which way.

---

8. More precisely, the state is a precondition for *civil* law, or human-made law. *Natural* law precedes the state.

9. I cite *The Elements of Law* (*EL*) according to the paragraph numbers.

Hobbes' idea of state personality was quickly overtaken and displaced by metaphysically thicker ideas of state personality, which have more in common with the agential theory. Although 'the Hobbesian view of the person of the state as the seat of sovereignty won immediate acceptance among a broad range of writers on natural jurisprudence in continental Europe' (Skinner, 2002: 407), these writers also abandoned the features that made this view of the state distinctly Hobbesian. Samuel von Pufendorf, whose work was 'the most important conduit for the transmission of [Hobbes'] doctrine', altered his idea of state personality in a crucial way. Whereas Hobbes understood the state as a fictional person, Pufendorf (1934: BVII II.13, 984) understood the state as a 'moral person'.[10] Skinner (2009: 349–52) takes this shift in terminology to be rather insignificant. He maintains that Pufendorf's theory of the state is little more than an 'adaptation of Hobbes's fictional theory' (ibid. 349). On the contrary, I argue, the shift from Hobbes' fictional personality to Pufendorf's moral personality marks a substantive shift.[11] For Hobbes, the state is a *fictional* person because it has no will of its own: 'a Common-wealth hath no Will, nor makes no Lawes, but those that are made by the Will of him, or them that have the Sovereign Power' (*L* XXXI. 570). For Pufendorf, the state is a *moral* person because it does have a will, as well as an intellect that guides this will. He describes the state as 'a single person with intelligence and will, performing other actions peculiar to itself and separate from those of individuals' (Pufendorf, 1934: BVII II.13, 983; see also Boucher, 2001: 566–67). One of Pufendorf's crucial moves was to reify the will of the state. He thus popularized Hobbes' theory of the state but stripped it of what made it distinctly Hobbesian.

The issue of whether non-rational entities can be persons illustrates the difference between Hobbes' theory of personhood and Pufendorf's theory of personhood. Hobbes thought there were 'few things, that are uncapable of being represented by Fiction' (*L* XVI. 246). Anything that has an authorized representative 'can be a person, that is, it can have possessions and other goods, and can act in law, as in the case of a temple, a bridge, or of anything whatsoever that needs money for its upkeep' (*DH* XV.4).[12] Just as 'Children,

---

10. I cite Pufendorf's *De jure naturae et gentium* according to the book number, chapter number, and paragraph number, as well as the page number from the 1934 edition of the Oldfather translation.

11. Skinner (2015) later acknowledges this. See Holland (2017: 6–14, 83–91, 199–207, 211–21) for a detailed account of the differences between Hobbes' theory of the state and Pufendorf's theory of the state.

12. I cite Hobbes' *De homine* according to the chapter and paragraph numbers.

Fooles, and Mad-men that have no use of Reason, may be Personated by Guardians, or Curators . . . Inanimate things, as a Church, an Hospital, a Bridge, may be personated by a Rector, Master, or Overseer'. Even 'An Idol, or meer Figment of the brain, may be Personated' provided that someone is authorized to speak and act in its name (*L* XVI. 248).[13] Pufendorf, on the other hand, argued that it was a mistake to ascribe personhood to non-rational entities.

> On this point Hobbes, *Leviathan*, chap. xvi, is mistaken in holding that in communities a man may frequently represent the person of an inanimate object, which in itself is not a person, such as a church, a hospital, a bridge, &c. For it is not necessary by a fiction of law to assign a personality to any of these things, since it is very much simpler to say that certain states have assigned to particular men the duty to collect the revenues for the preservation of such places, and to prosecute and defend any suits that arise on such account (1934: BI I.12, 11).

Pufendorf argues that ascriptions of personhood 'should presuppose such qualities as are appropriate' (ibid. I.14, 15)—namely, intelligence and will. For this reason, it was 'sheer madness and silly impudence' for Caligula to make his horse a Roman consul and a householder (ibid. I.15, 15–16), as it was for Hobbes to describe inanimate objects as persons. Whereas Hobbes thought anything that had an authorized representative could be a person, Pufendorf thought only rational agents could be persons. In List and Pettit's (2011: 170–73) terms, Hobbes' conception of personhood is 'performative', while Pufendorf's is 'intrinsicist'. For Hobbes, the state is a person because someone speaks and acts in its name. For Pufendorf, it makes sense to speak and act in the name of the state only because it has a will and an intellect. Hobbesian persons, unlike Pufendorfian persons, need not have any intrinsic capacity for rationality or agency.

Later ideas of state personality owe much more to Pufendorf than to Hobbes. Pufendorf's conception of the state as a moral person was taken up by many others, including Wolff, Vattel, Rousseau, and Kant,[14] and it remains common in Political Theory and International Relations to describe the state

---

13. A contemporary example of a Hobbesian fictional person is the Whanganui river in New Zealand, which has two guardians or representatives who speak and act its name (BBC, 2017b; Hutchison, 2014). The Whanganui can initiate court proceedings, assert its rights, and incur debts through its authorized representatives.

14. See Holland (2011: 439–41; 2017) on the influence of Pufendorf's idea of moral personhood on Wolff, Vattel, Kant, and others. See Derathé (1995: 397–410) on the relationship between Hobbes', Pufendorf's, and Rousseau's conceptions of state personality.

as a moral person (e.g., Vincent, 1989; Stilz, 2011; Wendt, 2004). What these disparate ideas of state personality have in common is that they take person-hood to be constituted by a set of intrinsic properties rather than by a process of social ascription. Hobbes' claim that bridges and idols can be persons falls strangely on modern ears because, like Pufendorf, we tend to take for granted that rationality and will are preconditions for personhood. Hobbes' theory of the state has thus been thoroughly eclipsed by Pufendorf's adaptation of it.

Hobbes' idea of state personality has no contemporary counterpart in the scholarship on state responsibility. In Political Theory, International Rela-tions, and Philosophy, it has been supplanted by the idea of the state as a moral agent. In International Law, it has been supplanted by the idea of the state as a functional legal person. However, there was one previous attempt to understand state responsibility in Hobbesian terms. E. H. Carr (1946) ap-provingly cites Hobbes in (of all places) his chapter titled 'International Morality' in *The Twenty Years' Crisis*. He describes Hobbes' idea of state per-sonality as 'an important step forward', which 'made possible the creation of international law on the basis of natural law' (ibid. 146). Hobbes' theory of the state helps to explain how states can have responsibilities—not just legal responsibilities, but *moral* responsibilities: 'States could be assumed to have duties to one another only in virtue of the fiction which treated them as if they were persons' (ibid.). For Carr, as for Hobbes, the personality of the state is 'a necessary fiction' (ibid.). It is a fiction because it has no factual or metaphysical basis, but it is necessary because it underpins sovereign debts, treaty obligations, and other corporate responsibilities (ibid. 149–51). Carr even describes the process of attribution in Hobbesian terms: 'The acts with which international morality is concerned are performed by individuals not on their own behalf, but on behalf of those fictitious group persons "Great Britain" and "Italy"' (ibid. 152). Attribution is a product of representation, not of agency, will, or function.

The only significant difference between Carr and Hobbes is one of empha-sis. Whereas Hobbes downplays the fictional character of the state, Carr em-phasizes it. His primary aim in doing so is to discredit 'utopian thinkers', who 'reject [state personality] with fervour, and are consequently led to deny that morality can be attributed to the state'. Carr's response is that the 'controversy about the attribution of personality to the state is not only misleading, but meaningless' (ibid. 148). The utopians have made the same mistake as the 'real personality' theorists (perhaps Otto von Gierke and the British Idealists), which is to assume that the question of whether states are persons can be an-swered by metaphysics. As he later adds: 'The hypothesis of state personality and state responsibility is neither true nor false, because it does not purport to be a fact, but a category of thought necessary to clear thinking about international relations' (ibid. 150). What drew Carr to Hobbes' idea of state personality is that it carries little metaphysical baggage.

Oddly, although Carr occupies a central place in the International Relations canon, his discussion of state personality and responsibility has been almost entirely overlooked in the literature on these subjects. One of the few passing mentions comes from Wendt (1999: 196), who invokes Carr to support his own theory of state personality: 'As Carr points out, it would be impossible to make sense of day-to-day IR without attributions of corporate actorhood.' The irony is that Wendt's theory, which aims to provide a metaphysical foundation for state personality, is exactly the kind of theory that Carr aimed to discredit. Carr's Hobbesian way of thinking about state responsibility has been misread on the rare occasions when it has been read at all. Although Carr's remarks on state responsibility are intriguing and suggestive, they are also brief and polemical, so they leave many important questions unanswered. What follows can be understood as an attempt to pick up where Carr left off—to develop a 'political' theory of state responsibility using Hobbes' theory of political representation.

§4 The Structure of the Book

The book has five main chapters. Chapter 1 reconstructs and critiques the agential and functional theories of state responsibility. I show that neither provides adequate answers to the Fundamental Questions. At best, the 'agent' and 'principal' models provide an incomplete set of answers. At worst, they blind us to important facets of state responsibility.

Chapter 2 lays the groundwork for the Hobbesian theory of state responsibility. It first sets out to determine what exactly Hobbes means when he says that the state is a person. Scholars of state and corporate responsibility, and even many Hobbes scholars, have failed to appreciate the novelty of Hobbes' idea of state personality because they have projected the idea of corporate agency—the core of the agential theory—back onto Hobbes. I show that it is possible to recover a novel understanding of state personality from Hobbes if we resist this urge to read him through the contemporary literature on corporate agency.

The next three chapters develop Hobbesian answers to the Three Fundamental Questions. Chapter 3 addresses issues of ownership, such as whether the actions of dictators and rogue officials ought to be attributed to states and whether states can commit crimes. I show that, with some modifications, Hobbes' account of attribution provides an intuitive and compelling answer to the Question of Ownership: an action counts as an act of state if and only if the agent who performed it was an authorized representative of the state.

Much of the chapter focuses on the conditions for authorization and representation.

Chapter 4 addresses issues of identity, such as whether changes in a state's population, territory, government, or constitution alter its personality and hence negate its responsibilities. According to Hobbes, the corporate identity of the state is created and sustained by representation. The state has a corporate identity because it has an authorized representative who speaks and acts in its name. This identity persists as long as the state has a continuous 'chain of succession', or an unbroken series of representatives. I show that this Hobbesian account of corporate identity solves many of the identity problems that arise in cases of revolution, annexation, secession, absorption, unification, and dissolution.

Chapter 5 addresses issues of fulfilment, such as why subjects ought to bear the costs of their state's debts and reparative obligations. I focus on intergenerational distributions of liability, in which the subjects who bear the costs were not yet born when their state incurred the responsibility. I use Hobbes' idea of 'representation by fiction' to explain how subjects can be implicated in acts of state that occurred before they were born.

The conclusion summarizes the implications of the Hobbesian theory of state responsibility and then looks to the future. There are three ongoing trends that are likely to alter both the nature and the scope of state responsibility: the development of international criminal law, the proliferation of treaties, and the replacement of human representatives with machines and algorithms. Although the practice of holding individuals responsible for acts of state might seem to render state responsibility redundant, I argue that the rise of international criminal law will not lead to the decline of state responsibility. The two forms of international responsibility are complementary rather than competitive. If anything, the domain of state responsibility will continue to expand in the coming decades because of the proliferation of treaties. As states continue to sign bilateral and multilateral treaties about everything from investor protection to environmental protection, political decisions will increasingly be circumscribed by international agreements. A sovereigntist backlash is already underway.

New technologies pose the greatest challenge to current understandings of state responsibility. Our theories of state responsibility are designed for a world in which the 'members' or 'organs' of states are flesh-and-blood human beings. But states are becoming 'cyborgs' as they rely more and more on algorithms to make decisions and on machines to execute them. Hobbes' theory of the state, which is mechanistic to begin with, is well suited to the emerging world of mechanized states.

1

The Agential and Functional
Theories of State Responsibility

THIS CHAPTER distinguishes, compares, and evaluates the two dominant theories of state responsibility.[1] According to the agential theory, states can be held responsible because they are moral agents like human beings. The model for state responsibility is an ordinary case of individual responsibility, such as a criminal trial. According to the functional theory, states are principals rather than agents. The model for state responsibility is a case of vicarious liability, such as when an employer is held liable for the actions of her employee. The primary distinction between the two theories of state responsibility is that they rely on different understandings of how corporate entities can act.

The agential and functional theories belong to parallel traditions of scholarship that often appear to be unaware of each other. While the agential theory is dominant in International Relations, Political Theory, and Philosophy, the functional theory prevails in International Law. Those on opposite sides of the ethical–legal division ask many of the same questions, but they tend to talk past each other because they employ different concepts and vocabularies.

This chapter uses the Three Fundamental Questions to bring the agential and functional theories into dialogue and to put them to the test. I argue that neither provides an adequate set of answers. While the 'agent' and 'principal' models of state responsibility are useful in some respects, each has important gaps and blind spots. Subsequent chapters will show that the Hobbesian theory provides a better set of answers to the Fundamental Questions.

---

1. This chapter expands on an earlier article, 'Moral Agents and Legal Persons: The Ethics and the Law of State Responsibility', which was first published in *International Theory* (Fleming, 2017b).

§5 States as Moral Agents: The Agential Theory

The core idea of the agential theory is that states can be held responsible for the same reasons that human beings are held responsible. Goodin (1995: 35) argues that 'the state is a moral agent, in all the respects that morally matter'. The state, 'like the natural individual, is capable of embodying values, goals and ends; it, too, is capable (through its legislative and executive organs) of deliberative action in pursuit of them' (ibid.). Erskine (2001: 69–70) argues that the disanalogy between states and human beings 'is often over-stated' and that states are 'capable of acting and knowing in a way that is analogous—but not identical—to that of most individual human beings'. Because states are capable of deliberating and of acting intentionally, they are 'moral agents in the same way that we understand most individual human beings to be moral agents' (Erskine, 2008: 2).[2]

The agential theory was developed by philosophers, most notably Peter French (1979, 1984, 1995, 1998), and later adopted by political theorists and International Relations scholars.[3] French argues that certain groups, which he calls 'conglomerate collectivities', are moral agents over and above their members and can therefore be held responsible separately from their members.[4] Conglomerate collectivities have two defining features: (1) corporate identities that do not depend on determinate memberships; and (2) corporate internal decision (CID) structures. First, unlike 'aggregate collectivities' such as mobs and crowds, conglomerates retain their identities despite changes in their memberships (French, 1984: 29–30). Ireland is the same state as it was yesterday even though some of its members have died and others have been born, and Microsoft remains the same company over time even though its employees and shareholders change. Second, conglomerate collectivities have CID structures that give them the capacity to deliberate and to combine the intentions of individuals into corporate intentions (ibid. 47–48). We might

2. The agential theory could alternatively be called the 'analogical theory' because it relies so heavily on the analogy between states and human beings. I call it 'agential' to emphasize the connection with 'moral agency'.

3. French belongs to an analytic and mostly American tradition of thought about collective action and responsibility. Seminal works include Feinberg (1968), Cooper (1968), and Held (1970).

4. French (1979, 1984) calls conglomerate collectivities 'moral persons' in his early work but 'moral actors' in his later work (1995, 1998). The reason for this terminological change is that he came to think 'calling corporations moral *persons* creates more confusion and misunderstanding than clarity' (1995: 10, emphasis added). His argument remains substantially the same throughout.

say that Ireland intends to raise taxes or that Microsoft intends to develop a new operating system. French concludes that conglomerate collectivities, such as states and corporations, are distinct agents that can be blamed, praised, punished, and obligated separately from their members. In an oft-quoted phrase that sums up his argument, he declares that corporate agents are 'full-fledged members of the moral community, of equal standing with the traditionally acknowledged residents: human beings' (ibid. 32).

O'Neill (1986) was the first to apply the agential theory to ethical issues in international affairs. She argues that many international ethical issues are intractable if individuals are assumed to be the only moral agents (ibid. 51–53). 'Individuals have remarkably few options to reduce nuclear dangers' (ibid. 55), so it is futile to say that they have duties to prevent nuclear war. Many responsibilities, such as duties to prevent war or climate change, must be assigned to states because states are the only agents with the power to act on them. The key premise of O'Neill's argument is that 'some institutions may be agents in the literal and unmetaphorical way in which individuals are agents' (ibid. 58). She argues that 'the two sorts of agents are similar enough to suggest that *if* ethical reasoning is accessible to individuals *then* it is not inaccessible to states' (ibid. 62, emphasis in original). The decision-making structures of states, like the minds of individuals, allow them to process ethical imperatives and set goals (ibid. 61–66). O'Neill thus uses the analogy between states and human beings to scale up Kantian moral agency.

Erskine (2001) introduced the agential theory to the discipline of International Relations, where she remains its most influential proponent (Erskine, 2003, 2004, 2008, 2010, 2014). Drawing from both French and O'Neill, she argues that a group is a moral agent if and only if it has five features:

> (1) an identity that is more than the sum of the identities of its constitutive parts, or what might be called a 'corporate identity'; (2) a decision-making structure that can commit the group to a policy or course of action that is different from the individual positions of some (or all) of its members; (3) mechanisms by which group decisions can be translated into actions (thereby establishing, with the previous characteristic, a capacity for purposive action); (4) an identity over time; and (5) a conception of itself as a unit (meaning simply that it cannot be merely externally defined) (Erskine, 2014: 119).[5]

These five criteria determine which groups are sufficiently analogous to human beings to count as moral agents. For example, mobs and crowds are not moral

---

5. For earlier formulations of the criteria for corporate moral agency, see Erskine (2001: 72; 2004: 26; 2010: 264–65).

agents because they do not have corporate identities or decision-making structures. Neither their personalities nor their intentions are distinct from the
personalities and intentions of their members. Nor do puppet states or shell
companies count as moral agents, since their identities are created and sustained by other agents. The class of corporate moral agents includes (most)
states, business corporations, unions, intergovernmental organizations, rebel
groups, and drug cartels.

For early proponents of the agential theory, corporate moral agency was
a contentious proposition that had to be defended at every turn. Erskine
(2003: 2) once lamented that there is a 'general reticence to accept that the
class of moral agent might extend from the individual human being to en-
compass certain types of groups'. However, since the mid-2000s, the agential
theory has ceased to require much justification, save for some obligatory
citations of the works of these early proponents. The next generation of
scholarship in the agential tradition focuses on applying the concept of corporate moral agency to particular issues, such as great-power responsibility
(Brown, 2004), evil (Lu, 2004), Europe's international citizenship (Dunne,
2008), national defence (Eckert, 2009), and state punishment (Erskine,
2010; Lang, 2007, 2008, 2011). Many works of international political theory
now take the idea of corporate moral agency as a basic premise (e.g., Collins,
2016; Collins and Lawford-Smith, 2016; Crawford, 2013b; Pasternak, 2013;
Stilz, 2011). As Valentini (2011: 133) declares, as if to state the obvious, 'states,
universities, churches, and hospitals clearly have a capacity for "collective
will formation" sophisticated enough to warrant attribution of *moral* agency'
(emphasis in original). The agential theory is almost uncontested in Political
Theory and International Relations. Its only significant rival is the lingering
(but waning) scepticism of corporate agency (e.g., Gould, 2009; Lomas,
2005, 2014; Wight, 1999, 2004, 2006). The remainder of this section uses the
Three Fundamental Questions to interpret and evaluate the agential
theory.

§5.1 The Agential Answer to the Question of Ownership

According to the agential theory, states take ownership of actions through
their wills or intentions. Just as an event constitutes an action of an individual
when it implicates his or her will, an event constitutes an action of a state when
it implicates that state's will. We say that Michael committed theft because he
intentionally took something that did not belong to him; we say that Russia
committed aggression because it *intentionally* invaded territory that did not
belong to it. The agential theory thus scales up the idea of intentional action
from human beings to states.

States form 'intentions' through their internal decision-making structures, which combine the intentions of individuals into corporate intentions. As Erskine (2001: 71) argues, a decision-making structure 'entails a degree of decision-making unity that would allow the collectivity in question to arrive at a predetermined goal, rather than simply display a spontaneous convergence of individual interests'. Whereas a mob or crowd has as many wills as it has members, a state or corporation has one will. Lang (2007: 244) similarly argues that 'states that have a deliberative body that determines not only instrumental actions but also overarching political aims can be said to have intentions' (see also Stilz, 2011: 195–96). According to the agential theory, it is not merely a figure of speech to say that 'Russia intends to annex Crimea' or that 'the US plans to roll back foreign aid'. States have intentions, goals, plans, and desires, just as individuals do.

Although corporate intentions may conjure up the idea of collective consciousness, they need not.[6] List and Pettit (2011) argue that corporate intentions 'supervene' on individual intentions, which means that the former are dependent on but irreducible to the latter. All that a group requires in order to form intentions is a unified decision-making structure. Tollefsen (2015: 60–62) uses the example of a PhD admissions committee to illustrate how corporate intentions can emerge from the combination of individual intentions. The committee's rules say that only applicants who have good test scores, grades, letters of recommendation, and writing samples can be admitted, and whether an applicant meets each criterion is to be determined by a majority vote. The committee votes as follows on Trevor's application.

TABLE 1. Tollefsen's Admissions Committee

	Good test score?	Good grades?	Good letters?	Good writing sample?	Accept the candidate?
Member #1	Yes	No	Yes	No	No
Member #2	No	Yes	Yes	Yes	No
Member #3	Yes	Yes	No	Yes	No
Committee	Yes	Yes	Yes	Yes	Yes

Although none of the committee members believe that Trevor meets all of the criteria for admission, the majority of them believe that he meets each

6. O'Neill (1986: 62–63) and Erskine (2003: 6–7) avoid 'intention' because of its mental connotations. However, for most proponents of the agential theory, 'intentions' are simply purposes or objectives (Wendt, 2004: 295).

criterion. As a result, after the votes are tallied, the committee decides to admit Trevor to the PhD programme even though none of its members think he is a suitable candidate. 'We intend to admit Trevor to the programme' is true even though 'I intend to admit Trevor' is false for each committee member. The decision-making structure of the committee thus produces a corporate intention that cannot be ascribed to any individual.

Even if the intention of the committee were shared by a majority of its members, its intention would not be reducible to the sum of theirs. Corporate intentions are 'multiply realizable', which means that the same corporate intention can result from different combinations of individual intentions (List and Pettit, 2011: 65–66; Tollefsen, 2015: 87–88). The committee might still have decided to admit Trevor if each of its members had voted differently, and even if the committee had entirely different members. List and Pettit's supervenience account of corporate intentionality is powerful because it begins from individualist premises. It implies that corporate intentions are irreducible to individual intentions even though they are entirely made up of individual intentions.

Several proponents of the agential theory of state responsibility have drawn on the supervenience account of corporate intentionality (Collins, 2016: 344; Erskine, 2014: 119; Stilz, 2011: 191; Wendt, 2004: 299–300, 2005). For instance, Wendt (2004: 300) argues that 'even though the intentions of a state person at any given moment are ontologically dependent on its constituent members, its intentions are not dependent on any *particular* members' (emphasis in original). A state's intention to wage war can be realized by different legislators, just as the committee's intention to admit an applicant can be realized by different members. The United States would still have intended to invade Iraq in 2003 if different members of Congress had voted for the invasion. Wendt (1999: 222–23) contends that the intentions of states are actually *less* mysterious than the intentions of individuals. While it is currently impossible to read another human being's mind, the intentions of states are often clearly described in their laws and policies.

According to the supervenience account, although states act only through individuals, states also exert higher-order control over what these individuals do. The intentions of states 'programme' the performance of certain actions, which can be 'implemented' by different individuals (List and Pettit, 2011: 160–63; Stilz, 2011: 191). The intention of the United States to invade Iraq was implemented by particular soldiers, but if some of these soldiers had refused to perform their duties, others would have been found to take their places. The United States is the agent that 'owns' the invasion because its intention to invade more or less guaranteed that the invasion would occur. While particular soldiers were the 'leading edge' of the invasion (Wendt, 1999: 217), the United

States was the force behind it. This is why it makes sense to say that 'the United States invaded Iraq' and to criticize the United States for the resulting calamity. Presumably (although proponents of the agential theory never address this point), states are also responsible for the unintended consequences of their actions, just as individuals are. The United States did not intend to kill thousands of Iraqi civilians, but it is nevertheless responsible for these deaths because they were a foreseeable consequence of its invasion of Iraq, which was an intentional action. In any case, an action must somehow be connected to a state's intention in order to count as an act of state.

An important implication of the agential theory is that only non-dictatorial states can truly own actions. As Lang (2007: 245) argues, 'when a dictatorial regime commits a crime, it makes more sense to attribute that crime to the head of state, in that the policy results from his individual intention'. Pettit (2014: 1649) likewise argues that a dictatorship ought to be treated 'not as a group agent that operates via an authorized individual, but as an individual agent whose reach and power is extended and amplified by the members of the authorizing group'. North Korea cannot own actions because its intentions are not genuinely corporate. Although we commonly say that 'North Korea conducted a nuclear test', the source of the intention, and thus the owner of the action, is really Kim Jong-un. Conversely, 'if a state is democratic and initiates a policy that leads to a crime, it makes more sense to attribute that crime to the state *qua* agent' (Lang, 2007: 245). Proponents of the agential theory are not clear whether oligarchic states can own actions. But since the actions of oligarchic states follow from collective decision-making, albeit by an exclusive decision-making body, it seems that they could have corporate intentions.

The central problem with the supervenience account of corporate intentionality is that it does not scale up. Even if we accept that a PhD admissions committee can have intentions, it does not follow that a state can have intentions. The archetype of a corporate agent is a small, participatory group, such as a committee or a panel of judges. This model does not easily scale up to large, non-participatory groups, such as states, corporations, or universities (Runciman, 2007: 104–5; Brito Vieira and Runciman, 2008: 95–96, 135). According to List and Pettit (2011: 35–36), a member of a corporate agent is someone who either actively participates in its decisions or authorizes others to participate. It is plausible, on this account, to say that Tollefsen's admissions committee intends to admit Trevor to the PhD programme because each member of the committee, whether he or she voted for or against admitting Trevor, actively participated in the decision. It is also plausible to say that the department intends to admit Trevor, provided that every member of the department authorized the admissions committee. However, it does not follow that the university intends to admit Trevor. The university cannot be the relevant corporate agent according to List and Pettit's criteria because many of its members, such as students, neither participate in admissions decisions nor authorize others to do so. Given that only participants and authorizers count as members of a corporate agent, the claim that the university is the relevant agent has the absurd implication that students are not members of the university. Committees and departments are the corporate agents that make admissions decisions; the university as a whole is a passive recipient of these decisions.

The committee model is even less applicable to the state. It is plausible to say that Cabinet intends to increase military spending, since every minister participates in budget decisions. It is also plausible to say that Parliament intends to increase military spending, since every member of Parliament gets to vote on the budget. The relevant corporate agent might also include members of the voting public, who authorize members of Parliament. However, it does not follow that the United Kingdom intends to increase military spending. Some members of the United Kingdom, such as children, neither participate in nor authorize budget decisions. While students might be considered to tacitly authorize admissions committees when they choose to enrol in the university, children certainly do not authorize governments (see §15.1, §24.1). Given that all members of a corporate agent are either participants or authorizers, the claim that the state is the relevant agent implies that children are not members of the state. It makes much more sense to think of Cabinet, Parliament, and the Treasury as the corporate agents that make budget decisions and of the state as a passive recipient of these decisions. The state appears not to be a single agent, but a collection of corporate agents, individual agents, and passive members. In other words, if we accept the dominant conception of corporate agency, then agency is a property of some parts of the state rather than a property of the whole.

List and Pettit's (2011) account of collective agency is only one of many (e.g., Bratman, 1999: 109–29; Gilbert, 1990; Tuomela, 2005, 2013), so the fact that it is not applicable to the state does not seem fatal for the agential theory. Yet the rival accounts are no more promising. As Poljanšek (2015: 185) points out, existing accounts of collective agency tend to 'presuppose the generalizability of small-scale cases of CA [collective agency], while they ignore the possibility of complex cases'. These accounts are based on examples, such as lifting a table or walking together, that have three common features: the members of the group share a goal; they interact face-to-face; and they act together simultaneously (ibid. 189).[7] States have none of these features: the goals of the

---

7. See Pettit and Schweikard (2006) on the relationship between 'joint action' and collective agency.

state are deeply contested; most of its members have never met; and many of its members are not even alive at the same time. If the committee model of collective agency does not scale up to the state, then the lifting-a-table model certainly does not. It is a mistake to make inferences about large, organizational groups from small, participatory groups.

At best, the agential theory provides a partial answer to the Question of Ownership. Although it provides a plausible explanation of how committees, courts, and legislatures can act in a way that is not reducible to the actions of their members, this explanation does not scale up to the state. There is a missing link between 'Parliament decided to wage war' and 'the United Kingdom decided to wage war'. What is missing is an account of how the actions of agents within the state—individual or corporate—can be attributed to the state as a whole. Chapter 3 explains how the Hobbesian theory fills this gap using the concepts of authorization and representation.

§5.2 The Agential Answer to the Question of Identity

Few proponents of the agential theory even acknowledge the importance of identity for state responsibility. In their treatise on corporate agency, List and Pettit (2011: 31–32, 172–73, note 20) mention corporate identity only in passing. The Questions of Ownership and Fulfilment have so far garnered almost all of the attention. Erskine is one of the few who address the Question of Identity at any length. According to her account, a corporate moral agent must have '[1] an identity that is more than the sum of the identities of its constitutive parts, or what might be called a "corporate identity" . . . [2] an identity over time; and [3] a conception of itself as a unit (meaning simply that it cannot be merely externally defined)' (Erskine, 2014: 119). She argues that most states satisfy these criteria, the exceptions being puppet states and some 'quasi-states' (Erskine, 2001; Erskine, 2010).

First, the identity of a state 'does not rely on a determinate membership' (Erskine, 2001: 72). 'The United Kingdom in 2018' is the same state as 'the United Kingdom in 2016' even though some of its members have died, others have been born, and still others have emigrated and immigrated. Just as a human being remains the same agent despite the gradual replacement of her cells, a state remains the same agent despite the gradual replacement of its members. This opens up the possibility that the state can have 'non-distributive' responsibilities. If the identity of the state is irreducible to the identities of its members, then the debts, obligations, and crimes of the state might also be irreducible.

Second, the identity of a state is temporally continuous. The territory and the laws of the United Kingdom have changed significantly since 1900, but we

still refer to it as the same state—the same United Kingdom that once colonized a large part of the globe. If the state 'has "a past accessible to experience-
memory and a future accessible to intention"' (Erskine, 2001: 75, quoting
Wiggins, 1976: 161), then it also has a past susceptible to blame and a future
susceptible to obligation. A state with an intergenerational identity can have
intergenerational responsibilities.

Third, the identity of a state is internally defined. Although the United
Kingdom, like all states, depends on the recognition of other states, it is not
simply a contrivance of other states. The identity of the United Kingdom
stands in contrast to that of the Republic of Transkei (1976–1994), which was
created and sustained by South Africa. In short, according to Erskine, the identities of states are *irreducible, intransient,* and *internal.*

The problem with Erskine's answer to the Question of Identity is that it is
purely negative. She tells us that the identity of the state does *not* depend on
its particular membership, is *not* transient, and is *not* externally defined, but
she does not tell us on what the state's identity *does* depend. If the identity of
the state does not depend on its population, territory, or government, then
what is the substratum that persists after subjects die, borders change, laws are
amended, and institutions are reformed? A positive criterion for corporate
identity is necessary in order to answer the central question: 'how are we to
tell whether a state is still the same state or a different one?' (Aristotle, 1992:
III.3, 175). For example, the Republic of Turkey has a different capital and even
a different constitution than the Ottoman Empire. Is it therefore a different
state?[8] We cannot even begin to answer this question until we identify the
locus of the state's corporate identity—the essential feature or features of a
state that distinguish it as *this particular state.* Erskine tells us which features
are not essential to a state's identity, but she does not tell us which features are
essential.

Because Erskine's answer to the Question of Identity is purely negative, it
is wide open to a riposte from sceptics who doubt that 'state' means anything
more than 'government'. Easton (1981: 316) famously argued that the state is
either 'no more than a substitute term for the political authorities' or 'some
kind of undefined and undefinable essence'. In response to the claim that the
identity of the state does not depend on its particular membership, he would
argue that this 'state' is nothing but 'a "ghost in the machine", knowable only
through its variable manifestations' (ibid.).[9] Easton's position amounts to the

8. I return to the issue of Turkish/Ottoman identity in Chapter 4.

9. Gilpin (1984: 301) and Jessop (1990: 366–67) are similarly doubtful that 'state' refers to
anything other than particular territory or people.

claim that no state satisfies Erskine's identity criteria—that there is no such thing as a corporate identity in the first place. Defining the identity of the state by what it is not reinforces the suspicion that it is vacuous and inscrutable.

Wendt (1999) uses an analogy between personal identity and corporate identity to develop a positive answer to the Question of Identity: 'what really distinguishes the personal or corporate identity of intentional actors from that of beagles and bicycles is a consciousness and memory of Self as a separate locus of thought and activity' (ibid. 225). What Wendt means by this is that the identity of a state is constituted by its members' shared narrative—for instance, their origin stories and national myths (ibid. 217). Subjects create a corporate identity by describing themselves as parts of a corporate 'Self' and by behaving as such. They give their state temporal continuity by passing down their shared narrative from one generation to the next.

> We normally think of states as persisting through time despite generational turnover, in part because their properties seem quite stable: boundaries, symbols, national interests, foreign policies, and so on. Such continuities help to give temporal continuity to the succession of governments, enabling us to call every national government in Washington, DC for 200 years a 'US' government (ibid. 217).

Wendt adds that 'these temporal and existential continuities are explained by structures of *collective* knowledge to which individuals are socialized, and which they, through their actions, in turn reproduce' (ibid. 217, emphasis in original). According to 'early Wendt', the identity of a state depends on the continuity of its members' shared narrative, much as the identity of an individual depends on the continuity of her mental states.

The problem with Wendt's account of corporate identity is that it assumes that the members of a state share a uniform and stable narrative. On the contrary, as Bell (2003: 73–74) argues, 'there is no singular, irreducible national narrative, no essentialist "national identity" . . . there will always be dissent and the story will never be accepted consistently and universally'. For example, Canada's dominant narrative at the moment is that it is the inclusive, peaceful, post-national cousin of the United States. One counter-narrative is that it is a settler-colonial state with a brutal and violent past; another is that it is an assimilationist, English-protestant state. There is no single narrative by which Canada's identity could be clearly defined. In addition, the narrative of inclusiveness serves to inoculate Canada against responsibility for genocide against indigenous peoples and for repression of minorities, such as the internment of Japanese-Canadians during the Second World War. The dominant narrative of a state often forecloses important questions of state responsibility, including historical reparations, from the outset.

Wendt (2015) doubles down on the analogy between personal identity and corporate identity in his later work. He argues that states are not just agents, but *conscious* agents. His first move is to embrace 'enactivism' in the philosophy of mind, which holds that 'consciousness is a transaction between the mind and its environment' (ibid. 277); it is not simply a function of the brain. An enactivist would say that, in the process of reading this chapter online, the Internet is as much a part of the relevant conscious system as is the reader's brain. Enactivism raises the possibility that there are conscious systems that are non-biological and spatially distributed.

Wendt's (2015: 277–78) second move is to employ the concept of 'We-feeling', or the idea that groups have shared points of view akin to first-person perspectives. Some experiences, such as national pride, are irreducibly collective. Wendt's explanation of these collective experiences is that, through 'quantum entanglement', each individual's experience is 'non-locally connected' to the experiences of other members of the group (ibid. 278–79). If, as 'later Wendt' argues, consciousness is not entirely a function of individual brains, and groups can have subjective experiences, then states can be conscious agents as well as intentional agents.[10]

Wendt's argument for collective consciousness gives new meaning to his claim that corporate identity depends on 'a consciousness and memory of Self as a separate locus of thought and activity' (1999: 225). For early Wendt, 'consciousness' and 'memory' were merely metaphors for the shared experiences and narratives of the members of the state. For later Wendt, states literally have consciousness and memory. The crucial implication of this shift is that the common criterion for personal identity—psychological continuity—now applies straightforwardly to the state. According to psychological accounts of personal identity (e.g., Garrett, 1998; Shoemaker, 1970), I know that I am the same person as I was yesterday because I remember what I did yesterday, or because my thoughts today are causally connected to my thoughts yesterday. If states are conscious, then they too are the same persons as long as their mental states follow a continuous train.

Wendt's use of psychological continuity as the criterion for corporate identity runs up against an epistemological problem: 'If such higher-order consciousnesses exist, how would we know it?' (Keeley, 2007: 428) I know that I am the same person I was yesterday because I experience a continuous 'train of thought'; you can verify your identity in the same way. Although we do not have access to each other's thoughts, we can make imperfect judgments about

---

10. See also Schwitzgebel (2015), 'If Materialism is True, the United States is Probably Conscious.'

the identities of other human beings by analogy with ourselves (Husserl, 1988: §44, 49–54). However, we cannot know whether Canada is psychologically continuous for the simple reason that none of us are states. Only Canada could really know whether it has subjective experiences at all. Even if we accept Wendt's argument for collective consciousness, it does not help us to make practical judgments about state identity, since we do not have access to the 'thoughts' of states. It might be possible to discern the state's 'intentions', construed as laws and policies (Wendt, 1999: 222–23), but its subjective experiences are beyond the bounds of what we could possibly know.

Ascribing psychological properties to states stretches the analogy between states and human beings beyond the breaking point. While the agential answer to the Question of Ownership is initially plausible because it requires only a thin notion of corporate intention, the agential answer to the Question of Identity requires collective consciousness, or something like it. Contra Wendt (1999: 225), the identities of states seem more like those of 'beagles and bicycles' than like those of human beings. However, analogies with 'animal identity' and 'object identity' also will not carry us very far. Beagles seem more like humans than like states. They may not be self-conscious in the way that humans are, but they do appear to have some form of subjectivity, and they clearly display signs of psychological continuity—they remember people, places, objects, and commands. States seem more like bicycles: they cannot think for themselves, nor do anything without human agents. Admittedly, Wendt's view of corporate identity is an outlier among proponents of the agential theory. But Wendt is the only one who has a positive account of corporate identity at all.

The broader point, which extends far beyond Wendt, is that analogies with personal and physical identity would often be unhelpful even if they were conceptually sound. Corporate identity raises a unique set of problems. States unite, divide, dissolve, and reconstitute in ways that human beings and physical objects simply cannot. Individuals cannot secede from or annex one another, and bicycle parts cannot reassemble themselves. I examine the conceptual differences between personal, physical, and corporate identity in Chapter 4.

§5.3 The Agential Answer to the Question of Fulfilment

An important implication of the agential theory is that the responsibilities of states are 'non-distributive' (Erskine, 2001: 73; Lang, 2007: 245). If states are moral agents over and above their members, then the responsibilities of states must exist over and above the responsibilities of their members. However, since states act only through individuals, states cannot fulfil their responsibilities without distributing them to individuals. The debts of states must be paid by their subjects, and the treaty obligations of states must be implemented by their legislators and officials. The challenge for proponents of the agential theory is to reconcile the idea that states are distinct agents with the fact that their members inevitably bear the costs and burdens of their responsibilities.

The idea that corporate responsibilities are non-distributive came out of the debates in analytic philosophy about collective responsibility in the 1960s and 1970s (e.g., Cooper, 1968; Feinberg, 1968; Held, 1970). An important insight that emerged from these debates is that the responsibilities of individuals often cannot be deduced from the responsibilities of groups. As Held (1970: 93) argues, 'from the judgment "Collectivity C ought (ought not) to have done A", judgments of the form "Member M of C ought (ought not) to have done A" cannot be derived'. For example, it may be the case that the United States owes its bondholders ten million dollars this week, but this does not imply that any particular American owes these bondholders ten million dollars. Nor does it imply that each American owes the bondholders a fraction of this sum. Despite what journalists sometimes say, the debt of the United States is not equivalent to 'what every man, woman, and child in America owes' (Tanner, 2012), because the United States does not owe less money whenever an American dies. A corporate responsibility is not equivalent to a conjunction of individual responsibilities. In this sense, corporate responsibilities are non-distributive.

Proponents of the agential theory of state responsibility initially adopted the idea that corporate responsibilities are non-distributive. In the beginning, Erskine (2001: 73) argued that 'some duties [of states] cannot be distributed among individuals at all', and Lang (2007: 245) argued that 'crimes can be attributed to states *without* attributing them to individuals' (emphasis in original). However, proponents of the agential theory have largely abandoned this idea. As Pasternak (2013: 361) argues, 'it is invariably the case that states pass their responsibilities on to their citizens' (see also Collins, 2016; Collins and Lawford-Smith, 2016; Stilz, 2011). Erskine (2010: 263), recognizing that states' responsibilities are inevitably distributive, later turned her attention to 'the danger of harming innocent individuals while ostensibly punishing delinquent states'. Although sanctions, treaty obligations, reparations, and debts attach to states in the first instance, the costs and burdens distribute to their subjects. The question that now concerns proponents of the agential theory is how these costs and burdens ought to be distributed. There are two rival answers to the Question of Fulfilment within the agential tradition.

The 'authorization account' of distribution focuses on the structure of the state. As Stilz (2011) argues, citizens should bear the burdens of their state's responsibilities provided that it is 'a *democratic legal state*—one that guarantees citizens' personal inviolability, basic subsistence, freedom of belief and expression, and legislates a system of private rights that treats them equally and in which they have a democratic voice and vote' (ibid. 204, emphasis in original; see also Parrish, 2009). Any state that meets these conditions counts as an authorized representative of its citizens, including citizens who do not personally support their state or identify with it: 'if a state that credibly interprets my basic right exists, then I *necessarily authorize* it—whether I agree to join it or not—since I require its system of law to secure me against others' interference' (ibid. 200, emphasis in original). The citizens of a democratic legal state can justifiably be burdened with its responsibilities because they are the authors of its actions. According to the authorization account, then, distributing the responsibilities of the state is justified as long as the structure of the state is just.

The 'participation account' of distribution focuses on the actions and intentions of the citizens of the state. Pasternak (2010, 2013) argues that the authorization account 'is grounded in a problematic understanding of the notion of authorization, which ignores citizens' own attitudes to their state, thus allowing them too little control over their liabilities' (2013: 362). She uses Kutz's (2000) notion of 'intentional participation' to develop a distributive principle that leaves room for individual attitudes. The members of a state count as its 'intentional members', and therefore can justifiably be made to bear the burdens of its responsibilities, provided that four conditions obtain:

> [1] they are members of the state according to its membership criteria; [2] they are reflectively aware of their citizenship status and that status informs some of their activities (e.g. applying for a passport, claiming state benefits, voting); [3] they are aware (or can be reasonably be expected to be aware) of their state's policies, or of the fact that there are some policies of which they are ignorant; [4] and their membership status is not imposed on them against their will (Pasternak, 2013: 371).

Although there is a strong presumption that the citizens of a state that respects human rights are its intentional members, this presumption is not absolute. Pasternak's (2013: 374–77) account allows citizens who publicly, consistently, and credibly disavow their citizenship—such as some ultra-Orthodox Jewish groups in Israel—to opt out of their share of the state's responsibilities. According to the participation account, what matters is not whether the structure of the state is just, but whether the members of the state are complicit in its actions.

I return to the authorization and participation accounts of distribution in Chapter 5. For now, the important point is that both employ the same structure of argument: states are corporate moral agents, distinct from the individual moral agents who compose them; but states cannot act on their own, so their responsibilities must be distributed to their members in order to be fulfilled; therefore, we need a principle that determines whether a given distribution of responsibility is just. The distributive principles that proponents of the agential theory propose are *ad hoc* amendments to the theory rather than logical implications of it. The idea of corporate moral agency does not help us to adjudicate between the authorization and participation accounts of distribution, and it is possible to accept one or the other without accepting the idea of corporate moral agency. *Ad hoc* amendments to the agential theory are necessary because the straightforward implication of corporate moral agency—that the responsibilities of states and individuals are mutually independent—is clearly false. If states and individuals are separate moral agents, then their responsibilities should also be separate—just as much so as the responsibilities of different individuals. The fact that the responsibilities of states and individuals are inextricable, and that the agential theory therefore requires patchwork amendments, is a reason to be sceptical of the agential theory.

The analogy between states and human beings is no more helpful for answering the Question of Fulfilment than it is for answering the Question of Identity. Although we might think that 'collective agents act by having their constituents act, in just the way that individual agents act by having parts of themselves act' (Collins and Lawford-Smith, 2016: 156), there is a crucial difference. The constituents of a state, unlike the constituents of an individual, are themselves moral agents. We depend on our members (i.e., appendages) to fulfil our responsibilities, but we do not distribute our responsibilities to them. Joyce's responsibility to pay back a loan does not imply that her arm has a responsibility to hand over an envelope of money. Corporate entities are unique in that they fulfil their responsibilities only by distributing them to others. This process of distribution does not have an individual-level analogue.

———

The appeal of the agential theory is that it promises a metaphysical foundation for state responsibility. Corporate moral agency eliminates the need to rely on juridical or political fictions. The line of argument, if it works, is powerful: if we think individuals are moral agents, then we should, for the same reasons, think states are moral agents. Yet there are reasons for doubt. First, although there are plausible accounts of corporate moral agency, they apply only to small, participatory groups, such as committees and teams. Corporate moral agency does not scale up to the state. Second, corporate identities are not closely analogous to personal identities. Even if states do have intentions, they do not have anything like consciousness or subjectivity, and the most important problems of corporate identity—secession, unification, and annexation—do not have interpersonal analogues. Third, unlike human beings, states are made up of moral agents. The relation between a state's responsibilities and its members' responsibilities has no individual-level analogue. The state–human analogy is of little help for answering the Questions of Identity and Fulfilment.

§6 States as Legal Persons: The Functional Theory

The international law of state responsibility has entirely different origins and influences. Whereas the agential theory grew out of Anglo-American philosophy, the law of state responsibility developed largely from post–First World War reparations law. As Crawford (2013a: 27–28) describes, the Treaty of Versailles 'placed issues of responsibility for the major events of international war and peace irrevocably within the domain of the "legal"'. Efforts to codify the law of state responsibility began in 1924, when the Assembly of the League of Nations convened a committee to identify and codify the most important areas of customary international law.[11] The United Nations International Law Commission (ILC) continued this work following the Second World War, and, after several decades, completed its *Articles on Responsibility of States for Internationally Wrongful Acts* (ILC, 2001).[12] Although the *Articles* have not yet been turned into a treaty or convention, they are widely considered to be an authoritative codification of the customary law of state responsibility (Crawford, 2013a: 42–44; Olleson, forthcoming). The *Articles* are of theoretical interest because they contain a 'functional' theory of state responsibility that has little in common with the agential theory.

The idea of corporate agency is notably absent from the international law of state responsibility. States are held legally responsible not because they are agents, but because they act vicariously through human agents. The ILC (2001: 35) makes this point in the Commentaries that accompany its *Articles*.

---

11. The resulting *Articles* have a very long and complicated drafting history that I cannot adequately address here. See Crawford (2013a: 3–44), Malekian (1985: 3–29), Matsui (1993), and Spinedi (1989).

12. International lawyers use 'state responsibility' narrowly to refer to responsibility for wrongdoing. As Crawford (2013a: 99) describes, 'the category "state responsibility" covers the field of the responsibility of states for internationally wrongful conduct, part of the international law of obligations'. The other major part is the law of treaties (UN, 1969).

The State is a real organized entity, a legal person with full authority to act under international law. But to recognize this is not to deny the elementary fact that the State cannot act of itself. An 'act of the State' must involve some action or omission by a human being or group: 'States can act only by and through their agents and representatives.'[13] The question is which persons should be considered as acting on behalf of the State, i.e. what constitutes an 'act of the State' for the purposes of State responsibility.

There are many similar remarks in the secondary legal literature and in the decisions of international courts. Cassese (2005: 246) writes that 'for a State to be responsible it is necessary first of all to establish whether the conduct of an individual may be attributed to it', and Nollkaemper (2003: 616) writes that 'in factual terms states act through individuals'. Crawford and Watkins (2010: 287) emphasize that 'states, lacking bodies of their own, can only act through the agency of others—in the end, of natural persons'. The relevant 'agents' for international lawyers are state *officials*.

The idea of corporate intentionality, which is foundational for the agential theory, is treated as both irrelevant and mysterious by international lawyers. The ILC's *Articles* include 'no requirement of *mens rea* on the part of a delinquent state: an act incurring state responsibility could occur even where a state did not undertake the act intentionally' (Crawford, 2013a: 37). Crawford later adds that 'the "intention" underlying state conduct is a notoriously difficult idea, quite apart from questions of proof' (ibid. 62). Even where proof of intent is necessary for state responsibility, it is the intent of state officials that counts (ILC, 2001: 34). Brownlie (1983: 38) similarly argues that 'metaphors based on intention (*dolus*) or negligence (*culpa*) of *natural* persons tend to be unhelpful' for understanding state responsibility, and he suggests that a more appropriate analogue is a principal–agent relation: 'the issues in inter-state relations are often analogous to those arising from the activities of employees and enterprises in English law, where the *legal* person held liable is incapable of close control over its agents' (ibid. 38, emphasis in original). In accordance with this analogy, international lawyers often describe state officials as 'state agents' (e.g., Cassese, 2007: 656, 661; ILC, 2001: 78–80; Momtaz, 2010: 237–38). States are like principals on behalf of which their officials act rather than like agents in their own right.

However, states differ from principals in one crucial respect. While principals authorize their own agents, and hence must be capable of acting on their own, states act *only* through their agents. An employer can authorize her own employees, but a state cannot authorize its own officials. International lawyers rely on the concept of function to explain how the agents of the state act on its

13. The ILC quotes from the *German Settlers in Poland* case (PCIJ, 1923).

behalf. The state is a 'community' or 'system of administration', and its agents are the 'organs' who perform its 'functions', such as controlling territory and entering into relations with other states (Brownlie, 1983: 135, 141; Crawford, 2013a: 113–15; Kelsen, 1970: 150). The language of 'organs' and 'functions' is a vestige of an organic conception of the state, which has since been replaced by the idea of the state as a system or organization.

Proponents of the agential theory have overlooked the functional theory entirely. The reason is that they have projected their own idea of corporate agency onto international law.[14] Lang (2007: 244) writes that 'since the heyday of positivism in the nineteenth century, states have been considered the primary agents of international law' and that 'the passage of the Articles on State Responsibility by the International Law Commission suggests that states can be considered responsible agents' (2008: 23). Wendt (1999: 10) declares that 'international politics as we know it today would be impossible without attributions of corporate agency, a fact recognized by international law'. Tollefsen (2002: 396) argues, more generally, that 'our practice of attributing responsibility to organizations . . . seems to presuppose that organizations literally have intentional states. For we could not hold them legally and morally responsible for an act unless they *intended* to commit the act' (emphasis in original). The agential theory is so dominant in International Relations, Political Theory, and Philosophy that its proponents cannot recognize an alternative theory of state responsibility when they see it.

I describe the functional theory's answers to the three Fundamental Questions in the next three subsections. But first, a word of caution is necessary. Proponents of the agential and functional theories have different aims, and any comparison must take this into account. Political theorists, International Relations scholars, and philosophers are concerned primarily with developing a normative justification for the practice of holding states responsible. International lawyers are concerned primarily with developing a set of procedures and criteria for making judgments about whether, in particular cases, a state is responsible. There is a danger here of criticizing international law for not being political philosophy. That said, the law of state responsibility is theoretically sophisticated, and it provides a unique set of answers to the Fundamental Questions. Comparing legal and ethical approaches to state responsibility is fruitful as long as we avoid evaluating one approach according to the aims of the other.

14. See Fleming (2017b) for a detailed analysis of how and why philosophers, political theorists, and International Relations scholars have misunderstood the international law of state responsibility.

§6.1 The Functional Answer to the Question of Ownership

According to the functional theory, states take ownership of actions through 'attribution', which refers to the process of attaching or imputing an action of an individual to a state (Condorelli and Kress, 2010). For example, in *United States v. Iran*, the International Court of Justice (1980: 35) ruled that the actions of the Iranian protesters who occupied the American embassy in 1979 were attributable to Iran; their actions were Iran's actions. All actions are performed by individuals, but some actions are attributable to states, meaning that they count as acts of state.[15]

The most basic rule of attribution is that 'the conduct of any State organ shall be considered an act of that State under international law, whether the organ exercises legislative, executive, judicial or any other functions' (ILC, 2001: Art. 4). The use of 'organ' rather than 'official' in the *Articles* is indicative of the post-organic or organizational conception of the state that underpins international law. Whereas 'official' implies an office, 'organ' implies a function (Kelsen, 1970: 150–58). For example, soldiers are state organs because they perform the function of defence. Other state organs include legislators, judges, diplomats, municipal officials, and police officers (Crawford, 2013a: 118–24; ILC, 2001: 41). Whether an entity is a state organ depends on its function: 'The key element is the role of the entity or official as part of the administration of the state' (Brownlie, 1983: 141).

The actions of private entities that 'exercise elements of the governmental authority' are also attributable to the state (ILC, 2001: Art. 5). The idea of governmental authority, although not functional on the face of it, ultimately collapses into the idea of function. Brownlie (1983: 136) uses 'authority' and 'function' interchangeably: 'state authority has been delegated to local traditional and religious authorities ... state functions have at other times been farmed out to private individuals'. Crawford (2013a: 129) notes that 'there is no consensus as to precisely what constitutes "governmental authority"', and he defines it primarily in terms of three sets of functions: detention and discipline, immigration control and quarantine, and seizure of property. Employees of private prisons exercise governmental authority because they perform the state functions of detention and discipline. In other words, they are '*de facto* organs' (Cassese, 2007: 656; Momtaz, 2010: 243). The rule is that the actions of entities that 'exercise functions of a public character' are attributable to the state, even if these entities do not have formal state authority (Brownlie, 1983: 162; see also ILC, 2001: 43).

---

15. The fact that an action is attributed to the state does not mean that the individual who performed it is off the hook. Some actions 'can be attributed twice: both to the state and the individual' (Nollkaemper, 2003: 618–19; see also ILC, 2001: Art. 58).

Actions can be attributed to the state even when the 'official authorities' are absent or incapable, such as in times of revolution or civil war (ILC, 2001: Art. 9). When private individuals perform state functions in the absence of an official government—for instance, by acting as police officers or border guards—their actions count as acts of state. The ILC (2001: 49) emphasizes that 'the nature of the activity performed is given more weight than the existence of a formal link between the actors and the organization of the State'. The decisive factor is, again, whether the action is performed to fulfil a state function.

The actions of a *de jure* or *de facto* state organ are attributable to the state 'even if it exceeds its authority or contravenes instructions' (ILC, 2001: Art. 7). For example, in *Caire v. Mexico,* two Mexican military personnel murdered a French citizen after trying to extort money from him. Although the personnel acted outside of their authority, the French-Mexican Claims Commission ruled that their actions were nevertheless attributable to Mexico because they acted under the guise of their status as state organs (UN, 2006: 517). What ultimately determines whether the actions of an individual are attributable to the state is not whether he acted under the authority of the state, but whether he 'acted by using the means and powers pertaining to his public function' (Cassese, 2005: 246). Function, not authority or agency, is thus the foundational concept in the international law of state responsibility.

Another important concept in the rules of attribution is consent. Even if an action is not performed by a state organ, it may be attributable to the state 'if and to the extent that the State acknowledges and adopts the conduct in question as its own' (ILC, 2001: Art. 11). This rule was at work in *United States v. Iran* (International Court of Justice, 1980). The protesters who occupied the American embassy in Tehran were neither *de jure* nor *de facto* organs of Iran, so their actions could not have been attributed to Iran on purely functional grounds. Their actions became acts of state when Ayatollah Khomeini endorsed them (ILC, 2001: 52–53).[16] Attribution by consent is uncommon for wrongful actions, but it is the norm for many other kinds of responsibilities, such as debts and treaty obligations. A state owes money that it borrows and is bound by treaties that it signs. Although the concept of consent is sometimes thought to be the foundational one in international law, it presupposes the concept of function, because a state can consent only through its organs. As the *Vienna Convention on the Law of Treaties* says, heads of state and foreign ministers can offer their state's consent 'in virtue of their functions' (UN, 1969:

---

16. In this case, the responsibility of Iran was overdetermined: Iran was responsible for the occupation of the US embassy both because it endorsed the protesters' actions and because it neglected its duty to protect the embassy. Either would have been sufficient.

Art. 7.1(a)). The functional relationship between the state and its organs is thus a precondition for the state's consent.

The rule regarding 'organs placed at the disposal of a State by another State' (ILC, 2001: Art. 6) follows from a combination of function and consent. If one state loans a diplomat to another, the diplomat's actions are attributable to the receiving state provided that she (1) performs a function for the receiving state (2) with the consent of the receiving state. As the ILC's (2001: 44) Commentaries describe, 'not only must the organ be appointed to perform functions appertaining to the State at whose disposal it is placed . . . the organ must also act in conjunction with the machinery of that State and under its exclusive direction and control'. The second condition is intended to exclude 'situations in which functions of the "beneficiary" State are performed without its consent, as when a State [is] placed in a position of dependence' (ibid.). One state cannot hijack another state by 'volunteering' its organs to perform the other state's functions. However, if the receiving state does give its consent, it becomes just as much responsible for the actions of its 'borrowed' organs as it is for the actions of its *de jure* organs.

An important implication of the functional theory is that there is a direct line of responsibility that runs to the state from each of its organs—whether *de jure, de facto,* or borrowed. Although the chain of command might matter for determining individual criminal responsibility, 'the position of an official in the internal hierarchy has no relevance to the question of state responsibility' (Brownlie, 1983: 134; ILC, 2001: 40). The actions of a corporal are attributable to the state no less than the actions of a general, since both perform the function of defence.

The functional theory also permits no distinction between legitimate and illegitimate organs. The actions of any insurrectional movement that successfully seizes power are attributable to the state. All of the insurrectional movement's actions, including during its struggle for power, count as acts of state (ILC, 2001: Art. 10). The ILC's (2001: 51) Commentaries insist that 'no distinction should be made . . . between different categories of movements on the basis of any international "legitimacy" or of any illegality in respect of their establishment as a Government'. As Crawford (2013a: 172) adds, 'Article 10 treats all insurrections generally and makes no attempt to distinguish between a struggle for national liberation on the one hand and a simple rebellion on the other'. Considerations of legitimacy also have no bearing on other kinds of responsibilities: debts and treaty obligations are attributable to the state regardless of what kind of government borrowed the money or signed the treaty. (I return to this issue in Chapter 3.) In short, the actions of any 'functioning' government are attributable to the state.

The functional account of attribution allows international lawyers to sidestep the thorny issue of legitimacy. What matters for the purpose of determining what counts as an act of state is whether the individuals in question perform state functions; attribution does not depend on whether they perform their functions well or badly. Nor does attribution depend on whether governments are democratically elected, have popular support, or respect human rights.

The problem with the functional answer to the Question of Ownership is that it allows the state to become a 'responsibility shield'. State organs can borrow money to enrich themselves, sign self-serving treaties, wage wars of conquest, and leave the state—and ultimately its subjects—with the resulting debts and obligations. For example, the Mobutu government borrowed about fourteen billion US dollars in the name of Zaire between 1965 and 1997 (Ndikumana and Boyce, 1998). Although much of the money was used for self-enrichment and nepotism, the debt was nevertheless attributed to Zaire, so the people of Zaire (later the Democratic Republic of Congo) were made to pay for their own oppression. Similarly, holding Iraq liable for reparations after Saddam Hussein's 1990 invasion of Kuwait effectively made many Iraqis—especially Kurds—pay for the wrongs of a regime of which they were also victims. Mobutu and Hussein were certainly state organs, since they did perform state functions, but it seems perverse to attribute their corrupt and self-serving actions to Congo and Iraq. The functional answer to the Question of Ownership fails to distinguish representation of the state from misrepresentation of the state.

§6.2 The Functional Answer to the Question of Identity

The rules of state continuity determine whether a state persists over time as the same legal person. These rules follow from what Crawford (2007: Chapter 2) calls 'the principle of effectiveness': an entity counts as a state provided that it effectively performs the functions of a state, such as controlling territory and concluding treaties. The corollary is that a state retains its identity as long as it continues to function as a state.

The first rule is that 'acquisition or loss of territory does not in itself affect the continuity of the State' (Crawford, 2007: 673; Marek, 1968: 15). Canada remained the same state after Newfoundland joined the federation in 1949, and Sudan remained the same state after South Sudan seceded in 2011. Even 'the total change of territory by a people which, under the same government and law, settles in a different territory, leaves the identity of the state intact' (Kunz, 1955: 72). A state cannot exist without territory,[17] since it needs territory in order to function as a state, but it does not need any particular territory.

---

17. There is one important exception: 'annexation of the territory of a State as a result of the illegal use of force does not bring about the extinction of the State' (Crawford, 2007: 690). I return to the issue of annexation and the related issue of relocated states in Chapter 4.

The second rule is that changes in population do not affect the continuity of the state (Crawford, 2007: 678; Kunz, 1955: 71–72). A state retains its identity despite births, deaths, immigration, and emigration, even if these changes alter the demographics of the state or result in a complete turnover in its membership: 'The young US with five million and the present US with one hundred and sixty million of inhabitants is, of course, the identical state in law' (Kunz, 1955: 71). A state needs a population in order to function as a state, but it does not need any particular population.

The third rule is that changes in government do not affect the continuity of the state (Crawford, 2007: 678–88; Marek, 1968: 24–40). The United States has a very different government than it did in the 1990s, but it is nevertheless the same state. Even 'the overthrow of a governmental system does not affect the continuity of the State' (Crawford, 2007: 679). Iran was therefore the same state before and after the Islamic Revolution. A state needs a government in order to function as a state,[18] but it does not need any particular government, nor any particular form of government.

The rules of state continuity, like Erskine's account of institutional moral agency (see §5.2), provide a purely negative account of corporate identity. They tell us that the identity of a state does *not* depend on its territory, population, government, or form of government, but they do not tell us on what the identity of a state *does* depend. However, Crawford (2007: 671) argues that the criteria for statehood can also be used as positive criteria for state identity. In his view, a state retains its identity as long as it has the same nucleus, or 'substantially the same constituent features': 'A State may be said to continue as such so long as an identified polity exists with respect to a significant part of a given territory and people' (ibid.). For example, the Russian Federation inherited the legal personality of the Soviet Union, including its seat on the United Nations Security Council, because Russia was the core of the Soviet Union in terms of both population and territory (ibid. 676–77). A state retains its identity over time insofar as its features remain 'substantially' the same.

There are two problems with using the criteria for statehood as criteria for state identity. The first is that the notion of 'substantial continuity' is of little help when two or more contemporary states share core features with the same antecedent state. Which state is identical with pre–Revolution China—Taiwan or the People's Republic of China? According to Crawford's criterion, both

---

18. As with territory, there is an important exception: 'belligerent occupation does not affect the continuity of the State' (Crawford, 2007: 688; see also Van Elsuwege, 2003). Occupied states retain their identities even when their governments are temporarily exiled or eliminated.

states seem to have equally valid claims to be the 'real' China. The People's Republic shares far more territory with pre–Revolution China, but Taiwan inherited the government of pre–Revolution China. (I return to this case in Chapter 4.) Unless different kinds of continuity carry different weight—for instance, territorial continuity matters more than governmental continuity (Kunz, 1955: 73–74)—there is no way to adjudicate cases in which multiple states are substantially continuous with the same antecedent state. Yet it is difficult to see how proponents of the functional theory could justify assigning different weights to different criteria for statehood, since territory, population, and government are equally necessary for a functioning state.

The deeper problem with using the criteria for statehood as criteria for state identity is that it confuses two kinds of identity: 'type identity' and 'token identity'. As Bartelson (1998: 297) explains, 'type identity concerns the identity of the state as a general concept, whereas token identity concerns . . . individual states'. The criteria for statehood are criteria for type identity, while state continuity concerns the identities of token states (such as China and Russia). The difficulty, as Craven (1998: 160) points out, is that an account of token identity cannot be derived from an account of type identity.

> 'Identity' assumes that individual states, whilst being members of a particular class of social or legal entities, also possess certain distinguishing features that differentiate one from another. Identity, therefore, presumes personality but is concerned with what is personal or exceptional in the nature of the subject. This can never be provided by reference to the traditional requirements of statehood.

Territory, population, and government are features that an entity must have in order to be a member of the *class* of states, not identifying features of particular states. A state must meet the conditions for statehood in order to retain its (token) identity over time; it cannot remain the *same* state if it ceases to be a state altogether.[19] However, if a state's territory, population, and government are not essential to its (token) identity, as the rules of state continuity imply, then the fact that a state has a particular population, territory, or government is not sufficient to identify it as a particular state. If the identity of the People's Republic of China does not depend on its particular configuration of territory, population, and government, then it is not possible to use these features to identify it over time, let alone to determine whether the People's Republic or Taiwan is continuous with pre–Revolution China.

---

19. However, as I argue in §21, a non-state entity can be continuous with a state. For instance, a state can become a province of another state while remaining the same corporate entity.

There is a deep tension, if not a contradiction, between the rules of state continuity (which are functional) and Crawford's 'substantial continuity' or 'nucleus' account of state identity (which is not). On one hand, the rules of state continuity say that a state's identity does not depend on its particular territory, population, or government. On the other, Crawford's account implies that a state's identity does depend on its particular territory, population, and government. He wants to maintain *both* that the features of a state are not essential to its identity *and* that it is possible to use these features to identify a state over time.

§6.3 The Functional Answer to the Question of Fulfilment

The ILC's (2001) *Articles* provide no specific guidance about how the costs and burdens of states' responsibilities should be distributed to their subjects. International law's answer to the Question of Fulfilment is implicit but clear: the laws of each state should determine the distribution of responsibility. There are currently only two pieces of legal literature about the Question of Fulfilment.

Crawford and Watkins (2010) argue that the practice of holding states responsible is justified despite the fact that 'the population that is eventually called upon to carry the costs of responsibility includes members who are, by any standard, morally blameless' (ibid. 290). They provide two justifications for distributing the costs of states' responsibilities to their subjects. The first is that these costs are usually 'so negligible as to be barely worth mentioning' (ibid. 293). The damages awarded against states by the International Court of Justice or by international tribunals or arbitrators have rarely been large enough to have any noticeable effects on their subjects. There have only been a few exceptions, such as the reparations levied against Iraq after its invasion and occupation of Kuwait (ibid. 294–95). Yet even when the costs are significant, Crawford and Watkins argue that subjects ought to bear them: 'In cases where one of two states must bear the costs of injury, then assuming that costs are always covered through general taxation, one of two populations is bound to end up worse off than it otherwise would have been' (ibid. 295). It is preferable, they suggest, to impose the costs on the population that has suffered less already.

One problem with this argument is that, in some cases, the population of the wrongdoer state has actually suffered more. Kuwaitis suffered greatly as a result of the Iraqi invasion and occupation, but Iraqis suffered triply from Saddam Hussein's rule, the American counter-invasion, and the sanctions against Iraq. Then, on top of it all, Iraqis had to bear the costs of reparations to Kuwait. If the goal is to shift losses to the population that has suffered the least, as

Crawford and Watkins suggest, then the population of the 'victim' state will sometimes be the one that should bear the costs.

Another problem is that the 'negligible burdens' argument applies only to some kinds of state responsibility, such as responsibility for wrongdoing. Although it is true that states' reparative obligations are rarely large enough to impose significant costs on their subjects, this is not true for other kinds of responsibilities (Murphy, 2010: 303). There are many cases in which sovereign debts have been so burdensome that they have severely diminished the life prospects of the debtor state's subjects. The International Monetary Fund (2016) lists 39 Heavily Indebted Poor Countries (HIPC), whose massive debt burdens hinder their development. Before the HIPC Initiative for debt relief, these countries 'were, on average, spending slightly more on debt service than on health and education combined' (ibid. 2). Even the populations of developed countries can be seriously harmed by sovereign debts.

> In Argentina, where life expectancy at birth is 75 years and approximately 97 percent of the population is literate, almost half the population was pushed below the poverty line by the trough of the economic crisis in 2002, the year following the country's debt default and collapse of its fixed exchange rate system (Ethics & International Affairs, 2007: 2).

Greece and Cyprus provide more recent examples of how the populations of developed states can be crushed by the burdens of their state's financial obligations. The costs that subjects bear are indeed negligible in some cases, but there are many cases in which the costs are burdensome.

Crawford and Watkins (2010: 296–97) also make a quasi-Rawlsian argument for distributing states' responsibilities to their members. They begin with the claim that a fair distribution of responsibility is one that 'would be chosen above any alternative in a position of partial ignorance, in which we were unaware of the particular state or population to which we belonged but we knew the various kinds of effects which different forms of liability had on different types of states and their populations' (ibid. 296). They argue that, behind this 'veil of ignorance', people would choose an international legal system that assigns responsibility to states: 'in the crucial choice between imposing remedial responsibilities on states or on assignable individuals (officials, leaders, etc.), we would choose the former over the latter' (ibid. 297). There are two reasons why people would prefer state responsibility to individual responsibility. First, they could be more confident that, if they were harmed, they would be able to seek compensation from someone or something that has the means to pay. States have much deeper pockets than individuals. Second, people would choose state responsibility because it provides means of redress for systemic wrongs, and in cases in which it is impossible to identify the individual wrongdoers.

People behind the veil of ignorance would no doubt choose an international legal system in which reparative obligations are assigned primarily to states rather than to individuals. Yet the 'crucial choice between imposing remedial responsibilities on states or on assignable individuals' (ibid. 296) is not the only relevant choice. If people were asked to choose a principle for distributing states' responsibilities, they would not choose the one that international law currently uses: let domestic law determine the distribution of responsibility within each state, and tough luck to those who happen to be stuck in states with corrupt or predatory governments. Instead, people behind the veil of ignorance would want to guard themselves against the possibility of ending up in Mobutu's Congo or Hussein's Iraq. They would choose a system that ensures that they would not be crushed by massive debts and reparations from loans and wars that they had nothing to do with. To this end, they would choose an international legal system in which responsibilities are assigned only to 'legitimate' states. (I return to the issue of legitimacy in Chapter 3.) They certainly would not choose the system that currently exists.

Crawford and Watkins (2010: 297–98) recognize that their quasi-Rawlsian argument does not justify the current practice of state responsibility in its entirety. They admit that people behind the veil of ignorance would be unlikely to expose themselves to the risk of having to pay enormous reparations, such as the reparations that Germany was saddled with after the First World War. Their suggestion is to create a special insurance scheme for aggression that spreads the costs of reparations among all states (ibid. 298). But if it makes sense to spread the costs of reparations for aggression, then why not spread the burdens of other obligations as well? After all, as Crawford and Watkins (2010: 290) recognize, most subjects of 'wrongdoer' states bear no more personal responsibility than the subjects of 'victim' states. The same applies to the subjects of debtor states and creditor states.

Murphy (2010) takes up this instrumentalist line of argument in a reply to Crawford and Watkins. He doubts that distributing the state's responsibilities to its subjects can ever be justified on grounds of fairness or hypothetical consent. The justification will 'have to be instrumental—not justifying the imposition of burdens on people because they are morally responsible, but in spite of the fact that they are not' (ibid. 306). The costs that subjects bear for the responsibilities of their states are necessary evils that must often be tolerated in the pursuit of some greater objective, such as peace or stability (ibid. 311). If, at some point in the future, a better mechanism for distributing costs becomes feasible, then the current mechanism should be abandoned.

Like the agential answers to the Question of Fulfilment, the functional answers are *ad hoc* amendments to the theory rather than logical implications of it. The functional theory implies nothing about how the responsibilities of states should be distributed to their subjects. On the contrary, the very structure of the functional theory excludes the Question of Fulfilment. By focusing entirely on the relation between the state and its organs, the functional theory obscures the equally important relation between the government and its subjects.

———

The appeal of the functional theory is that it allows us to set aside many difficult metaphysical and normative questions. It does not matter whether states are corporate agents; all that matters is that states have organs that act on their behalf. Nor does it matter whether these organs are legitimate; all that matters is that they perform state functions. While issues of agency and intentionality can be sidestepped without adverse consequences, sidestepping issues of legitimacy has turned the practice of holding states responsible into a tool of the wicked. The functional theory allows corrupt governments to rack up debts, line their pockets, and leave the state with the bill. On top of that, because international law defers to domestic law in determining how states' responsibilities ought to be distributed, the victims of corrupt and predatory regimes are made to pay for their own exploitation. Another problem with the functional theory is that its account of state identity is conceptually confused. Although statehood can be defined in terms of functions, such as controlling territory and entering into relations with other states, the identities of particular states cannot be. The functional theory is dysfunctional without an account of legitimacy and an account of corporate identity.

§7 The Limitations of the Agential and Functional Theories

The agential and functional theories are both incomplete. Neither provides adequate answers to the Three Fundamental Questions, because neither the 'agent' analogy nor the 'principal' analogy fully captures the conceptual structure of state responsibility.

States are like human agents in two important respects: actions are attributed to them, and they have unique identities that are denoted by proper names. But there are also two important differences between states and human agents: states merge and divide in ways that human beings cannot, and the process of distributing a state's responsibilities to its subjects has no individual-level analogue. The agential theory is best thought of as a heuristic. It is sometimes useful to think of states as giant individuals. For instance, it might be useful for the sake of simplicity to think of a treaty between two states as a contract between two individuals, or to think of war reparations as torts paid by a single perpetrator to a single victim. But these analogies are bound to lead us astray if we take them too far. Treaties are like interpersonal contracts in that they are voluntary agreements, but they are unlike contracts in that treaties can outlive the individual signatories.[20] War reparations are like torts in that they are payments to compensate for wrongdoing, but reparations are unlike torts in that most of the people who bear the costs are not the people who committed the wrongs. The state/human analogy that underpins the agential theory does not need to be pressed very hard before it breaks down.

The same warning applies to the functional theory. States are like principals in one important respect: they act vicariously through representatives or agents. It is sometimes useful to think of the relation between the state and its officials as a principal–agent relation. A treaty between two states is a bit like a contract between two principals, each of whom signs the contract through a lawyer. Reparations against states for the actions of their officials are a bit like torts against employers for the actions of their employees. However, these analogies also have limits. States differ from principals in two important respects: they are incapable of authorizing their own agents, and they are made up of agents. Focusing on the relation between the state and its officials obscures the role of subjects, both in authorizing these officials and in bearing the costs of the state's responsibilities. If a war is waged on behalf of one state and against another, then it seems obvious that the 'perpetrator' state should compensate the 'victim' state. Yet the subjects of the 'perpetrator' state may or may not be the authors of the war; they may even be among its victims.

The broader point is that we should be careful with analogies between state responsibility and individual responsibility. Although these analogies are sometimes helpful, and perhaps even unavoidable, they should be used for illustration rather than for demonstration. An analogy between state responsibility and some other form of responsibility (individual or collective) is merely suggestive; it proves nothing. Every such analogy should be supplemented with a principled argument that can stand on its own. It is a mistake to try to transplant any theory of individual responsibility onto the state. What is needed is a theory of responsibility that is designed for the state. As I argue in the next chapter, Hobbes lays the groundwork for a theory of this kind.

---

20. See Fleming (2020) on the disanalogy between treaties and contracts.

2

Hobbes and the Personality
of the State

ONE OF the central claims that Hobbes makes in each of his major political works is that the state is a person.[1] The state can be said to make laws, sign treaties, borrow money, and wage war. Proponents of the agential and functional theories of state responsibility would agree. However, Hobbes' state is not the kind of person that proponents of the agential theory or the functional theory have in mind. Hobbes does not mean that the state is a corporate agent, despite the fact that he sometimes equates 'person' with 'actor' (see §11.1 below). Nor does he mean that the state is a principal or an organism, despite the fact that he describes the state as an 'Author' and an 'Artificial Animal' (see §11.2). This chapter intervenes in the debate in Hobbes scholarship about what kind of person his state is. It then proceeds to lay out the structure of the Hobbesian theory of state responsibility.

My analysis of Hobbes in this chapter is rather long, fine-grained, and text-focused, but it is necessary for the broader argument. Readers who are solely interested in contemporary issues of state responsibility can get away with reading only this introductory section and the last two sections of this chapter (§11, §12), provided that they are willing to take my interpretation of Hobbes for granted.

The chapter has five sections. The first describes the tension in *Leviathan* between Hobbes' definition of 'person' and his claim that the state is a person. On one hand, he says that persons are actors or representatives. One the other, he says that the state is a person but *not* an actor or representative. The second section resolves this tension using Hobbes' alternative definition of 'person'

---

1. The chapter expands on an earlier article, 'The Two Faces of Personhood: Hobbes, Corporate Agency, and the Personality of the State', which was first published online in October 2017 in the *European Journal of Political Theory* (Fleming forthcoming b).

from Chapter 42 of *Leviathan*, which instead defines persons as represented things, or representees. I show that this sense of personhood is essential for understanding how Hobbes uses 'person' throughout his political works. The third section revisits Hobbes' theory of the state in light of the Chapter 42 definition. I argue that, in terms of his theatrical metaphor, Hobbes' state is best understood as a character rather than an actor. Whereas a Hobbesian assembly, such as a legislature, is a fictional actor, Hobbes' state is a fictional character. The fourth section explains how Hobbes' theory of the state differs from the agential and functional theories. I show that it is neither a rudimentary theory of corporate agency, as it is often described, nor an organicist theory of the state, as it might also be interpreted. The fifth section explains how Hobbes' idea of state personality translates into a theory of state responsibility. What makes Hobbes' idea of personhood unique and valuable is that it decouples personhood from metaphysical conceptions of agency; it explains how states and other entities can be persons even though they do not have any intrinsic capacity for rationality, intentionality, or action.

§8 The Skinner–Runciman Debate

Hobbes defines the state or 'Common-wealth' as a 'Multitude [of men] united in one Person' (*L* XVII. 260).[2] Although he had developed an elaborate typology of persons in the previous chapter, he does not tell the reader what type of person the state is. Nowhere does he provide an explicit answer. His many descriptions of the state invite confusion: 'by Art is created that great LEVIATHAN called a COMMONWEALTH, or STATE, (in latine CIVITAS) which is but an Artificiall Man' and, as he later calls it, a 'Mortall God' (*L* Intro. 16, XVII. 260).

Skinner (1999) and Runciman (2000b) have tried to figure out where in Hobbes' typology of persons the state fits. The focal point of their debate is the definition of 'person' at the beginning of Chapter 16 of *Leviathan*.

> A PERSON, is he, whose words or actions are considered, either as his own, or as representing the words or actions of an other man, or of any other thing to whom they are attributed, whether Truly or by Fiction.
>
>   When they are considered as his owne, then is he called a *Naturall Person*: And when they are considered as representing the words and actions of an other, then is he a *Feigned or Artificiall person* (*L* XVI. 244).

2. Hobbes provides similar definitions of the state in his earlier works (*EL* XX.1, XIX.8; *DC* V.9, X.5). I cite *De cive* according to the chapter and paragraph numbers.

Hobbes uses an analogy with representation in the theatre to illustrate this rather convoluted definition. He points to the common etymology of 'person' and the Latin '*persona*', which 'signifies the *disguise*, or *outward appearance* of a man, counterfeited on the Stage' and 'more particularly that part of it, which disguiseth the face, as a Mask' (ibid.). The person is not the mask itself, but the actor who wears it: 'a *Person*, is the same that an *Actor* is, both on the stage and in common Conversation'—that is, a 'Representer of speech and action' (ibid.). To 'personate' someone or to 'beare his person' is to speak or act in his name.

Skinner and Runciman agree on many points of interpretation: (1) persons are actors or representatives; (2) natural persons are those that act in their own names, such as defendants who represent themselves in court; and (3) artificial persons are those that do not act in their own names (but a subtle disagreement remains, as I discuss below). Their main point of contention is whether the state is represented 'truly' or 'by fiction'. Skinner (1999: 21–22) argues that Hobbes' state is best described as a 'purely artificial person'. Like a character in a play, the state is *purely* artificial because it is incapable of being a natural person, or of acting in its own name. The state acts only through its representatives. But whereas a character in a play is represented only by fiction, the state is represented truly because it is truly considered to be responsible for its representatives' actions. Actions performed in the name of the state generate real responsibilities, such as debts and treaty obligations; actions performed in the name of Harry Potter do not. Runciman (2000b: 271–73) counters that Hobbes' state is a 'person by fiction'. Although we attribute actions to the state, we do so only by fiction, since the state cannot truly 'own up' to these actions any more than Harry Potter can. The costs of the state's debts and treaty obligations must be borne by human beings. Following Skinner's (2005: 178; 2009: 346–47) concession on this point, I take it to be settled that the state is represented by fiction.[3] I focus instead on Skinner and Runciman's side-debate about the meaning of 'artificial person', which points to a more fundamental issue about what kind of person Hobbes' state is.

Skinner (1999: 11–12) argues that an artificial person is someone who is represented by someone else, such as a defendant who is represented by a lawyer. He points to the grammar of the following sentence: 'when [the words and actions of a person] are considered as representing the words and actions of an other, then is he a *Feigned* or *Artificiall person*' (*L* XVI. 244). While the

---

3. However, as Douglass (2014: 141) points out, 'what the [Skinner–Runciman] exchange is lacking is a clear definition of "fiction"'. This is an important problem that I cannot adequately address here.

structure of the paragraph suggests that the referent of 'he' in the second clause is 'a person', which implies that an artificial person is a representative, Skinner argues that the referent of 'he' should be 'an other', which implies that an artificial person is instead a representee. According to the common reading of this passage, a lawyer is an artificial person when she represents a client. According to Skinner's reading, her client is the artificial person.

Skinner acknowledges that his interpretation does not fit well with the remainder of Chapter 16. As Hobbes (*L* XVI. 244) later writes, 'Of Persons Artificiall, some have their words and actions Owned by those whom they represent'. The artificial persons that Hobbes refers to here are clearly representatives. Moreover, if a person is 'a Representer, or Representative' (ibid.), then an artificial person should be an artificial representative. To justify his unconventional reading, Skinner (1999: 12) relies heavily on Chapter 15 of *De homine*, where Hobbes inverts his definition: '*a person is someone to whom the words and actions of men are attributed, whether they are his own or those of someone else. If they are his own, then the person is a natural one. If they are those of someone else, then the person is a fictional one*' (Skinner's translation).[4] Whereas Chapter 16 of *Leviathan* defines an artificial person as someone whose words or actions are attributed to someone else (a representative), Chapter 15 of *De homine* defines a fictional person—which Skinner in this case takes to be the same as an artificial person—as someone to whom someone else's words or actions are attributed (a representee). The latter, he suggests, is Hobbes' considered definition of 'artificial person'.

Runciman (2000b: 269–72) replies that Skinner has artificial personhood upside down: 'artificial person' ought to be read as 'artificial representative' rather than as 'artificial representee'. The artificial person in a lawyer–client relationship is the lawyer, not the client. Runciman argues that Skinner's reading puts more weight on Hobbes' later works than they can bear. He points out that the crucial distinctions between natural and artificial persons, and between true and fictional representation, are either missing or muddled in *De homine* and the Latin *Leviathan* (ibid. 274–77). He contends that the accounts of personhood in these works are not careful clarifications of the one in the English *Leviathan*, as Skinner assumes, but simplified accounts of personhood that serve Hobbes' political aim: to rule out the possibility that the state could act

---

4. Skinner (1999: 12) also appeals to the Latin *Leviathan*. Although he claims that 'the persons whom Hobbes had initially classified as artificial are now contrasted rather than equated with representatives', his own translation of the relevant passage suggests otherwise: 'if [a person] acts in the name of someone else, then the person is *Representative* of the one [i.e., the person] in whose name he acts' (ibid.). The representative and the representee are *both* persons.

independently of the sovereign. Runciman therefore gives priority to the more detailed account of personhood from Chapter 16 of *Leviathan,* where Hobbes defines persons as representatives: natural persons represent themselves; artificial persons represent others; artificial persons 'represent truly' when they are authorized by the entities that they represent; and artificial persons 'represent by fiction' when they are authorized by third parties (ibid. 269–70).

Runciman has the vast majority of Hobbes scholars on his side. Most, both before and after Runciman, also follow the definition of 'artificial person' as 'representative' from Chapter 16 of *Leviathan* (Forsyth, 1981: 197; Gauthier, 1969: 121–22; Hood, 1964: 164; Pitkin, 1967: 15–16; Tukiainen, 1994: 46; cf. Copp, 1980: 582–83; Green, 2015: 27). Pettit (2008: 56) neatly summarizes the standard interpretation of Hobbesian personhood: 'Hobbes's view, to put it in a slogan, is that there are no persons but spokespersons. Natural persons are spokespersons for themselves, acting and speaking in their own name, and artificial persons are spokespersons for another'.

Yet if 'there are no persons but spokespersons', it is difficult to see how the state could be a person of any kind. The state can speak neither for itself nor for anyone else. It *requires* a representative—a sovereign—precisely because it cannot *be* a representative. As Hobbes takes great pains to show, the state 'can do nothing but by the Person that Represents it', and the words and actions that are attributable to it are the words and actions 'onely of the Soveraign' (*L* XXIV. 388).[5] Skinner (1999: 11, note 65) clearly recognized the problem here: 'If we adopt Hobbes's initial proposal and call representatives artificial persons, then sovereigns are artificial persons while states are not.' This is the thought that led Skinner to question the standard interpretation of Hobbesian personhood: the state is an artificial person (hence 'Artificiall Man'); but the state is a representee, not a representative; so at least some artificial persons must be representees rather than representatives.

Runciman (2000b: 272–73; 2009) is well aware that Hobbes' state is not really a representative or actor. But unlike Skinner, he does not recognize the tension between Hobbes' definition of 'person' as 'actor' and his claim that the state is a person. He relies on the phrase, 'by fiction', to fill the gap. The state is not a natural actor like a human being, nor an artificial actor like an assembly, but an actor 'by fiction'. Runciman compares the state to other 'persons by fiction', such as 'bridges and madmen', which are likewise 'incapable of responsible action' (ibid. 271). For a bridge to be a person, 'both the owners and the representative of the bridge [must] act in such a way as to ensure that it appears

---

5. See Hobbes (*L* XXI. 332, XXXI. 554) for additional statements to the effect that the state acts only through the sovereign.

that the bridge is itself acting responsibly' (ibid. 272). Similarly, the actions of sovereigns and subjects together sustain the fiction that states 'truly are persons, truly capable of the actions that personal responsibility requires' (ibid.).

Emphasizing 'by fiction' does not solve the problem. As Sagar (2018) points out, Hobbes never uses the phrase, 'person by fiction'; he refers only to things that are 'represented by Fiction' (*L* XVI. 246). 'Persons by fiction' are Runciman's invention, just as 'purely artificial persons' are Skinner's invention. Further, it is not clear from Chapter 16 that things that are represented by fiction are therefore persons, as Runciman assumes (Sagar 2018: 79). Hobbes says that 'Inanimate things, as a Church, an Hospital, a Bridge', 'Children, Fooles, and Mad-men', and even 'An Idol, or meer Figment of the brain, may be *Personated*' (*L* XVI. 246–48, emphasis added). As Martinich (2016: 228) points out, only in *De homine* and the Latin *Leviathan* does Hobbes say that 'an inanimate thing can be a person' (*DH* XV.4; *LL* XVI. 246–47). In Chapter 16 of the English *Leviathan*, there is only one instance in which Hobbes clearly says that something becomes a person by being represented: 'A Multitude of men, are made *One* Person, when they are by one man, or one Person, Represented' (*L* XVI. 248). But the definition of 'person' as 'representative', which Runciman follows, is not sufficient to decipher this crucial passage: Hobbes does not mean that a multitude becomes a representative when it is represented by a representative. As I argue in the following sections, Hobbes uses 'person' in two opposite ways, and it is necessary to recognize this in order to fully understand what kind of person the represented multitude is.

In sum, while Runciman provides decisive reasons to reject Skinner's interpretation of Hobbesian personhood, his own interpretation is also untenable. On one hand, he maintains that all persons are representatives. On the other, he maintains that states (and other incapable entities), which are not representatives, are nevertheless persons. This inconsistency is a problem not only for Runciman, but for anyone who exclusively follows Hobbes' definition of 'person' from Chapter 16 of *Leviathan*. If we take persons to be representatives, as most Hobbes scholars do, then Hobbes' state is no person at all. As I show in the next section, the source of the problem is that many Hobbes scholars have focused too narrowly on the definition of 'person' from Chapter 16 of *Leviathan*.

§9 The Two Faces of Personhood

In his discussion of the Holy Trinity in Chapter 42 of *Leviathan*, Hobbes provides another definition of 'person': 'a Person, (as I have shewn before, chapt. 13.) is he that is Represented, as often as hee is Represented' (*L* XLII. 776). He then draws the inference that God is 'three Persons in the proper signification of Persons; which is, that which is Represented by another' (ibid.). God is one person as represented by Moses, another person as represented by Christ, and yet another person as represented by the Apostles and their successors. Whereas Chapter 16 says that a person is a representative, Chapter 42 says that a person is a representee.

Hobbes' inversion of his definition of 'person' has not gone unnoticed (Abizadeh, 2012: 131, note 85; Brito Vieira, 2009: 169, note 69; Martinich, 2005: 228; Pettit, 2008: 73). Although the Chapter 42 definition has a prominent place in discussions of Hobbes' theology (Abizadeh, 2017; Brito Vieira, 2009: 213–14; Wright, 2006: 198), it is rarely mentioned in discussions of his political thought, and it is entirely absent from Skinner and Runciman's debate about what kind of person the state is. This neglect of the Chapter 42 definition is especially odd given that Hobbes' theological and political thought are so closely connected (Lessay, 2009; Runciman, 2009: 15, note 1). The principle that underpins his doctrine of the Holy Trinity—'it is consequent to plurality of Representers, that there bee a plurality of Persons' (*L* XLI. 772)—also underpins his claim that the state must have a single representative. For the same reason that 'God, who has been Represented (that is, Personated) thrice, may properly enough be said to be three persons' (*L* XLII. 776), a multitude with three representatives is 'not one Person, nor one Soveraign, but three Persons, and three Soveraigns' (*L* XXIX. 512). I argue that the Chapter 42 definition is just as important as the Chapter 16 definition for understanding how Hobbes employs the concept of personhood in his political thought.

The parenthetical reference to Chapter 13 in the Chapter 42 definition presents a puzzle. The former chapter ('Of the Naturall Condition of Mankind') does not provide a definition of 'person', so the reference must be an error. Hobbes most likely meant to refer to Chapter 16.[6] However, this makes the reference even more puzzling. He appears to have defined 'person' as 'representee' and directed the reader to the opposite definition all in the same sentence. One possibility is that he contradicted himself in a moment of uncharacteristic carelessness. A more plausible explanation is that the Chapter 16 and Chapter 42 definitions describe two sides of the same concept. Hobbes' concept of personhood is ambivalent: persons can be representatives, representees, or (as natural persons are) both at the same time.

There are already hints of this ambivalence in Chapter 16 of *Leviathan*. Hobbes claims that '*persona*', which denotes 'a Mask or Visard', 'hath been translated to any Representer of speech and action, as well in Tribunalls, as Theaters' (*L* XVI. 244). As Brito Vieira (2009: 168–69) points out, 'the

6. Malcolm takes Chapter 16 to be the intended referent. See Hobbes (*L* XLII. 776).

inference is troubling because the theatrical mask is not the actor, but he whom the actor represents: more correctly, a representation of the represented (fictional) character'. The abrupt switch from '*persona* as mask' to 'person as actor' is indicative of Hobbes' ambivalence about whether persons are representatives or representees.

This ambivalence is borne out in Hobbes' usage of 'person'. His usage in Part II of *Leviathan* ('Of Commonwealth') corresponds as often to the Chapter 42 definition as it does to the Chapter 16 definition. For example, when Hobbes writes, 'every man, or assembly that hath Soveraignty, representeth two Persons' (*L* XXIII. 376), he does not mean that every sovereign represents two representatives. The sovereign *is* the representative. The persons in this context are the things that the sovereign represents, or the roles that the sovereign plays—namely, himself and the state.[7] A monarch, for example, represents the state in public and himself in private. Similarly, when Hobbes writes, 'in their Seats of Justice [judges] represent the person of the Soveraign' (*L* XXIII. 380), he means that judges represent the sovereign. He does not mean that judges represent the representative of the sovereign. The person is the role that the judges play, not the actor who plays the role. Even in the phrase 'bear a person', the person is the representee. In Hobbes' favourite example, Cicero is the representative, and the three persons that he bears are the three roles that he plays: the role of himself, the role of his adversary, and the role of the judge (*L* XVI. 244). Representatives bear persons; they are not the persons that are borne. Hobbes' neglected definition of 'person' from Chapter 42 is indispensable for understanding how he uses the word.

However, the Chapter 16 definition is equally indispensable. Hobbes often uses 'person' as a synonym for 'representative', such as when he describes the sovereign as 'the Person of the Common-wealth'. For instance, he says that 'In all Courts of Justice, the Soveraign (which is the Person of the Common-wealth,) is he that Judgeth' (*L* XXVI. 422) and that 'they that give Counsell to the Representative person of a Common-wealth, may have, and have often their particular ends, and passions' (*L* XXV. 404). He uses 'person' to mean 'representative' even in Chapter 42. Although he defines persons as representees near the beginning of the chapter (*L* XLII. 776), he equates '*the Publique Person*' with 'the Representant of the Common-wealth' near the end (*L* XLII. 920). The only way to determine whether any given instance of 'person' in *Leviathan* refers to a representative or a representee (or both) is to use the context as a guide.

---

7. See Brito Vieira (2009: Chapter 2) and Pettit (2008: 55–58) on the theatrical or role-based character of Hobbes' concept of personhood.

Hobbes' usage of 'person' in his early works displays the same ambivalence. Although he did not introduce the concept of representation until *Leviathan* (Malcolm, 2012: 15–17; Skinner, 2007: 168; cf. Douglass, 2018), he did use the concept of personhood in *The Elements of Law* and *De cive,* where he associates personhood with will rather than with representation. Hobbes does not provide italicized definitions of 'person' in these early works, so we have to rely solely on his usage. In some parts of *The Elements*, Hobbes uses 'person civil' to refer to the state, as in 'a multitude of persons natural are united by covenants into one person civil' (*EL* XX.1, see also XIX.8, XXVII.7). In other places, he equates the 'person civil' with the sovereign: 'a person civil [is] either one man, or one council, in the will whereof is included and involved the will of every one in particular; as for example: in this latter sense the lower house of parliament' (*EL* XXI.11). Both the sovereign and the state—both the giver and the receiver of the will—are persons. The same ambivalence is present in *De cive.* On one hand, Hobbes describes the state as 'one *person* formed from several men' (*DC* X.5, see also V.9, XIII.3). On the other, he describes an aristocratic assembly, or 'council of optimates', as a person: 'without a fixed schedule of the times and places at which the *council* of optimates may meet, there is no longer a *council* or a single person, but a disorganized crowd without sovereign power' (*DC* VII.10). Hobbes' concept of personhood was Janus-faced from the very beginning.

Once we recognize that Hobbesian persons can be representatives or representees, we can begin to make sense of his later accounts of personhood, which have often puzzled Hobbes scholars. Hobbes' definition of 'person' as 'representee' in Chapter 15 of *De homine* is apparently the opposite of his definition in Chapter 16 of *Leviathan*: '*a person is he to whom the words and actions of men are attributed, either his own or another's:* if his own, the person is *natural;* if another's, it is *artificial* [fictitia]' (*DH* XV.1).[8] Hobbes inverts his theatrical analogy to match. He begins by describing the distinction in Latin between *facies* and *persona*: '*facies* if they wished to indicate the true man; *persona* if an artificial one' (ibid.). He does not mention *facies* in *Leviathan*, where he quickly jumps from saying that a *persona* is a mask to saying that 'a *Person*, is the same that an *Actor* is' (*L* XVI. 244). The point of the distinction between *facies* and *persona* is that the actor is distinct from the person, or character, that he plays. When an actor wears a mask, the audience considers his words and actions to be the words and actions of the character that the mask depicts: 'the actor playing Agamemnon in a false face ... was, for that time, Agamemnon' (*DH* XV.1). However, after the play is over, the actor is 'understood without

8. Compare Skinner's (1999: 12) translation, quoted in §8.

his false face, namely being acknowledged as the actor himself rather than the person he had been playing' (ibid.). It is clear from Hobbes' definition and his usage in *De homine* that the person is the character that the actor plays rather than, as Chapter 16 of *Leviathan* says, the actor who plays the character.

Hobbes scholars have struggled to reconcile the *De homine* and Chapter 16 definitions. Simendić (2012: 153–55) argues that 'artificial person' in *De homine* ought to be read as 'representative', as in Chapter 16. While Skinner and Runciman take '*he to whom the words and actions of men are attributed*' to be the representee, Simendić contends that '"words and actions" of the represented are attributed to the representative and not *vice versa*' (ibid. 155). But if we follow Simendić's interpretation of 'attributed', we then need to explain why Hobbes uses 'attributed' in the opposite way in Chapter 16 of *Leviathan*, where he says that the thing to which words and actions are attributed is the representee (*L* XVI. 244). Further, if the *De homine* and Chapter 16 definitions are equivalent, then why did Hobbes invert his theatrical analogy in *De homine*? Martinich (2016: 329–30), seeing no way to make the two definitions compatible, suggests that Hobbes' definition in *De homine* 'may have been different simply because it had a different purpose' and concludes that it 'is of little value to his political theory'. This is implausible given that Hobbes explicitly discusses the state in Chapter 15 of *De homine*, which is suggestively titled '*De homine fictitio*'—Of Fictional Man. As Hobbes says, 'Not only can a single man bear the person of a single man, but one man can also bear many' (*DH* XV.3). The definition of 'person' in *De homine* cannot be rendered congruent with the definition in Chapter 16 of *Leviathan*, nor can it be disregarded.

What has gone almost entirely unnoticed is that the definition of 'person' in *De homine* matches the one from Chapter 42 of *Leviathan*.[9] Hobbes defines a person as '*he to whom the words and actions of men are attributed*' in the former and 'he that is represented' in the latter. The two definitions are equivalent: someone who is represented is, by definition, someone to whom words and actions are attributed. There is clear continuity between *Leviathan* and *De homine*—just not between the Chapter 16 definition and *De homine*. The *De homine* definition, like each of the *Leviathan* definitions, is best read as one side of a double-sided concept.

The definition of 'person' from Hobbes' Latin translation of *Leviathan* is explicitly double-sided: 'A PERSON, is he who does things in his own or another's name. If in his own, he is a proper or natural person; if in another's, he is the representative person of the one [i.e., the person] in whose name he acts' (*LL* XVI. 244–45). Here, as Runciman (2000b: 277) points out, 'a person is

---

9. The lone exception is Abizadeh (2012: 131, note 85; 2017: 923, note 40).

TABLE 2. Hobbes' Theory of Personhood

Person	Representative	Represented
Natural	Represents itself	Represented by itself
Artificial	Represents another	Represented by another
True	Represents truly	Represented truly
Fictional	Represents by fiction	Represented by fiction

defined both as an actor and as a non-actor to whom actions are attributed'—
'both as he who acts and whatever is acted for' (see also Martinich, 2016:
330–32). This definition, which Runciman says 'introduces confusion', is actually a symptom of the confusion that was there all along. The definition of
'person' from the Latin *Leviathan* is the only one that captures the ambivalence
of Hobbes' usage. A complete account of Hobbesian personhood must take
both senses of 'person' into account. Hobbes' key distinctions apply to both
representative and represented persons.

Natural persons are both representatives and representees, so it does not
make a difference which side of personhood we start from. The class of natural
persons by the *De homine* definition is coextensive with the class of natural
persons by the Chapter 16 of *Leviathan* definition even though the definitions
are opposite in meaning. However, the distinction between representative
persons and represented persons becomes crucial when we consider artificial
persons. While artificial persons in the first sense represent others, artificial
persons in the second sense are represented by others. True artificial persons are
those that are simultaneously natural persons: on the representative side, lawyers
and estate agents; on the represented side, their clients. Fictional artificial persons are those that are not also natural persons: on the representative side, assemblies; on the represented side, corporate and incapable entities. The next
section explains how each type of person figures in Hobbes' theory of the state.

§10 Hobbes' Theory of the State

A complete understanding of Hobbes' theory of the state requires both senses
of personhood, as well as the distinctions between natural and artificial persons and between true and fictional representation. His explanation of how
the multitude becomes a person involves several types of persons.

> A Multitude of men, are made *One* Person, when they are by one man, or
> one Person, Represented; so that it be done with the consent of every one
> of that Multitude in particular. For it is the *Unity* of the Representer, not

the *Unity* of the Represented, that maketh the Person *One*. And it is the Representer that beareth the Person, and but one Person: And *Unity*, cannot otherwise be understood in Multitude (*L* XVI. 248).

In other words, many persons become one person when they authorize one person to bear their person. This passage means hardly anything until we distinguish the types of persons involved.

The members of the multitude are natural persons. Each individual, acting in his or her own name, authorizes another person to represent the group. The multitude as a group cannot authorize its own representative because it 'naturally is not *One*, but *Many*; they cannot be understood for one; but many Authors, of every thing their Representative saith, or doth in their name' (*L* XVI. 250). As Hobbes puts it in *De cive*, 'a crowd cannot make a promise or an agreement, acquire or transfer a right, do, have, possess, and so on, except separately or as individuals, so that there are as many promises, agreements, rights, and actions, as there are men' (*DC* VI.1a). A multitude is incapable of acting as a unit, which is why it is necessary for each natural person to authorize a representative to act in the name of the multitude.

The person that the members of the multitude authorize is a representative artificial person. If this person is an individual (i.e., a monarch), then he or she is a true representative. If this person is made up of several natural persons (i.e., an assembly), then it is a fictional representative. An assembly is, as Hobbes says, 'artificiall, and fictitious' (*L* XVII. 352): the artifice of majority rule sustains the fiction that the assembly has a single will. The fictitious character of an assembly explains why it cannot commit a crime or an injustice: 'a body politic [in this context, meaning 'assembly'], as it is a fictitious body, so are the faculties of will thereof fictitious also. But to make a particular man unjust . . . there is required a natural and very will' (*EL* XXI.4; see also *DC* VII.14). An assembly can serve as a representative only insofar as its members maintain the fiction that they have a single will, or speak with a single voice. They do this through majority rule, which cancels out contradictory wills or voices.

[I]f the Representative consist of many men, the voyce of the greater number, must be considered as the voyce of them all. For if the lesser number pronounce (for example) in the Affirmative, and the greater in the Negative, there will be Negatives more than enough to destroy the Affirmatives; and thereby the excesse of Negatives, standing uncontradicted, are the only voyce the Representative hath (*L* XVI. 250).

However, if the assembly has an even number of members, or if each member has a veto, then the fiction that it has a single voice may break down. The assembly will be 'oftentimes mute, and uncapable of Action' (ibid.).

The common claim that Hobbes made 'no formal distinction between a democratic sovereign and a monarchical one' (Tuck, 2016: 100) is not entirely true. A monarch is a true representative, or one whose 'civil will' is simultaneously a 'natural will'; a democratic or aristocratic sovereign is a fictitious representative, or one whose 'civil will' depends on the fiction that it speaks with a single voice (*DC* VII.14). Hobbes' worry about sovereign assemblies is that this fiction is fragile: 'a Monarch cannot disagree with himselfe, out of envy, or interest; but an Assembly may; and that to such a height, as may produce a Civill Warre' (*L* XIX. 290). Although Hobbes thought democratic and aristocratic assemblies could be just as sovereign as monarchs, he did draw a conceptual distinction between representative individuals and representative assemblies.

The act of authorizing a single representative person transforms the multitude of natural persons into a represented person by fiction. Whereas an assembly is '*Many men made One* [person] *by Plurality of Voyces*', a state is many men made one person when they are 'by one man, or one Person, Represented' (*L* XVI. 248–50). An assembly is a person in the Chapter 16 sense: a 'Representer of speech and action' (*L* XVI. 244). A state is a person in the Chapter 42 sense: 'that which is Represented by another' (*L* XLII. 776). Hobbes scholars frequently overlook the fact that there are two ways in which a group can become a person (but see Copp, 1980). An assembly is a person because it *is* a representative; a state is a person because it *has* a representative. To use Hobbes' theatrical analogy, an assembly is a fictional actor, while a state is a fictional character. An assembly is like the chorus in an ancient Greek tragedy: it plays a single role, but only by the fiction that it speaks with one voice. A state is like the character that the chorus represents, such as the Elders of Argos in *Agamemnon*: it is incapable of playing a role on its own, so it must be brought to life by an actor. The state cannot act apart from the sovereign any more than the Elders of Argos can act apart from the chorus. The difference between a state and a character in a play is not that they are different kinds of persons, but rather, as Runciman (2000b: 275–76) puts it, that 'one is a person by fiction whose attributed actions are backed up by the actions of real persons, and the other is not'. Whereas subjects are ultimately liable for the actions that the sovereign performs in the name of the state, no one is liable for the actions that the chorus performs in the name of the Elders of Argos.

While the sovereign represents the state, the sovereign is also represented by public ministers. Ambassadors and messengers 'represent the Person of their own Soveraign, to forraign States' (*L* XXIII. 382), and 'in their Seats of Justice [judges] represent the person of the Soveraign; and their Sentence, is his Sentence' (*L* XXIII. 380). The sovereign is therefore both a representative artificial person and a represented artificial person. Public ministers represent the sovereign truly, since they are authorized by the sovereign in whose name they act: 'Publique Ministers . . . serve the Person Representative, and can doe nothing against his Command, nor without his Authority' (*L* XXIII. 378).

Runciman (2016: 373–74) argues that public ministers represent the state rather than the sovereign. Hobbes does sometimes suggest this reading, such as when he says that public ministers represent 'the Person [*qua* representee] of the Commonwealth' (*L* XXIII. 376), but he also provides a decisive reason to reject it. Given that 'it is consequent to plurality of Representers, that there bee a plurality of Persons' (*L* XLI. 772),[10] the state would be multiple persons if it had multiple representatives. Further, when Hobbes provides examples of public ministers, he says that they act 'in the name of the Soveraign', 'represent the person of the Soveraign', 'represent the Person of their own Soveraign', and 'serve the Person Representative' (*L* XXIII. 378–82). Although every action that public ministers perform is ultimately 'the act of the Common-wealth' (*L* XXIII. 382), their actions are attributable to the state only through the sovereign: public ministers represent the sovereign, and the sovereign, in turn, represents the state. Hobbes confirms this reading in his reply to John Bramhall: 'All that he objecteth is, that it followeth hereupon, that there be as many Persons of a King, as there be petty Constables in his Kingdom. And so there are, or else he cannot be obeyed' (*AB* 393). If a king has as many persons as he has ministers, then public ministers must represent the sovereign rather than the state. Hobbes had a good reason not to allow public ministers to represent the state directly: they might claim to represent the state independently of the sovereign, as Parliament did around the time of the English Civil War. Portraying public ministers as deputies of the sovereign makes it clear that they are subordinate to the sovereign.

In sum, Hobbes' formula for making a person out of a multitude involves five types of persons. When the multitude of (1) natural persons authorize a representative artificial person, whether (2) an individual (who is a true representative) or (3) an assembly (which is a fictional representative), the members of the multitude are united into (4) a represented artificial person (by fiction). The representative artificial person is simultaneously (5) a represented artificial person (truly) when she (or it) authorizes public ministers to act on her (or its) behalf. Figure 1 describes how all of these persons hang together. Subjects (i.e., the multitude) authorize the sovereign; the sovereign authorizes public ministers; public ministers represent the sovereign; and the

---

10. Although the 12 Apostles represent the same person of God, this is possible only because the Apostles are a 'councell' or assembly (*L* XLII. 824–28).

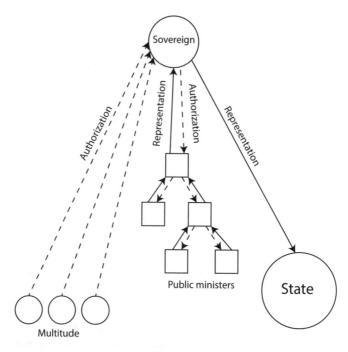

FIGURE 1. Hobbes' Theory of the State

sovereign represents the state. The state neither authorizes nor represents; it is only passively represented.

Representation of the state is conceptually similar to representation by fiction of other artificial persons, such as 'Children, Fooles, and Mad-men that have no use of Reason' and 'Inanimate things, as a Church, an Hospital, a Bridge' (*L* XVI. 246–48). Like 'Fooles' and bridges, states 'may be personated . . . but cannot be Authors, nor therefore give Authority to their Actors' (*L* XVI. 246). Just as the representatives of 'Fooles' and bridges must be authorized by their 'Owners, or Governours' (ibid.), the representatives of states must be authorized by their subjects. As Skinner (1999: 22) and Abizadeh (2012: 133–34) argue, Hobbes' state is most similar to 'An Idol, or meer Figment of the brain', such as the 'Gods of the Heathen' (*L* XVI. 248). Although 'Idols cannot be Authors: for an Idol is nothing', the Roman Gods 'were Personated, and held Possessions, and other Goods, and Rights, which men from time to time dedicated, and consecrated unto them' (ibid.). 'Fooles' and bridges exist regardless of whether anyone represents them, but the state, like a figment of the imagination, ceases to exist if it ceases to be represented: 'a Common-wealth, without Soveraign Power, is but a word, without substance, and cannot stand' (*L* XXXI. 554).

§11 Artificial Men and Artificial Animals

What Hobbes provides is an account of how the state can be a person—that is, an entity to which actions, rights, and responsibilities are attributed—even though it is not an actor. Although the state has no more agency than a bridge or an idol does, it can properly be said to make laws, sign treaties, borrow money, and exercise the rights of sovereignty as long as the agents who in fact perform these actions have been duly authorized to act in the name of the state. I turn to the question of who or what counts as an authorized representative in Chapter 3.

But before that, there are two rival interpretations of Hobbes' theory of the state that must be addressed. First, since Hobbes frequently anthropomorphizes the state, it is possible to interpret his theory of the state as a predecessor of the agential theory. Second, since Hobbes compares the parts of the state to the organs of the body, it is possible to interpret his theory of the state as a predecessor of the functional theory. I argue that both of these interpretations are mistaken. If we resist the urge to project contemporary theories of the state back onto Hobbes, it is possible to recover a unique and valuable conception of state personality from his political thought.

§11.1 Hobbes' State as a Corporate Agent

Like proponents of the agential theory, Hobbes employs an analogy between states and human beings. He describes the state as an 'Artificiall Man' (*L* Intro. 16), and the frontispiece of *Leviathan* depicts the state as a large man composed of many smaller men. In addition, Hobbes sometimes equates 'person' with 'actor'. If the state is a person, and 'a *Person,* is the same that an *Actor* is' (*L* XVI. 248), then it seems to follow that the state is an actor. It is therefore plausible to read Hobbes' theory of the state as a predecessor of the agential theory.

Many International Relations scholars, political theorists, and philosophers interpret Hobbes' theory of the state as a rudimentary theory of corporate agency. According to List and Pettit (2011: 7), Hobbes' '"authorization theory" of group agency . . . distinguished three ways a multitude or collection of individuals might form a group agent, particularly a state or commonwealth'. They argue that Hobbes' state is 'a degenerate group agent' because it fails to meet the standard of collective rationality (ibid. 76). As Pettit (2014: 1648) later writes, 'Hobbes takes the group agent that individuals constitute by recruiting an individual spokesperson to be an agent or person only "by fiction"'. Erskine (2001: 75) similarly portrays Hobbes' state as a crude imitation of a corporate agent: 'For Hobbes, the agency of the state is a useful "fiction".

Conversely, my aim is to establish the institution as a moral agent in a way that is not simply metaphorical.' Even some Hobbes scholars have interpreted him in this way. Baumgold (1988: 43, 51) describes what she calls 'Hobbes' nominalist analysis of corporate agency', which explains how 'the multitude forms itself into a "people", or corporate agent'. Garsten (2010: 525) likewise reads 'person' as 'agent': 'to speak of a "people" as if it could want anything, or do anything, was to speak of it as an agent—or, in Hobbes's vocabulary, a "person"—an entity capable of being responsible for words and actions'.

Yet Hobbes' state is not an agent in the sense that contemporary philosophers, political theorists, and International Relations scholars use the term. Agents, in this sense, are 'intentional—purposive or goal-directed—systems' (Wendt, 2004: 295). In List and Pettit's (2011: 20) terms, an agent is an entity that 'has representational states, motivational states, and a capacity to process them and to act on their basis'—that is, an entity that acts according to its own will and its own conception of its environment. Hobbes' state is not an agent, or even a fictional agent, by these definitions. As I have previously argued (§10), his state is not a fictional actor or agent, but a fictional character; the sovereign is the (true or fictional) actor that acts in its name.

Hobbes' state lacks the defining feature of a corporate agent: a will that is distinct from the wills of its members and representatives (see §5.1). He repeatedly denies that the state has a distinct will. Although he occasionally refers to 'the Will of the Common-wealth', he insists that it is nothing more than 'the Will of the Representative' (*L* XXVI. 420). Just as the will of a bridge is nothing but the will of its caretaker, the will of a state is nothing but the will of its sovereign: 'a Common-wealth hath no Will, nor makes no Lawes, but those that are made by the Will of him, or them that have the Soveraign Power' (*L* XXXI. 570). Similarly, in *De cive*, Hobbes says that 'a commonwealth has a will, and can assent and refuse through the holder of *sovereign power*, and only so' (*DC* VI.19, see also VI.1a). This claim plays a crucial role for Hobbes. If the state had a will of its own, then two seditious possibilities would arise: the state could act independently of the sovereign, or the subjects could object that the sovereign has misrepresented the will of the state. The idea that the state is an agent in its own right is precisely what Hobbes wanted to rule out.

However, Hobbes does allow that assemblies have wills of their own. The will of an assembly, as Hobbes says, must be 'understood as the *will of the greater part* of the men who make up the assembly' (*DC* V.7). It cannot be identified with the will of any particular individual. An essential part of Hobbes' theory of the state is that a sovereign representative, which must have a will of some kind, can be an assembly. Whereas states and other 'characters' cannot be said to act unless they are represented by third parties, an assembly can be its own representative, just as an individual can: 'a Monarch, hath the person not onely of the Common-wealth, but also of a man; and a Soveraign Assembly hath the Person not onely of the Common-wealth, but also of the Assembly' (*L* XXIII. 376). If there are any rudimentary corporate agents in Hobbes' political thought, they are assemblies, not states.[11]

Yet a Hobbesian assembly differs in some important respects from a corporate agent. Whereas a corporate agent can have intentions that none of its members share, a Hobbesian assembly cannot. If an assembly uses majority rule to decide every issue, as Hobbes suggests, then it cannot have an intention unless the majority of its members also have that intention. Recall Tollefsen's example of the admissions committee (§5.1, Table 1). It is possible for the committee to intend to admit an applicant to the PhD programme against the wills of most or even all of its members only because the decision-making procedure of the committee is not strictly majoritarian. The members of the committee vote on four 'premises'—whether the applicant has a good test score, good grades, good letters, and a good writing sample—and then let their votes on these premises dictate the committee's decision about whether the applicant will be admitted. Conversely, a Hobbesian version of this committee would vote directly on whether to admit the applicant. Its members' judgments about whether he satisfies each criterion for admission would not be aggregated. If the majority of the members of the committee voted against admitting the applicant, then the committee would decline to admit him. The will of a Hobbesian assembly, unlike the will of a corporate agent, can never be anything more than the will of the majority.

Pettit (2008: 82–83) argues that Hobbes fails to appreciate the limitations of majoritarian decision-making (see also List and Pettit, 2011: 43–46). If the members of an assembly decide every issue using majority voting, then they are likely to end up making an inconsistent set of decisions. Pettit uses the example of a three-member assembly that must decide four issues: whether to balance the budget, whether to increase taxes, whether to increase military spending, and whether to increase other spending. Table 3 describes the assembly's votes.

Although each member of the assembly makes a consistent proposal, the decision of the majority is inconsistent. It is impossible to simultaneously balance the budget, increase military spending, and increase other spending without increasing taxes. This example illustrates a more general problem with

11. Hobbesian corporations are, oddly enough, not 'corporate agents' either: like states, they will and act only through their representatives. Hobbes repeatedly suggests that states and corporations are persons of the same kind, such as when he describes the latter as 'many lesser Common-wealths in the bowels of a greater' (*L* XXIX. 516; see also *EL* XXVII.7; *DC* V.10).

TABLE 3. Pettit's Sovereign Assembly

	Balance the budget?	Increase taxes?	Increase military spending?	Increase other spending?
Member #1	Yes	No	Yes	No (reduce)
Member #2	Yes	No	No (reduce)	Yes
Member #3	Yes	Yes	Yes	Yes
Assembly	Yes	No	Yes	Yes

majoritarian decision-making. Any assembly that tries to follow the will of the majority on every issue, as Hobbes proposes, will face a '"discursive dilemma": they can be responsive to individuals, in which case they will risk collectively [*sic*] irrationality; or they can ensure collective rationality, in which case they may fail to be responsive to individuals' (Pettit, 2008: 83). Pettit argues that assemblies have little choice but to take the second horn of the dilemma. They must follow the minority on some issues—for instance, by increasing taxes against the will of the majority—in order to ensure that their decisions are consistent and actionable.

Hobbes had obviously never heard of the discursive dilemma, but he would not have been troubled by it. He would simply have grasped the other horn of the dilemma. List and Pettit (2011: 56–58) solve the dilemma through a 'sequential priority procedure', which means letting the assembly's decisions on temporally or logically prior issues determine its decisions on later or derivative issues. In the example above, the assembly might let its decisions on the other three issues dictate its decision about whether to raise taxes. Hobbes would solve the dilemma in precisely the opposite way: by letting later votes overturn earlier votes. He is deeply hostile to the idea that sovereigns, or even subordinate judges, can be bound by the decisions of their predecessors: 'mens Judgements have been perverted, by trusting to Precedents . . . though the Sentence of the Judge, be a Law to the party pleading, yet it is no Law to any Judge, that shall succeed him in that Office' (*L* XXVI. 434). If the assembly first voted to balance the budget, then to increase military spending, then to increase other spending, and then to keep taxes the same, the vote to keep taxes the same would overturn one of the three earlier decisions. The assembly would have to vote again to decide which to overturn.

The underlying principle is that 'the Soveraign of a Common-wealth, be it an Assembly, or one Man, is not Subject to the Civill Lawes. For having power to make, and repeale Lawes, he may when he pleaseth, free himself from that subjection' (*L* XXVI. 416). Anything that the majority decides to do can be undone by a subsequent majority. This Hobbesian solution to the discursive dilemma follows from his theory of sovereignty. States are 'Absolute, and *Independent*, subject to none but their own Representative' (*L* XXII. 348), which means that this representative cannot be bound—not by subjects, nor by other sovereigns, nor by the decisions of its predecessors, nor even by its previous decisions (see §12 below). Hobbes might have to admit that this solution to the discursive dilemma will not work for subordinate assemblies, such as the boards of companies and universities, which are legally bound by their prior actions and agreements. In any case, the discursive dilemma presents no problem for Hobbes' theory of the state.

The main problem with describing Hobbes' state as a corporate agent is not that it is anachronistic, but that it is simply misleading. Hobbes' state does not have a distinct will, as 'agency' implies; its will is its sovereign's will. If there are any primitive corporate agents in Hobbes' political thought, they are assemblies, not states. It is difficult to fault readers for taking Hobbes at his word in Chapter 16 of *Leviathan* when he says that persons are actors. Yet focusing too narrowly on this passage, and subsequently ignoring his definitions of 'person' from Chapter 42 and from his later works, leads them to project the idea of corporate agency onto Hobbes' state.

What makes his idea of state personality novel and valuable is precisely that it decouples personhood from agency. It therefore allows us to sidestep the protracted debates about the metaphysics of corporate agency and intentionality. If we follow Hobbes, then whether corporate entities (and also other entities, such as robots, animals, and natural entities) should have rights and responsibilities need not depend on whether they are really agents. Hobbesian personhood is created out of political processes of authorization and representation, not discovered through metaphysical speculation. After all, even 'An Idol, or meer Figment of the brain, may be Personated' (*L* XVI. 248). All that an entity requires in order to be a Hobbesian person is an authorized representative who acts in its name.

§11.2 Hobbes' State as an Organism

Hobbes' theory of the state could also be interpreted as a predecessor of the functional theory. He gives some credence to this interpretation when he describes the state as an 'Artificiall Animal' and when he compares the parts of the state to the organs of the body (*L* Intro. 16). For example, he describes public ministers as the 'parts Organicall' of the state, which 'resembleth the Nerves, and Tendons that move the severall limbs of a body natural' (*L* XXIII. 376–78). Hobbes also suggests, much as international lawyers do, that the relation between a state and its organs is akin to principal–agent relation. He says that the actions of public ministers must have 'the Common-wealth for Author' (*L* XXIII. 382), as if the state is the principal and its ministers are its agents. It is therefore plausible to interpret Hobbes' theory of the state as a predecessor of the quasi-organic theory of the state that underpins international law. Hobbes is rarely interpreted this way (but see Baumgold, 1988: 39). At the risk of knocking over a straw man, it is worthwhile to show that this interpretation is mistaken, if only to clearly distinguish Hobbes' theory of the state from the functional theory.

Hobbes' state is more like a machine than it is like an organism (Runciman, 1997: 21–24; Sagar, 2018). Although he describes the state as an 'Artificiall Animal', he conceives of animals, including human beings, as nothing more than machines: 'For seeing life is but a motion of Limbs, the beginning whereof is in some principall part within; why may we not say, that all *Automata* (Engines that move themselves by springs and wheeles as doth a watch) have an artificiall life?' (*L* Intro. 16). The heart is a spring, nerves are strings, and joints are wheels; the artificial heart (treasury), nerves (justice system), and joints (magistrates) of the state are artificial springs, strings, and wheels. As Runciman (1997: 24) points out, 'Hobbes's organicism is as applicable to the watch to which the Leviathan is first of all compared as it is to the commonwealth itself'. The relation between the state and its organs is thus more mechanical than organic or teleological. Hobbes' theory of the state is a mechanistic theory rather than a functional theory. His use of the organic metaphor was, above all, rhetorical. Describing the state in terms of the body was ubiquitous in early modern political thought (Holland, 2017: 3–5), and Hobbes used this trope to give his readers a familiar heuristic with which to grasp his arguments about the proper roles of the parts of the state.

The relation between the state and its representatives bears only a superficial resemblance to a principal–agent relation. Whereas a principal authorizes his or her own agents, the state has representatives authorized for it by third parties (namely, subjects and the sovereign). Although Hobbes occasionally says that the state authorizes public ministers (*L* XXIII. 382), he makes it clear that the state grants authority only through its sovereign: 'For such Protectors, Vice-Roys, and Governors, have no other right, but what depends on the Soveraigns Will' (*L* XXIII. 378). Since the state 'can do nothing but by the Person that Represents it' (*L* XXIV. 388), the state cannot grant authority except through the sovereign. The sovereign, in turn, receives her (or its) authority from the members of the multitude. Representation of the state is thus structurally different from a principal–agent relation. The relation between a lawyer and a client is dyadic: the client authorizes the lawyer, and the lawyer represents the client. The state is much more complex: subjects authorize the sovereign, the sovereign authorizes public ministers, public ministers represent the sovereign, and the sovereign represents the state.

———

Hobbes uses a variety of analogies for the state—artificial animal, artificial man, mortal god—because the state is not perfectly analogous to anything. Like an animal, the state is a kind of automaton or mechanical system. Unlike a non-human animal, but like a man, the state is capable of speech and action. Unlike a man, however, the state is not an agent in its own right; it needs a representative to speak and act in its name. In this way, Hobbes' artificial man is more like an artificial 'Foole', although he clearly would have balked at this suggestion. Like God, the state is the highest power in its respective domain. Just as God is supreme in the spiritual world, the state is supreme in the temporal world. In addition, as Abizadeh (2012, 2017) argues, the state and God are both represented by fiction: neither is capable of acting except through the sovereign and her ministers. Unlike God, however, the state cannot have multiple representatives: 'In the Kingdome of God, there may be three Persons independent, without breach of unity in God that Reigneth; but where men Reigne, that be subject to diversity of opinions, it cannot be so' (L XXIX. 512). Multiple representation of God is the Holy Trinity; multiple representation of the state is civil war. Each of Hobbes' analogies captures some aspect of the state but obscures others. The only way to precisely describe Hobbes' state is to describe the relations of authorization and representation that constitute it (see Figure 1).

Hobbes' claim that states are 'persons' tends to provoke skepticism among contemporary readers. Some readers will understandably be hesitant to accept that the category of persons includes corporate entities as well as flesh-and-blood human beings. But Hobbesian personhood is metaphysically thin and fairly innocuous. Ascribing Hobbesian personhood to states does not entail that they are intrinsically valuable or that they are deserving of human (or human-like) rights. To say that states are persons is simply to say that actions, rights, and responsibilities can be attributed to states via their authorized representatives—again, like 'Fooles' or idols. The word, 'person', is ultimately dispensable. Instead of saying that states 'are' persons, one could change the verb and say that states 'have' *personae* (or identities). Alternatively, one could say that states are 'entities' or 'bearers of responsibility'. I use 'person' for ease of expression, because I will be referring back to Hobbes repeatedly, but readers who are uncomfortable with this person-talk can easily paraphrase that word away. The concepts of authorization and representation do all of the important work in Hobbes' theory, as in mine.

§12 The Hobbesian Theory of State Responsibility

What I have shown so far is that Hobbes had a unique idea of state personality and that this idea has no counterpart in contemporary Political Theory, International Relations, or International Law. I argue in the remainder of the book that this idea of state personality provides a helpful way of conceptualizing state responsibility in the present. However, there is one apparent problem with this argument that must be addressed at the outset.

Although Hobbes thought corporations could and should be held responsible by the state (*L* XXII. 352), his theory of sovereignty rules out the possibility that states could be held responsible. When companies misbehave, the state can fine or even dissolve them, but there is no higher authority that can fine or dissolve states. What distinguishes states from other corporate entities is that they are 'Absolute, and Independent, subject to none but their own Representative' (*L* XXII. 348), which implies that there is no one to whom states can be responsible. A state cannot be responsible to another state because there is no higher authority that can compel states to fulfil their responsibilities to each other. As Malcolm (2002: 438–39) points out, Hobbes did think states had 'natural' duties to uphold their agreements, as long as these agreements remain compatible with their survival and security: 'if a weaker Prince, make a disadvantageous peace with a stronger, for feare; he is bound to keep it; unlesse (as hath been sayd before) there ariseth some new, and just cause of feare, to renew the war' (*L* XIV. 212). But because 'all men are equall, and judges of the justnesse of their own fears' in the state of nature (*L* XIV. 210), this effectively means that sovereigns have a right to repudiate their state's agreements whenever they see fit. Further, if there were a higher authority that were capable of enforcing agreements between states, then this authority would, by Hobbes' definition, be the lone state; there would consequently be no other states to which it could be responsible.

A state also cannot 'be obligated to a citizen; for since [the sovereign] can release it from its obligation, if he so wishes (since the will of each citizen is comprehended in the will of the commonwealth in all matters), the commonwealth is free whenever it so wishes' (*DC* VI.14). An agreement between the state and a subject would be of no consequence. If the state (acting through the sovereign) violated the agreement, the subject would have no reason to complain, because he 'is Author of every act the Soveraign doth' (*L* XXI. 330), including the act that violated the agreement. According to Hobbes, states can be responsible only in a weak sense. States have responsibilities that derive from natural law, but they can never be *held* responsible because they are not subject to any higher authority.

However, as Runciman (2009) points out, Hobbes' absolutism is not a consequence of his theory of representation.[12] The core structure of this theory of representation is equally applicable to modern democracies: subjects *qua* individuals authorize political representatives, and these representatives act in the name of the state as a whole (see Figure 1). Nothing about individualistic authorization or corporate representation implies that the authority of the representatives must be absolute. Hobbes' absolutism is a consequence of his theory of *sovereignty*, which says that there must be a supreme representative whose authority is limitless and irrevocable. This theory of sovereignty is what precludes holding states responsible.[13] If we retain the structure of Hobbes' theory of representation but reject the idea that states are 'subject to none but their own Representative' (*L* XXII. 348), then a Hobbesian theory of state responsibility becomes possible.

As I explain in subsequent chapters, the Hobbesian theory of state responsibility provides better answers to the Three Fundamental Questions than do the agential and functional alternatives. But one might wonder why it is necessary to go all the way back to Hobbes to find an adequate theory of representation. The virtue of Hobbes' theory is that it is 'triadic' rather than 'dyadic'. For Hobbes, political representation is not a two-way relation, as it is usually understood, but a complex set of three relations: (1) between subjects and representatives, (2) between these representatives and the state, and (3) between the state and its subjects. (There is also a fourth, more basic relation between the state and itself over time—identity.) A theory of state responsibility requires a triadic theory of representation because it has to account for all of these relations. The choice of a structurally Hobbesian theory of representation is thus necessary rather than arbitrary.

The three possible dyadic understandings of representation are all dead ends. First, if representation is understood as a relation between subjects and their representatives, like a group of principals with one agent, then the state is written out of the picture. It is difficult to see how actions undertaken in the names of present-day subjects could generate responsibilities for a totally different group of subjects with different representatives three generations from

---

12. I return to this point in §15.3.

13. Tuck (2016: Chapter 2) argues that Hobbes' theory of sovereignty is more amenable to democracy than is usually thought. The people can be a 'sleeping sovereign' that retains sovereignty even though they have appointed a monarch or an assembly to wield power. Yet a Hobbesian democracy, unlike a modern democracy, is still absolutist; it cannot be limited, either by constitutional constraints or by international law. The absolutist aspect of Hobbes' theory of sovereignty is what precludes a more robust notion of state responsibility.

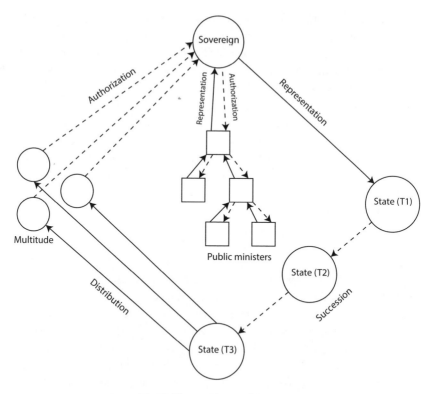

FIGURE 2. The Hobbesian Theory of State Responsibility

now. Second, if representation is understood as a relation between the state and its representatives—or 'organs', as in the functional theory—then subjects are written out of the picture. Their role in determining who represents the state is obscured, as is the fact that subjects ultimately bear the burdens of the state's responsibilities. Whereas the first dyad elides the corporate character of the state, the second elides the issues of legitimacy and distribution. Third, if representation is understood as a relation between subjects and the state, then the representatives of the state—legislators, presidents, soldiers, and civil servants—are written out of the picture. The state becomes a monolithic 'agent' that is assumed to act as a unit. The third dyad elides the fact states act through individual representatives, and that these representatives sometimes act at cross-purposes.

Hobbes' theory of representation simultaneously illuminates all four of the important relations: subjects authorize representatives; these representatives act in the name of the state; the state retains its identity over time; and the responsibilities of the state are distributed to its subjects.

The Hobbesian theory of state responsibility has three parts, which correspond to the Three Fundamental Questions. The first part is 'attribution': subjects (i.e., the multitude) authorize the sovereign, and the sovereign represents the state (directly and through public ministers). The consequent responsibilities, such as debts and treaty obligations, are attributable to the state. The second part is 'succession': the state (along with its responsibilities) persists over time as long as it has a continuous series of representatives. The identity of the state is sustained by representation, just as it is created by representation. The third part is 'distribution': the costs and burdens of the state's responsibilities are distributed to its subjects. Insofar as subjects are the authors of the sovereign's actions, it is legitimate to distribute the resulting costs and burdens to them. The next three chapters explore the issues of attribution, succession, and distribution in depth.

3

Attribution

THE QUESTION OF OWNERSHIP

'Men cannot distinguish, without study and great understanding, between one action of many men, and many actions of one multitude' (*L* XI. 158).

HOW CAN actions be attributed to a state? Hobbes' answer is deceptively simple: an action counts as an act of state provided that the agent who performed the action was an authorized representative of the state. For example, an airstrike is attributable to Israel if and only if the pilot who carried out the airstrike was, at that time, an authorized representative of Israel. It is not necessary to determine the 'intentions' of the state, as the agential theory suggests. Nor is it necessary to determine whether the individuals who performed the action were 'organs' of the state, as the functional theory suggests. The familiar concepts of authorization and representation do all of the work.

However, there are many boundary cases and complications. Can dictators be authorized representatives? Hobbes thought so, but most of us would now doubt this. What about parastatal entities, such as state-owned companies? Hobbes thought of corporations, public and private, as little more than extensions of their parent states, but present-day corporations are much more autonomous. This chapter reconstructs Hobbes' account of attribution and shows that, with some modifications, it provides an elegant and intuitive answer to the Question of Ownership.

The chapter has five sections. The first section distinguishes two types of responsibilities and two corresponding modes of attribution. Whereas *general* responsibilities are attributed to states according to their types (such as 'wealthy' or 'democratic'), *personal* responsibilities are attributed to states according to the actions of their authorized representatives (such as signing a treaty or borrowing money). The second section divides Hobbes' account of attribution into its two components: representation and authorization. The third section addresses problems and complications with this account, such as whether dictators count as authorized representatives and whether the actions of rogue officials count as acts of state. The fourth section translates Hobbes' account of attribution into an account of state responsibility. The state, its representatives, and its subjects are all implicated in acts of state, but in different senses: ownership lies with the state; accountability and culpability lie with its representatives; and liability lies with its subjects. The final section develops an account of misattribution, or 'impersonation', which determines who or what is responsible for misrepresentation and unauthorized representation of the state.

§13 General and Personal Responsibilities

There are two ways in which persons can incur responsibilities. The first is simply by being persons, or persons of a particular type. For example, it is often said that the rich have a responsibility to help the poor. The claim is that rich people have responsibilities because they belong to the type, 'rich'. It does not matter how they got rich or whether they agreed to help the poor; the responsibility is attributed to them on the basis of their class alone. *General* responsibilities are prospective and, as the label suggests, general in form: 'all persons (of type F) ought (not) to do X'. These include role-based responsibilities, which are attributed to persons according to their statuses (such as 'police officer'), and relational responsibilities, which are attributed to persons according to their relations to other persons (such as 'parent of' or 'neighbour of').

The second way in which persons can incur responsibilities is through their actions. If Margaret owes money to a creditor, it is because she borrowed the money. The amount of money she owes does not depend on how much money she has. The responsibility to repay the creditor is attributed to her on the basis of her actions rather than her class. *Personal* responsibilities have a simple subject–predicate form, and they can be either prospective or retrospective: 'P ought (not) to do X' or 'P ought (not) to have done X'. Whereas general responsibilities are attributed to persons according to their types, personal responsibilities are attributed to persons according to their actions.

Many of the responsibilities of states are general. For example, the United Nations General Assembly proclaimed in 2005 that 'each individual State has the responsibility to protect its populations from genocide, war crimes, ethnic cleansing and crimes against humanity' (UN, 2005: Art. 138). The claim is that all persons that belong to the type, 'state', have a responsibility to protect their populations. Other general responsibilities apply to types of states, such the responsibility of wealthy states to help poor states. Customary international law is the main source of states' general responsibilities.

Attributing general responsibilities to states is theoretically unproblematic. There are often definitional issues, such as whether Romania counts as a wealthy state. But once the content of a general responsibility is specified precisely enough, the attribution of it is almost automatic. If states with per capita GDPs above forty thousand US dollars have a responsibility to devote ten per cent of their GDPs to helping states with per capita GDPs below ten thousand US dollars, it follows logically that Luxembourg has this responsibility and that Romania does not. Problems of attribution that involve general responsibilities can be solved only by refining first-order normative theories and by codifying customary international law. A better theory of state responsibility will not make attribution any easier.

Most of the theoretical issues of attribution arise from personal responsibilities, such as debts, reparations, and treaty obligations. These responsibilities presuppose the attribution of particular actions to particular states. For example, the controversy about whether Russia was responsible for the 2014 missile attack on Malaysian Airlines Flight MH17 hinged on whether the act of launching the missile was attributable to Russia or only to particular pro-Russian rebels (Gibney, 2015). Issues of attribution are also central to the debate about whether states can commit crimes. It makes sense to hold Serbia (rather than individual Serbians) criminally responsible for ethnic cleansing during the Yugoslav Wars only if both the act of ethnic cleansing and the corresponding intent can be attributed to the state (Lang, 2011). Any theory of state responsibility must begin with an account of attribution—an account of what constitutes an act of state.

§14 The Conditions for Attribution

Hobbes drew a sharp distinction between acts of state and private acts. Actions of the state, or 'the people', are those performed by its authorized representatives: 'Whenever we say that a People . . . is willing, commanding or doing something, we mean a commonwealth which is commanding, willing and acting through the will of one man or [assembly]' (*DC* VI.1a). Private actions are those performed by subjects, or members of 'the multitude'. He saw the failure to distinguish 'between one action of many men, and many actions of one multitude' (*L* XI. 158) as a cause of sedition and conflict. Subjects 'are disposed to take for the action of the people, that which is a multitude of actions done by a multitude of men' (ibid.), which leads them to misattribute private actions to the state. What Hobbes had in mind was the rebellion against Charles I during the English civil wars. Subjects mistook the actions of the Parliamentarians for actions of England because they 'speak of a *large number* of men as the *people*, i.e. as the *commonwealth*; they speak of the *commonwealth* having rebelled against the *king* (which is impossible)' (*DC* XII.8). According to Hobbes, there are two individually necessary and jointly sufficient conditions for attributing actions to the state: representation and authorization.

§14.1 Representation

The first condition for attribution is that the action must be performed in the name of the state. The fact that the action is performed by a state official, or even by the sovereign, is not sufficient. As Hobbes says, 'a Monarch, hath the person not onely of the Common-wealth, but also of a man; and a Soveraign Assembly hath the Person not onely of the Common-wealth, but also of the Assembly' (*L* XXIII. 376).[1] When the sovereign acts (e.g., buys property or signs a contract) as a natural person, or in his own name, the action is attributable to him as an individual. But when the sovereign acts as an artificial person, or in the name of the state, the action is attributable to the state. Whether an act of the sovereign counts as a private act or as an act of state depends on which person—his own person, or the person of the state—he purports to represent at that time.

Similarly, subordinate officials or 'ministers' may represent either the natural person or the artificial person of the sovereign. Ministers 'that be servants to [sovereigns] in their naturall Capacity, are not Publique Ministers; but those onely that serve them in the Administration of the Publique businesse' (*L* XXIII. 376). Public ministers include judges, treasurers, provincial and colonial governors, ambassadors, civil servants, police officers, and soldiers. They represent the artificial person of the sovereign and, indirectly, 'the Person of the Commonwealth' (ibid.). For example, 'in their Seats of Justice [judges] represent the person of the Soveraign; and their Sentence, is his Sentence' (*L* XXIII. 380); his sentence is, in turn, the state's sentence. Sentencing a criminal is therefore an act of state. Conversely, private ministers represent the natural person of the sovereign (*L* XXIII. 382). When a servant makes tea for the sovereign, the act of making tea is not an act of state. Nor would making tea for the sovereign be an act of state if a judge or an ambassador did it, even though judges and ambassadors are normally public ministers. To represent the artificial person of the sovereign is to act for a public purpose.

If Hobbes' distinction between natural and artificial representation seems obvious, it is because something like it is taken for granted in modern politics. We still distinguish private acts from acts of state in much the same way

---

1. For the sake of brevity, I refer to the sovereign as if it is always an individual.

that Hobbes did. When Justin Trudeau signs a contract in his natural capacity, we say 'Trudeau signed a contract'. But when Trudeau signs a contract in his artificial capacity, we say 'Canada signed a contract'.[2] The only significant difference between Hobbes' notion of political representation and the modern notion is that we are less clear about where sovereignty is located. (As I explain in the next section, where we fundamentally diverge from Hobbes is on the issue of *authorization*.) Hobbes insists on a sharp distinction between the sovereign, who represents the state directly, and the public ministers, who represent the state indirectly by representing the artificial person of the sovereign (see §10 above). This distinction remains fairly sharp in constitutional monarchies. Trudeau is the prime (public) minister, and he represents Canada through the Queen, who is the sovereign. One might doubt that the Queen is the sovereign of Canada, or even of the United Kingdom, in anything but an empty, formal sense. But if the Queen is not really the sovereign, then who is? Parliament? The subjects? One might even doubt that there is a sovereign—much less a Hobbesian sovereign—in a modern, democratic state.

The elusiveness of the modern sovereign matters little for the issue of attribution, since the actions of both the sovereign and the public ministers are ultimately attributable to the state. A contract that Trudeau signs in his artificial capacity binds Canada regardless of whether he is the sovereign or merely a minister. The important distinction is not between the sovereign and the public ministers, but between people who act in the name of the state and people who do not. In other words, what matters is who represents the state, not which of its representatives is sovereign. In what follows, I often collapse the distinction between the sovereign and public ministers by referring to both together as 'the government'.[3]

The concept of representation puts limits on the kinds of actions that can be attributed to the state. As Runciman (2009: 23) points out, 'even the representatives of things that have no independent existence are limited by the need to keep up appearances'. An actor has to provide a plausible portrayal of the character that he plays, even if this character is fictional. He might portray Robin Hood as a gunslinger instead of an archer, but he cannot portray Robin Hood as a greedy executive. The first portrayal is conceivable, albeit anachronistic;

2. See Fleming (2017a) for a Hobbesian analysis of the semantics of action-sentences about states. I show that Hobbes' account of attribution allows us to make sense of these locutions without the idea of corporate agency.

3. I elide the distinction between sovereign and government with recognition that it is important for purposes other than attribution, such as determining who has the final say on constitutional questions (Tuck, 2016).

the second is so far 'out of character' that the audience will probably reject it. Political representatives are similarly constrained by the need to play the state's role in a plausible way. Although Hobbes insists that sovereigns can never be held accountable by their subjects, he argues that it is nevertheless important for sovereigns to provide a portrayal of the state that is acceptable to their subjects. The sovereign should always appear to be acting to preserve '*the safety of the people* . . . [and] all other Contentments of life, which every man by lawfull Industry, without danger, or hurt to the Common-wealth, shall acquire to himselfe' (*L* XXX. 520). It is especially important 'that Justice be equally administred to all degrees of People; that is, that as well the rich, and mighty, as poor and obscure persons' (*L* XXX. 534). If the sovereign routinely acts in his own interest or in the interest of a certain class of subjects, then his subjects will come to see him as a natural person who is merely pretending to be an artificial person, and they may cease to accept his actions as acts of state. The inevitable result of 'partiality toward the great' is 'the ruine of the Common-wealth' (*L* XXX. 536), both metaphorically and literally: the idea that the state is a distinct person will be lost, and the political union will be torn apart by faction and rebellion.

The representatives of modern states are similarly bound by the constraints of representation. Justin Trudeau can sign a treaty in the name of the Canada, but he cannot take a vacation in the name of Canada. States do sign treaties; they do not take vacations. Nor can he buy his children a palace in the name of Canada. The more tenuous the connection is between an action and 'the safety of the people', the less plausible it is to attribute that action to the state.

§14.2 Authorization

Representation is necessary but not sufficient for attribution. Anyone can act in the name of the state, but only the actions of those who are authorized to do so are attributable to the state. As Hobbes says, 'a Souldier without Command [of the sovereign], though he fight for the Common-wealth, does not therefore represent the Person of it' (*L* XXIII. 378). The Parliamentarians acted in the name of England; what distinguishes them from Charles I is that they lacked authority (at least, in Hobbes' view, before the King was executed). Authority likewise distinguishes the Provisional Irish Republican Army (IRA) from the Irish Army. Members of the Provisional IRA acted in the name of the Republic of Ireland, but, because they were not authorized to do so, their actions were not attributable to the state. We therefore say that the Provisional IRA assassinated Lord Mountbatten, not that the Republic of Ireland did. Much as Hobbes did, we use the concept of authority to distinguish person-ation of the state from *im*personation of the state.

For Hobbes, authorization of the state's representatives proceeds in two steps. The individual members of the multitude first 'Authorise all the Actions and Judgements, of [one] Man, or Assembly of men' (*L* XVIII. 264); this individual or assembly becomes the sovereign. The sovereign then parcels out this authority to public ministers, who 'have no other right, but what depends on the Soveraigns Will' and therefore 'can doe nothing against his Command, nor without his Authority' (*L* XXIII. 378). As with representation, we no longer make such a stark distinction between sovereign authority and the authority of public ministers, but we still tend to think of political authority as a roughly hierarchical chain. Authority is initially granted by subjects and then distributed among the representatives of the state. For example, in the Westminster system, subjects authorize members of Parliament, members of Parliament authorize the prime minister, the prime minister authorizes cabinet ministers, cabinet ministers authorize political staff, and so on. The important distinction is not between sovereigns and public ministers, but between representatives who are part of the chain of authority and representatives who are not.

Identifying the authorized representatives of the state is in most cases straightforward. Some, such as police officers and soldiers, literally wear their authority on their sleeves. Others, such as bureaucrats, have titles that indicate their authority. As Hobbes says, 'if the question be of Obedience to a publique Officer; To have seen his Commission, with the Publique Seale, and heard it read; or to have had the means to be informed of it, if a man would, is a sufficient Verification of his Authority' (*L* XXVI. 428). But a 'Publique Seale' is not a necessary sign of authority: a spy is a 'Minister of the Common-wealth' even though he does not display his authority publicly (*L* XXIII. 382). The authority of spies, undercover police, and other secret agents can be inferred from the fact that they take orders from authorized representatives of the state.

So far, so simple. In order to count as an act of state, an action must (1) be performed in the name of the state, as well as constitute a plausible performance of the state's role; and (2) be performed by an agent who has been authorized, directly or indirectly, by the subjects of the state. Omissions can be attributed to the state in the same way. For instance, we say that the United States failed to ratify the Rome Statute of the International Criminal Court because its authorized representatives failed to do so. As obvious as Hobbes' account of attribution might seem, it differs greatly from the accounts of attribution that underpin the agential and functional theories of state responsibility. It relies on the concepts of representation and authorization rather than agency or function, and it therefore eliminates the need to identify the 'intentions' or 'organs' of the state. However, as I explain in the next section, Hobbes' account of attribution has several problems of its own.

§15 A Hobbesian Account of Attribution

There are five problems with Hobbes' account of attribution: (1) his conception of 'voluntary' action is flawed; (2) he assumes that subjects must authorize the sovereign unanimously; (3) he assumes that political authority must
be limitless and therefore irrevocable; (4) he does not distinguish the actions
of unauthorized representatives from *ultra vires* actions; and (5) his view of
subordinate corporations as extensions of the state is no longer realistic. What
is needed in each case is a more refined notion of authorization. Although the
structure of Hobbes' account of attribution can be retained, his understanding
of authorization is no longer adequate, if it ever was.

It should not be surprising that Hobbes does not provide a ready-made
theory of state responsibility. On the contrary, we should be surprised—and
sceptical—whenever someone claims that a thinker from a radically different
time provides a grand solution to a contemporary problem. What Hobbes
provides is simply the right way of conceptualizing attribution. This section
makes the transition from Hobbes' account of attribution to a 'Hobbesian'
account of attribution.

§15.1 The Background Conditions for Authorization

Hobbes' account of authorization is superficially similar to modern, democratic accounts of authorization (e.g., Parrish, 2009; Stilz, 2011). The representatives of the state are authorized through voluntary actions of its subjects:
'The way by which a man either simply Renounceth, or Transferreth his Right,
is a Declaration, or Signification, by some voluntary and sufficient signe, or
signes, that he doth so Renounce, or Transferre' (L XIV. 202). However, what
counts as a voluntary action for Hobbes is very different from what we would
consider to be voluntary. In his view, actions that are performed under the
threat of violence count as voluntary (L VI. 92, XIV. 212), so authority that is
granted under duress is valid. A sovereign who threatens his subjects into submission is nevertheless their authorized representative.

> A Common-wealth by Acquisition, is that, where the Soveraign Power is
> acquired by Force; And it is acquired by force, when men singly, or many
> together by plurality of voyces, for fear of death, or bonds, do authorise all
> the actions of that Man, or Assembly, that hath their lives and liberty in his
> Power (L XX. 306).

Hobbes places only one limit on what counts as valid authorization. People
who are kept in prisons or chains cannot authorize their captors (L XX. 312–
14), because a person can be bound by his words only if he is not already

bound by force. The necessary background condition for valid authorization is thus that the author must have 'corporall liberty allowed him' (*L* XX. 312).

Hobbes' account of authorization follows from his theory of the will. He defines the will as 'the last Appetite, or Aversion, immediately adhaering to the action, or to the omission thereof' (*L* VI. 92).[4] An appetite is an inclination toward something (such as hunger or lust), while an aversion is an inclination away from something (such as fear or disgust). An agent's hunger is her will when it causes her to eat; an agent's aversion to gaining weight is her will when it causes her to refrain from eating. Since 'A *Voluntary Act* is that, which proceedeth from the Will' (ibid.), and since the will can be an aversion, it follows that 'those [actions] that have their beginning from Aversion, or Feare of those consequences that follow the omission, are *voluntary actions*' (ibid.). Hobbes considers authority that is granted under the threat of violence to be valid because, by his definition, it has been granted voluntarily. Although subjects of the Khmer Rouge might have pledged allegiance to the government because they were afraid of being killed, they nevertheless pledged allegiance voluntarily according to Hobbes, because their pledges proceeded from their wills. The only subjects of the Khmer Rouge who did not voluntarily pledge allegiance to the government were those who were compelled to do so through torture or imprisonment. Mere threats of torture, imprisonment, or even death do not suffice to make their pledge involuntary or their authorization invalid.

Hobbes' account of authorization looks repugnant to the modern reader, and for good reason. It implies that Pol Pot was an authorized representative of Cambodia no less than Tony Blair was an authorized representative of the United Kingdom. An adequate account of authorization requires a more refined conception of voluntary action. What makes an action voluntary is not just that it proceeds from the agent's will, but that it proceeds from the agent's *authentic* will—a will that follows from the agent's own deliberation and judgment. It is obviously true that no agent's will ever perfectly satisfies this condition, even in the most favourable circumstances. Our wills are always doubly tainted by natural impulses and by social influences. First, habits and emotions impinge on our deliberation and judgment. Second, even if we can resist the force of impulse, the content of our deliberations and judgments is largely determined by socialization. The latter is the Rousseauian problem of authenticity: 'the man accustomed to the ways of society is always outside himself and knows how to live only in the opinion of others' (Rousseau, 1987 [1754]: 81).

Although our wills are never fully authentic, some wills are more authentic than others. Voluntary action requires only a *minimally* authentic will, or, put

---

4. See Overhoff (2000) on Hobbes' theory of the will.

the other way around, a will that has not been entirely corrupted or hijacked. A will that follows from habit, such as the desire to buy a product of a certain brand, seems authentic enough for voluntary action. So does a will that is shaped by social pressure, such as the desire to wear certain clothes to fit in with one's peers. Even a will that follows from compulsion, such as the desire to gamble or take drugs, is authentic enough for voluntary action in all but the most pathological cases. A will that follows from violent threats, systematic deception, or insanity, on the other hand, is not sufficiently authentic for voluntary action, because it is not mediated by the agent's deliberation and judgment. There are three necessary conditions for voluntary action and hence for valid authorization: the agent's will must not be a product of (1) coercion, (2) indoctrination, or (3) incompetence.

First, the 'coercion condition' says that an action is involuntary if the agent performs it under the threat of violence.[5] If subjects pledge allegiance to a government only to avoid imprisonment, torture, or death, then they do not pledge allegiance voluntarily. The flaw in Hobbes' argument to the contrary is not as obvious as it seems. He is right that actions performed out of fear are not necessarily involuntary: 'when a man throweth his goods into the Sea for *feare* the ship should sink, he doth it neverthelesse very willingly' (*L* XXI. 326). His mistake is that he elides the difference between performing an action to avoid a negative consequence and performing an action to avoid a negative consequence that *another agent* threatens to inflict. The man who throws his goods into the sea acts out of fear, but his actions are voluntary because the only will involved is his own. The subject who is threatened into pledging allegiance to a government does so involuntarily because her actions follow from *someone else's* will. She is effectively an instrument of the government. What makes coerced authorization involuntary and therefore invalid is not that it is driven by fear, but that it is driven by the will of another agent.

The first background condition for valid authorization is thus that the authors must not be compelled to authorize; otherwise, their authorization could not be said to follow from their own wills. At a minimum, subjects must be able to express dissent without violent consequences. This must be understood as a general standard rather than an absolute rule, since all governments occasionally use violence against dissenters. The fact that an otherwise liberal-democratic government has deployed police to arrest peaceful protesters does not make it an unauthorized government. Even more violent and frequent repression of dissenters does not automatically disqualify the government

---

5. See Nozick (1969) for an influential account of coercion. While all kinds of threats can be coercive according to Nozick, I use 'coercion' more narrowly to refer to threats of violence.

from being authorized. A government that uses violence in response to certain kinds of dissent (such as protests) or certain kinds of dissenters (such as separatists) might still count as authorized if it allows other kinds of dissent, such as genuine opposition parties, public criticism, or independent opinion polling. The coercion condition only disqualifies governments that systematically and violently repress dissenters to such a degree that dissent is not a viable option. There are all too many examples of governments of this kind. The Maoist government, the Khmer Rouge, and, more recently, the governments of North Korea and Turkmenistan might be taken as archetypical examples. Governments that threaten their subjects into submission are *ipso facto* unauthorized because they make it impossible to know whether their subjects grant authority voluntarily.

Second, the 'indoctrination condition' says that an action is involuntary if it is a consequence of systematic manipulation. If subjects pledge allegiance to the government because it has used its power to indoctrinate or brainwash them, then they pledge allegiance to the government involuntarily. What makes manipulated authorization involuntary is not that it proceeds from ignorance, but that it proceeds from an inauthentic will. Someone who supports a certain party out of habit, without knowing much about the party's platform or candidates, supports that party out of ignorance but nevertheless voluntarily, since the only will involved is his own. Someone who supports a certain party because the party has indoctrinated him (as in North Korea) does so involuntarily, since his will has been hijacked by other agents. Like the subject who is threatened into submission, the indoctrinated subject is little more than an instrument of the government.

The second background condition for valid authorization is thus that subjects must have access to information. This is not to say that governments that control information or spread misinformation cannot count as authorized, but only that subjects must have some sources of information that are not controlled by the government that they are supposed to authorize. Although Putin's Russia and Erdoğan's Turkey make extensive use of censorship and propaganda, their subjects still have other sources of information, restricted as they are. Russian and Turkish subjects are not indoctrinated, much less brainwashed, though their governments have indeed deceived many of them. The governments of Turkmenistan and North Korea, on the other hand, have effectively monopolized information and used this power for systematic manipulation. Governments that indoctrinate their subjects are *ipso facto* unauthorized because they make it impossible for subjects to form the authentic wills that are necessary for valid authorization.

The indoctrination condition is similar to Williams' (2005: 6) 'critical theory principle', which says that 'the acceptance of a justification [for exercising power] does not count if the acceptance itself is produced by the coercive power which is supposedly being justified'. Yet there is an important difference. Williams (2002: 226) argues that a 'belief is not necessarily discredited just because it is caused through the power of someone'. The belief, and the consequent acceptance of the power that brought it about, is nevertheless valid as long as the agents would still accept the belief 'if they were to understand properly how they came to hold this belief' (ibid. 227). Williams uses the example of compulsory education. Although the beliefs of a student are brought about through the power of her teacher, this power is legitimate insofar as the student, after coming to understand the power relation between student and teacher, would continue to believe what the teacher taught her. The same test applies to the beliefs that subjects hold about their government: 'If they were to understand properly how they came to hold this belief, would they give it up?' (ibid. 227)

The indoctrination condition eschews this counterfactual and accordingly makes a stronger claim. Authorization that is a consequence of systematic manipulation, or indoctrination, is *necessarily* invalid because it does not follow from the authors' own deliberation and judgment. For example, suppose that a government used an extensive system of propaganda, censorship, and reeducation in an attempt to eliminate all forms of inequality. This government might pass the critical theory test, because most subjects might still believe in human equality and even continue to support the government if they understood how their beliefs were brought about.[6] However, the authority of the 'egalitalitarian' government would be invalidated by the indoctrination condition. Since subjects' beliefs were brought about through indoctrination, any action that follows from these beliefs is involuntary. Subjects are incapable of voluntary action and hence of granting authority if their wills have been hijacked by other agents. What subjects *would* do if they had the opportunity to exercise their capacities for deliberation and judgment has no bearing on whether their actions are *in fact* voluntary, nor therefore on the validity of their authorization. Nor does it matter whether their belief in human equality is sound; the issue of 'false consciousness' is also irrelevant. The point of this admittedly artificial example is that indoctrination of subjects renders their authorization invalid, regardless of the content of the doctrine.

---

6. 'Might' is the crucial word here. The critical theory principle requires speculative counterfactuals about what people would believe under radically different conditions, which makes it easy for the speculators to smuggle in their own values. Libertarians and socialists would reach different conclusions about what the members of the 'egalitalitarian' state would believe if they understood how their beliefs were brought about. An advantage of the indoctrination condition is that it makes these wild counterfactuals unnecessary.

What makes this artificial example necessary is that pure cases of indoctrination do not really exist. Coercion and indoctrination inevitably go together. It is difficult to see how a government could indoctrinate its subjects without tightly controlling information, and it is equally difficult to see how a government could tightly control information without using violence to silence dissenters. Governments that are disqualified by the indoctrination condition are very likely to be disqualified by the coercion condition. However, although indoctrination initially requires coercion, successful indoctrination renders subsequent coercion unnecessary. I treat the coercion and indoctrination conditions separately to emphasize that manipulated authorization is invalid even if it is no longer backed up by force. A cult-like government that indoctrinates its subjects into submission could not be authorized any more than a government that threatens its subjects into submission.

Third, the 'competence condition' says that an action is involuntary if the agent lacks the ability to comprehend its consequences. A child who recites a pledge that she cannot understand has not pledged allegiance voluntarily. Hobbes himself makes this point:

> naturall fooles, children, or mad-men . . . had never power to make any covenant, or to understand the consequences thereof; and consequently never took upon them to authorise the actions of any Soveraign, as they must do that make to themselves a Common-wealth (*L* XXVI. 422).

'Incompetent' subjects, and especially children, pose a serious problem for any theory of state responsibility. If children cannot be counted as authors of the government's actions, then why should subjects bear the costs of debts and other obligations that the government incurred before they reached the age of majority—let alone before they were born? I put this problem aside until Chapter 5 because it pertains to the distribution of liability rather than to authorization of the state's representatives. For now, it suffices to say that the fact that some subjects are incapable of granting authority does not imply that the government is unauthorized. I argue in the next section that unanimous authorization is unnecessary.

In sum, the background conditions for authorization follow from the principle that authorization requires a minimally authentic expression of the author's will. A government cannot possibly count as an authorized representative of the state if it suppresses or hijacks subjects' wills through systematic coercion or indoctrination. At a minimum, an authorized government must permit some dissent and some exchange of information among subjects. This account of authorization may appear to depend on a 'liberal' conception of the individual, which assumes that human beings have inherent capacities for independent thought and action. Although my account of authorization is indeed individualistic, it does not assume that individuals are metaphysically free, let alone freedom-loving. The distinction between voluntary and involuntary actions does not require anything like the notion of free will (Harris, 2012: 12–13). A will need not be 'free', in the sense of 'undetermined' or 'agent-determined', in order to be authentic. I take for granted (as Hobbes does) that agents' wills are ultimately determined by some combination of forces beyond their control, such as education, socialization, and genetics. What makes an action voluntary is simply that it is mediated by the agent's subjectivity, influenced as it is by many external factors. An involuntary action, on the other hand, is one that the agent performs because of the direct influence of *some other specific agent or agents,* rather than a diffuse set of social and biological influences.

The background conditions for authorization tell us very little by themselves. It is one thing to specify the conditions that must be met in order for authorization to be possible, but it is quite another to determine whether a particular government is actually authorized. The next two sections fill in the form and content of authorization.

§15.2 The Form of Authorization

According to Hobbes, every single subject authorizes the sovereign. They are 'many Authors, of every thing their Representative saith, or doth in their name; Every man giving their common Representer, Authority from himselfe in particular' (L XVI. 250). Although the members of the multitude might initially disagree about whom to authorize, they must authorize the sovereign unanimously: 'every one, as well he that *Voted for it,* as he that *Voted against it,* shall *Authorise* all the Actions and Judgements, of that Man, or Assembly of men' (L XVIII. 264). A dissenter can either 'consent with the rest' or remain in the state of nature, 'wherein he might without injustice be destroyed by any man whatsoever' (L XVIII. 268). Authorization is therefore binary: a representative of the state is authorized by all subjects or by none of them.

The idea that authorization must be unanimous clearly served Hobbes' political aim—to encourage absolute obedience to the sovereign—but it is both unrealistic and unnecessary. For one thing, political authorization is always partial and contested. Subjects inevitably disagree about whether a government is authorized, and dissenters cannot simply be cast back into the state of nature (if there is even such a place to cast them). In any case, it is unnecessary for the government to be authorized by every single subject. Unanimous authorization would be necessary if the government represented subjects as individuals, because individuals who are not 'fooles, children, or mad-men' could not legitimately be represented by agents whom they did not authorize.

Presidents and legislators could not represent competent adults who have not authorized them, any more than lawyers and accountants could. But the government represents the state, not each subject; it need not be authorized by every individual because it does not represent any individual.[7]

There is a tendency to think that governments represent individual subjects. For example, some Americans have disavowed Donald Trump using the phrase 'not my president', with the implication that Trump does not personally represent them (Gold, Berman, and Merle, 2016). This is certainly true, but it is equally true of Trump's supporters, because the president does not represent Americans as individuals.[8] This point is borne out in our common language (see Fleming, 2017a). Although we attribute the actions of presidents to their states, we do not attribute their actions to individual subjects. When Trump announced his plan to withdraw from the Paris Climate Change Agreement, the act of withdrawing was attributable to the United States. Headlines accordingly read that the 'US withdraws from Paris climate change agreement' (Sharman, 2017). However, the act of withdrawing was not attributable to any particular American other than Trump himself. We would not say of a Trump supporter—say, Michael from Pittsburgh—that *he* withdrew from the Paris Agreement. The fact that Trump represents the state, not individual Americans, explains why he need not be authorized by every single American. Political authorization is not and need not be unanimous. This is what makes it political.

Williams' (2005) idea of the Basic Legitimation Demand (BLD) provides an account of authorization that recognizes the fact that political authority is always partial and contested. Although he mainly uses 'legitimacy' rather than 'authority', his account of legitimation is essentially an account of authorization. For Williams, legitimate power *is* authority.[9] The BLD fits well into a Hobbesian framework, not least because Williams identifies 'the "first" political question in Hobbesian terms as the securing of order, protection, safety, trust, and the conditions of cooperation' (ibid. 3). What follows is a

7. Hobbes sometimes says that the sovereign is the 'representative of all and every one of the Multitude' (*L* XIX. 284; see also Martinich, 2016), which suggests that the sovereign represents each subject in addition to the state. Be that as it may, unanimous authorization is not logically or conceptually necessary for representation of the state.

8. This point is inspired by Runciman's (2007: 101–2) discussion of the 'not in my name' campaign against the 2003 Iraq War.

9. For instance, Williams (2005: 11) writes that 'what we acknowledge as LEG [legitimate], here and now, is what, here and now, MS [makes sense] as a *legitimation of power as authority*' (emphasis added; see also Williams, 2005: 135).

Hobbesian adaptation of the BLD.[10] It might alternatively be called the Basic Authorization Demand (BAD) if not for the unfortunate acronym.

The BLD says that there must be 'an "acceptable" solution to the first political question' (ibid. 4). In order to count as authorized, the government must provide a justification of its power that its subjects accept—one that 'makes sense' to them according to their own culture, history, and political vocabulary (ibid. 10–11). There are three insights that we can take from Williams about the form that authorization must take: (1) it requires 'acceptance' of the government (as opposed to explicit consent or mere acquiescence); (2) acceptance is never unanimous, so the criterion for authorization is whether a 'substantial number' of subjects accept the government; and (3) authorization depends on whether subjects *actually* accept the government, not on whether they would or should accept it.

First, 'acceptance' is more demanding than acquiescence but weaker than consent. Acquiescence, or the absence of resistance against the government, is not sufficient for authorization because it need not be voluntary (see §15.1). Merely obeying someone who exercises power—whether a police officer or a highway robber—does not make one an author of that power. If acquiescence were sufficient for authorization, then victims of robbery would become authors of their robbers' actions when they hand over their goods. Consent, or endorsement of the government, is sufficient but not necessary for authorization. It is too demanding, not least because most subjects have never consented to be governed at all (Simmons, 2009). The criterion for authorization is whether subjects *accept* the government, or recognize it as a legitimate representative of the state. Whereas consent requires a specific action, acceptance is an attitude or disposition. Subjects can accept a government (e.g., by recognizing an election result as legitimate), and thus authorize it, without consenting to it (e.g., by voting for it or taking a pledge of allegiance). For example, although most Canadians did not vote for the Liberal Party in 2015 or 2019, the vast majority of them accept that the Liberal government legitimately represents Canada. Dissenters often question the wisdom of the government's policies but rarely its right to govern. If consent—or even the consent of the majority—were the standard for authorization, then the government of Canada would not count as authorized, since the majority of voters (to say nothing of Canadians in general) did not vote for the Liberal Party or consent to be governed by it in any other way. The fact that most Canadians accept the Liberal government as legitimate is sufficient to implicate their wills and hence to make them its authors. I say more below about how it is possible to judge whether subjects accept the government.

10. See Hall (2015) and Sagar (2017) for analyses of Williams' BLD.

Second, given that acceptance is never unanimous, the criterion for authorization is acceptance of the government by 'a substantial number of the people' (Williams, 2005: 136). Ideally, this 'substantial number' should include a diverse cross-section of the subjects, including some members of minority and opposition groups. But as Williams argues, it is not possible to be more precise than this. What counts as a sufficient number of the people 'is a political question, which depends on the political circumstances' (ibid.). Judgments about whether a government passes the threshold for authorization are contextual and difficult, and this is what makes the assumption of unanimous authorization so tempting. It allows the political theorist to eliminate the need for messy political judgments. Stilz's (2011: 200) 'authorization account' of state responsibility succumbs to this temptation: 'if a state that credibly interprets my basic right exists, then I *necessarily authorize* it' (emphasis in original). With the claim that no subject can possibly withhold authority from a 'democratic legal state', she eliminates the need to consider whether subjects actually accept their government as legitimate. It is not obvious that the subjects of present-day Oman, for example, would accept the legitimacy of a 'democratic legal state', which is an essentially Western construction. Stilz also eliminates the need to consider subjects who credibly and consistently disavow the government (Pasternak, 2013: 367). Many indigenous peoples want nothing to do with the 'democratic legal states' that have been imposed on them. The problem with Stilz's argument is that it conflates the issue of whether the state is just with the issue of whether its government is authorized.[11]

Although the governments of just states are almost always authorized, there are countless examples of authorized governments that represent unjust states. The pre–Civil War United States was obviously unjust, but the governments that represented it were nevertheless authorized. A substantial number of Americans accepted these governments as legitimate representatives of the United States, even though a substantial number of Americans were enslaved and disenfranchised. If we deny that these slavery-era governments were authorized, and hence deny that the actions of these governments were attributable to the state, then the United States could not be responsible for slavery. Conflating just states with authorized governments rules out state responsibility for historical injustice from the outset. Justice concerns whether the structure of the state meets some moral standard of fairness. Authorization concerns whether subjects accept the government as a legitimate representative of the state.

---

11. Stilz (2011) does, however, restrict the scope of her argument to 'democratic authorization'. She leaves open the possibility that a non-democratic government might be authorized in some other way.

Third, authorization requires actual rather than hypothetical acceptance of the government. Whether subjects would or should accept the government as legitimate under idealized conditions might matter for determining whether the state is just (e.g., Rawls, 1971), but it has no bearing on whether the government of the state is authorized. Thought experiments and counterfactuals—even of the modest sort, as in Williams' (2002, 2005) critical theory principle—are irrelevant to the question of authorization. So, too, are universal moral principles, such as human rights. Subjects certainly *should* not authorize governments that do not respect human rights, but this does not mean that they do not. The claim that only rights-respecting governments can be authorized implies that states cannot be responsible for violations of human rights. For example, if the Milošević government's treatment of minorities disqualified it from being authorized, then Serbia could not be responsible for ethnic cleansing during the Yugoslav Wars, because the actions of the Milošević government would not be attributable to the state. We must not fall into the trap of thinking that an authorized government is necessarily a 'good' one.[12] An authorized government is one that a substantial number of subjects actually accept; it need not be democratic, liberal, or even rights-respecting.

Although there is no precise test for determining whether subjects accept the government as legitimate, it is possible to sketch some general principles, which might more accurately be called 'presumptions'. They indicate where the burden of proof lies, but they must be supplemented by contextual judgments.

The first presumption is that elected governments are authorized. Where there are institutionalized procedures for allocating political authority, there is a presumption that the representatives who are chosen by these procedures are authorized representatives of the state. Institutionalized procedures typically reflect a shared idea of what constitutes 'acceptance' in a given society (although these procedures are also, to some extent, products of power). There is also a presumption that the subordinates of these political representatives, such as civil servants, police officers, and soldiers, are authorized representatives of the state. The less democratic and less institutionalized the authorization procedures are, the weaker the presumption of authorization becomes. Restricted suffrage weakens the presumption in proportion to the restriction, because it makes the authorization procedure a less accurate measure of whether subjects actually accept the government as legitimate. Similarly, unreliable or rigged elections weaken the presumption of authorization in proportion to the extent of the unreliability or rigging. In short, there is a

---

12. The distinction between 'good' governments and authorized governments is central to contemporary political realism. E.g., Galston (2010), Horton (2012), Rossi (2012), and Sleat (2014).

presumption that elected governments are authorized governments, but the strength of the presumption depends on the character of the elections.

The presumption of authorization is reversed for unelected rulers, such as hereditary monarchs and military dictators. If a government circumvents the institutionalized authorization procedures (as in a coup), or if the authorization procedures do not provide a role for subjects (as in hereditary rule), then there is a presumption that the government is not authorized. Democratic authorization procedures have a privileged status only because, unlike other procedures, they purport to *measure* whether subjects accept the government as legitimate. The presumption of non-authorization for military and hereditary governments can be overturned if there is compelling evidence that subjects do accept the government. For example, although Oman is a hereditary monarchy, subjects' apparent loyalty to the Sultan (even through the Arab Spring) is evidence that he is an authorized representative (Tennent, 2015). Democratic elections provide especially strong evidence of authorization, but they are not the only possible evidence.

The picture of political authorization so far is as follows. In order to count as authorized, a government must first meet the coercion and indoctrination conditions, which, in practice, means that it must allow some dissent and some exchange of information among subjects. In addition, there must be evidence that a substantial number of subjects actually accept the government as a legitimate representative of the state. Elected governments are presumably authorized, but the strength of this presumption depends on how institutionalized and how democratic the elections are. Unelected governments are presumably unauthorized, but this presumption can be overturned if there is compelling evidence that subjects do accept the government as legitimate. There is one part of the Hobbesian account of authorization that remains to filled in: the content of authorization, or what the representatives of the state are authorized to do.

§15.3 The Content of Authorization

According to Hobbes (*L* XVII. 260), subjects authorize the sovereign to do anything that is necessary for their 'Common Peace and Safetie'. Since the sovereign is the sole judge of what is necessary, this effectively means that subjects authorize 'all the Actions, and Judgments of the Soveraigne' (*L* XVIII. 270). The authority of the sovereign is absolute; he is authorized to do anything that he sees fit.[13]

---

13. This does not mean that subjects must obey every command of the sovereign. As Hobbes later adds, subjects are not obligated to kill, injure, or accuse themselves. Nor are they obligated

One important implication of Hobbes' absolutism is that the authority of the sovereign is irrevocable. Subjects cannot withdraw their authority because, once they have authorized a sovereign, the right to revoke this authority belongs exclusively to the sovereign (*L* XVIII. 264). Nor can the sovereign forfeit his authority by exceeding it, because his authority has no limits (*L* XVIII. 266). Subjects do not even get their authority back when the sovereign dies, since the authority to choose a successor belongs to the current sovereign (*L* XIX. 298).

There is no reason why we must accept Hobbes' absolutism or the implication that political authority is irrevocable (see §12). As Runciman (2009: 26) points out, Hobbes' absolutism can be separated from the structure of his theory of representation.

> What can be dispensed with from Hobbes's account is the idea that authorization must be a once-for-all event, rather than an ongoing process. But what can be retained is the idea that those whom we authorize to act for us act not in our name as individuals, but in the name of the state, though it is as individuals that we pass judgment on their actions.

Political authority is always temporary, both because the conditions under which authorization occurs are temporary and because the subjects themselves are temporary. Although it is not possible to precisely specify the shelf-life of authority, there are two universally relevant considerations. The first is the human lifespan. Authority cannot possibly outlive the authors, so it fades with the passage of time. The fact that Alexander Lukashenko, president of Belarus, was democratically elected in 1994 has little bearing on whether he is authorized today. Many of the Belarusians who authorized him in 1994 have since died, and others have emigrated. Even those who did authorize him then might not authorize him now. The second consideration is that there are always new subjects. Reauthorization is necessary in order to account for children who have come of age and immigrants who have become subjects. Given that the voting age in Belarus is eighteen, Belarusians who were born after 1976 have never had the opportunity to vote in a fair election, so they cannot be counted as authors of the government unless they have authorized it in some other way. All governments must be reauthorized every few years, but what counts as 'a few' is determined by the conventions in each state. In the United Kingdom, there must be an election every five years; in Canada, every four years. The 'reauthorization interval' varies even though the requirement for reauthorization is universal.

---

to refrain from defending themselves against force, even when the force is that of the sovereign (*L* XXI. 336–40).

In addition to being temporary, political authority is always limited and conditional. The limits and conditions are prescribed by the role of each representative. For example, the role of 'British prime minister' has different limits than the role of 'British soldier'. A British prime minister has the authority to negotiate treaties but not the authority, which a British soldier has, to kill enemy combatants. These role-specific limits to authority are also context-specific. A British soldier in Afghanistan had different rules of engagement than a British soldier in Northern Ireland during the Troubles. We can usually defer to the laws and policies of a state in determining the precise limits of each representative's authority. Where laws and policies are silent, or where they are manifestly corrupt, we can turn to the inherent limits of each role, such as 'prime minister' and 'soldier'. A soldier acts outside of his authority if he extorts money from civilians, and a prime minister acts outside of her authority if she buys herself a sports car using public funds, regardless of whether the laws say otherwise. The concept of representation imposes limits on the kinds of actions that can plausibly be performed in the name of the state (see §14.1).

A less obvious consequence of Hobbes' absolutism is that it vitiates the distinction between representatives who exceed their authority, or act *ultra vires,* and representatives who are not authorized at all. This distinction is simply inapplicable to sovereign representatives. 'Unauthorized sovereign' is a contradiction in terms, and a Hobbesian sovereign cannot exceed his authority because his authority is limitless. A distinction between unauthorized and *ultra vires* actions could be drawn for public ministers, but Hobbes refuses to do so. He insists that public ministers 'can doe nothing against [the sovereign's] Command, nor without his Authority' (*L* XXIII. 378). If a minister exceeds his authority, then his actions are not attributable to the sovereign, nor therefore to the state. The underlying principle is that the actions of agents bind their authors 'so far-forth as is in their Commission, but no farther' (*L* XVI. 246). According to Hobbes, ministers who exceed their authority are no different than private individuals who usurp the sovereign's authority.

Although the principle that *ultra vires* actions are not attributable to the state might seem obvious and unobjectionable, it has some counterintuitive and troublesome implications. For one thing, it makes the distinction between authorized and unauthorized actions too sharp. If a police officer has jurisdiction only within a particular city, but he arrests a suspect a few metres outside city limits, is the act of arresting the suspect not an act of state? The police officer clearly exceeded his authority, but it would be inappropriate to treat him as a private individual. A police officer who acts *ultra vires* is not the same as a vigilante. Further, if *ultra vires* actions are not attributable to the state, then it is difficult to see how states could commit wrongful actions.

Suppose that the police officer used excessive force against the suspect—say, by Tasering him after he had already surrendered. Since the police officer did not have the authority to Taser the suspect, we would have to conclude that Tasering him was not an act of state. The fact that the police officer exceeded his authority would mean that the state is not in any way responsible for his actions. The suspect could sue the officer, just as he could sue a private individual who Tasered him, but he could not sue the state. Much less could the state be responsible for atrocities that its soldiers commit, such as abusing civilians or committing genocide, because no one has the authority to do these things. The absence of a distinction between unauthorized actions and *ultra vires* actions effectively makes the state an 'artificial angel': it can do no wrong, because the wrongs that its representatives commit are never attributable to the state.

The root of the problem is that Hobbes considers authority to be a licence to perform specific actions. The verb, 'to authorize', takes an agent (such as John Smith) as its direct object and an action (such as signing a contract) as its indirect object, as in 'I authorize John Smith to sign a contract in my name' (Martinich, 2016: 317). Although authorization of accountants and estate agents works this way, political authorization does not. Political representatives are not authorized to perform specific actions; they are authorized to perform roles. The indirect object of the verb, 'to authorize', is a role rather than an action, as in 'the people of France have authorized Emmanuel Macron to be president'. Within the limits of their roles, political representatives are authorized to use discretion and judgment. The same is true of subordinate representatives, such as police officers and civil servants. In Pettit's (2009: 65) terms, representatives of the state are 'trustees' rather than 'delegates'. Instead of 'delegating' the performance of specific actions to political representatives, subjects 'entrust' these representatives with the authority to make judgments about how to perform their roles.

This role-based notion of authorization makes it possible to distinguish *ultra vires* actions from unauthorized actions. Since political representatives are authorized to perform roles, not to perform specific actions, it is possible for them to exceed their authority in a particular instance while remaining authorized representatives. The difference between an *ultra vires* action and an unauthorized action is the difference between performing a role poorly and not performing it at all. The police officer who acts outside of his territorial limit is still acting as a police officer, and his actions are still attributable to the state, because he is still plausibly performing the role of a police officer. The same goes for the police officer who uses excessive force against a suspect. However, a police officer who extorts money from civilians is no longer acting as a police officer, because he is no longer performing his role; he is a 'rogue official'.[14] While the actions of representatives who act *ultra vires* are attributable to the state, the actions of rogue officials are not. I examine the consequences of misrepresentation and unauthorized representation of the state in §17.

§15.4 Non-State Corporate Entities

So far, I have assumed that the representatives of states are all individuals. Yet the actions of other corporate entities can also be attributed to the state. Just as it is necessary to distinguish the public and private actions of individuals, it is necessary to distinguish the public and private actions of corporate entities.

Hobbes distinguishes two types of non-state corporate entities. First, there are private bodies, 'which are constituted by Subjects amongst themselves, or by authoritie from a stranger [i.e., a foreign sovereign]' (*L* XXII. 348). Some private bodies, such as 'Corporations of Beggars, Theeves and Gipsies' (*L* XXII. 368), are prohibited by law. Others, such as families, are permitted (though not recognized or chartered) by law. In neither case are the actions of private bodies attributable to the state.

Second, there are '*Bodies Politique*' or '*Persons in Law* . . . which are made by authority from the Soveraign Power of the Common-wealth' (*L* XXII. 348). These include provinces, colonies, cities, universities, churches, and companies, all of which are chartered by 'Letters from the Soveraign' and regulated by law (*L* XXII. 350). Hobbes' account of subordinate corporate bodies appears to be similar to the 'concession theory' of corporations (Dewey, 1926: 666–68). Like proponents of the concession theory, he considers most corporate bodies to be creations of the sovereign. However, going well beyond the concession theory, he considers the actions of these bodies to be *attributable* to the sovereign. As Hobbes says, 'the act of [a representative of a corporate body] that recedes not from the Letters of the Soveraign, is the act of the Soveraign' (*L* XXII. 352). The clear implication is that an act of a corporate body is an act of state. What makes these bodies 'Politique' is that they are extensions of the state. It is striking that Hobbes puts 'colonies' and 'companies of merchants' in the same category; both are political bodies. For Hobbes,

---

14. Contemporary international law makes a similar distinction, though in functional terms: 'Cases where officials acted in their capacity as such, albeit unlawfully or contrary to instructions, must be distinguished from cases where the conduct is so removed from the scope of their official functions that it should be assimilated to that of private individuals, not attributable to the State' (ILC, 2001: 46).

chartered corporations are much like public ministers: they are authorized by the sovereign, and their actions are attributable to the artificial person of the sovereign and hence to the state. It is not coincidental that he discusses corporate bodies and public ministers in successive chapters.

Hobbes' account of corporate bodies made sense in his time, when many corporations were extensions of the state. He was intimately familiar with the corporations of his day, having held shares in the Virginia Company and the Somer Islands Company (Malcolm, 2002: 54–79). His experience with these companies probably shaped his understanding of corporations as 'political' bodies that are—or, at least, should be—controlled by the state. The Virginia Company was headed for a time by Sir Edwin Sandys, a prominent Parliamentarian whose sons served as colonels in the Parliamentary Army. As Malcolm writes, 'the Virginia Company must have seemed, to Hobbes, tainted with anti-royalism' (ibid. 57).

Modern corporations are still 'political' in the sense that the state creates the conditions for their existence (Ciepley, 2013), but they are not merely extensions of the state. It makes little sense to treat the actions of Apple and Google as actions of the United States simply because these corporations are incorporated under, and thus authorized by, American law. The fact that a corporation is authorized by the government does not necessarily mean that it represents the state. Hobbes' account of subordinate corporate bodies is far too simplistic: if the body is authorized by the sovereign, then its actions are acts of state; if it is not so authorized, then its actions are not acts of state. What is needed for attribution, in addition to authorization, is representation. The best evidence of representation is control. If a state controls another corporate entity, then there is a presumption that the entity represents the state. This presumption applies to the full range of sub-state and non-state corporate entities, from government agencies to private companies, from puppet states to rebel groups, and from intergovernmental organizations (IGOs) to nongovernmental organizations (NGOs).

At one end of the spectrum are government agencies, or corporate entities that are parts of the state. Some of these bodies are representative assemblies, such as legislatures, courts, cabinets, committees, boards, and tribunals. Others are represented by fiction, like the state itself; they are like 'many lesser Common-wealths in the bowels of a greater' (L XXIX. 516). The latter include departments, cities, armies, police forces, and the dozens of subunits within each. The representatives of the state often represent several of these fictional persons simultaneously. For example, a constable might simultaneously represent the Royal Canadian Mounted Police (RCMP), the Drug Squad, and Canada. His act of arresting a suspect is attributable to all three of these corporate bodies. In some contexts, we say that the Drug Squad arrested the suspect, such as when we count how many people the Drug Squad arrested in a given year. In other contexts, we say that the RCMP arrested the suspect, as a journalist probably would if she were writing a story about the case. In still other contexts, we say that Canada arrested the suspect, such as when we count how many people Canada has arrested for drug offences. Since a corporate body normally controls its subunits, attribution normally runs from the smallest body to the largest. The constable's actions are attributable to the Drug Squad, the Drug Squad's actions are attributable to the RCMP, and the RCMP's actions are attributable to Canada. There is a strong presumption that the actions of government agencies are attributable to the state.

At the other end of the spectrum are private companies. Although private companies are incorporated, and thus authorized, by the laws of their parent states, this does not imply that they represent their parent states. Authorization does not necessarily imply representation. Being incorporated under the laws of a state does not make a corporation a representative of that state, any more than being licensed to drive makes a driver a representative of the state that issued the licence. Although British Petroleum bears the name of Britain and is headquartered in London, it does not represent the United Kingdom because it is not controlled by the United Kingdom. It would obviously have been a mistake to say, after the 2010 *Deepwater Horizon* oil spill, that the United Kingdom spilled 4.9 million barrels of oil into the Gulf of Mexico. There is a strong presumption that the actions of private companies are not acts of state.

There are many corporate bodies that lie somewhere between government agencies and private companies. Near the former end of the spectrum are state-owned companies. Ownership creates a presumption of attribution to the state, because ownership allows the state to control the company as well as profit from it. The strength of this presumption varies according to how much equity the state has and how much control it exercises. The presumption of attribution is weaker for Norway's Equinor, which is only two-thirds state-owned, than for Malaysia's Petronas, which is wholly state-owned. There is a similar presumption of attribution for private companies that states have hired or contracted. Inmates of private prisons would obviously be counted among the people whom the United States has incarcerated. For the same reason, it makes sense to count Iraqi civilians killed by Blackwater, a private security company hired by the United States, among those killed by the United States. If a state commissions another corporate entity to act on its behalf, then the actions of that corporate entity are attributable to the state.[15]

---

15. Contemporary international law recognizes a similar principle: 'The conduct of a person or group of persons shall be considered an act of a State under international law if the person

This principle applies equally to rebel groups. Since Iran funds, arms, and gives orders to Hezbollah, the actions of Hezbollah are presumptively attributable to Iran. In other words, Hezbollah is presumed to represent Iran unless there is a compelling reason (such as disobedience of Iranian orders) to believe that Hezbollah is acting independently. This is not to say that the actions of all rebel groups that are associated with a state are presumptively attributable to that state. The Provisional IRA does not represent the Republic of Ireland, which has outlawed the Provisional IRA for decades. The presumption of attribution applies only to rebel groups that are, at least in part, controlled by a state.

The actions of puppet states are presumptively attributable to their puppeteer states. Since the 'Independent' State of Croatia was created, sustained, and partly controlled by Fascist Italy and Nazi Germany, the atrocities that the Independent State committed were also attributable to Italy and Germany. For the same reason, the actions of apartheid South Africa's Bantustans were attributable to South Africa. However, the presumption of attribution is much weaker for client states, which are partly dependent on but not created or controlled by their patron states. Although Israel receives financial and military support from the United States, it is also substantially autonomous. It would be a mistake to say that the United States invaded Gaza in 2014. However, if the United States did, in certain instances, exercise control over Israel, then Israel's actions would also be attributable to the United States. The primary consideration in each case is control.

The case is more complex and varied for international organizations. There is a presumption that the actions of NGOs, like the actions of private companies, are not attributable to the states in which the organizations are based or in which they operate. After all, they are *non*governmental. The exception is when a state exercises control over an NGO or commissions it to act. Under normal circumstances, the actions of the American Red Cross are not attributable to the United States. But if the United States commissions the American Red Cross to distribute aid, then the act of distributing aid is an act of state.

The actions of an IGO are not normally attributable to its member states. Rather, attribution normally runs from member states to the IGO. The relation between an IGO and its member states is structurally similar to the relation between a state and its agencies. If subordinate corporate bodies are like 'many lesser Common-wealths in the bowels of a greater' (*L* XXIX. 516), then IGOs are like greater commonwealths made up of many lesser. Just as a government

---

or group of persons is in fact acting on the instructions of, or under the direction or control of, that State in carrying out the conduct' (ILC, 2001: Art. 8).

department represents its parent state, a member state can represent the IGO of which it is a member. For instance, when Canada sent troops to Kosovo in 1999, it did so in the name of NATO. The act of sending troops was therefore attributable to NATO, just as the actions of Canadian soldiers were attributable to Canada. However, the connection between an IGO and its member states is much weaker than the connection between a state and its agencies. Government agencies almost always represent their parent states, but the member states of an IGO only represent the organization in certain cases and in very narrow domains. Although the actions of the Canadian Army are almost always attributable to Canada, the actions of Canada are rarely actions of NATO or the United Nations. It is necessary to distinguish the 'sovereign' from the 'intergovernmental' actions of states. For instance, the United States acted in the name of NATO when it invaded Afghanistan in 2001, but not when it invaded Iraq in 2003. The question in each case is whether the representatives of the state also acted as authorized representatives of the IGO.

Responsibility for the actions of an IGO is distributed among its member states, much as responsibility for the actions of a state is distributed among its subjects. Yet the justification for distributing responsibility is different in each case. Participatory accounts of collective responsibility do not apply within the state because most subjects do not directly participate in acts of state (see §1). As I argue in Chapter 5, subjects are liable as 'authors' of acts of state rather than as participants. The member states of an IGO, on the other hand, usually do participate directly in its actions. Responsibility for the actions of an IGO can simply be parcelled out among the member states in proportion to the control that they exert over the organization. For instance, the members of NATO bear responsibility for the 1999 intervention in Kosovo in proportion to their roles in authorizing, planning, and executing the intervention. Although the United States looms large among NATO members, decisions of the organization are made by consensus, which calls for a fairly broad distribution of responsibility. The United States bears a much greater share of responsibility for the intervention in Kosovo than does Poland, which did not participate in the intervention, but every member of NATO bears some share of the responsibility.

The actions of organizations that are neither intergovernmental nor nongovernmental, such as international courts and tribunals, are not normally attributable to states. Judgments of the International Court of Justice are sometimes directly authorized by states, as when two states submit a dispute to the Court, but these judgments are made only in the name of the Court. Its fifteen judges represent neither the states who submit disputes to them nor the United Nations General Assembly, which elects them. The Court is the only corporate person to which the decisions of its judges can be attributed.

However, if a judicial body is coopted or controlled by a state, then its actions ought to be attributed to that state. For example, although the International Narcotics Control Board (2018) purports to be 'an independent, quasi-judicial expert body' whose 'members serve impartially in their personal capacity, independently of Governments', it has been described as a 'conservative mouth piece of the US State Department' (Koutsoukis and Riley, 2000) on matters of drug policy. As one expert confirms, the claim 'that the US has exceptional and direct influence upon the operation of the Board is plausible' (Bewley-Taylor, 2012: 271). To the extent that the United States exerts control over the Board, the Board's actions ought to be attributed to the United States. The actions of a 'puppet organization', like those of a puppet state, are attributable to the puppeteers.

––––––

The Hobbesian account of attribution provides a set of principles and guidelines for determining what counts as an act of state. The same heuristic applies to every case: was the agent, at the time of the action, an authorized representative of the state? This heuristic can be used to fill in any remaining gaps and to guide our contextual judgments in particular cases.

§16 From Attribution to Responsibility

A person to which an action is attributed is always, in some sense, responsible for it. However, responsibility can take several different forms: (1) ownership, meaning that nominal responsibility for the action attaches to the person; (2) culpability, meaning guilt or blame; (3) accountability, meaning an obligation to explain or justify the action; and (4) liability, meaning an obligation to bear the costs. These four kinds of responsibility are seldom distinguished because they usually go together in cases of individual responsibility.[16] For example, holding a thief responsible involves all four kinds of responsibility: we simultaneously attribute ownership to him (by calling him a thief and putting the theft on his record), hold him culpable (by sentencing and punishing him), hold him accountable (by asking him to explain his actions or to apologize), and hold him liable (by making him return the stolen goods or compensate the victim).

Yet there are a variety of circumstances in which the kinds of responsibility come apart. One is when an employer delegates authority to an employee. If the employee is reckless and injures someone on the job, both she and her

---

16. See Shoemaker (2011) for an influential attempt to distinguish the components of responsibility.

employer are responsible, but in different ways. The employee owns the reckless act (it goes on her criminal record), and she is both accountable (must apologize) and culpable (guilty and punishable) for it, but the employer may be partly liable (for compensating the victim). The kinds of responsibility often come apart in principal–agent relationships. They come apart to an even greater extent for persons that are represented by fiction, such as states and corporations. The state, its representatives, and its subjects are all responsible for acts of state, but in different ways: ownership lies with the state; accountability and culpability lie with its representatives; and liability is distributed among its subjects.

States 'own' the actions of their authorized representatives, which means that nominal responsibility for these actions attaches to the state. When the government of Canada borrows money, Canada owes the money; the debt does not belong to the government or to individual Canadians (see §1). Likewise, when the chancellor of Germany signs a treaty, Germany is bound by the treaty; the obligation does not belong to Angela Merkel, even though she was the one who signed her name on the page. Nor does the obligation belong to the subjects of Germany or to any subset thereof, past or present. In some cases, ownership lies with both the agent who performed the action and the state that she represents. Since an action can be attributed to more than one person (see §15.4), ownership can be shared. For example, when soldiers carry out ethnic cleansing, we say both that the soldiers committed ethnic cleansing and that their state did. Ownership is non-exclusive: assigning responsibility to state officials for their part in wrongdoing does not preclude assigning that wrongdoing to the state, and vice versa. Nor, as I argue below, does holding individuals responsible render state responsibility redundant. Although ownership is a very thin and ephemeral kind of responsibility, the fact that states can be ownership-responsible has important consequences.

States cannot be culpable, accountable, or liable any more than bridges, rivers, or other persons that are represented by fiction can. First, culpability requires intent, and states do not have intentions, or 'natural wills'. As Hobbes says,

> if a decision contrary to a *natural law* is made in the case of a *people* [democracy] or a *council of optimates* [aristocracy], the offender is not the commonwealth itself, i.e. the civil person, but the citizens who voted for the decision. For an offence issues from an expression of natural will, not from a political will, which is artificial (*DC* VII.14).[17]

17. Hobbes makes the same point in *The Elements*, except he describes the wills of sovereign assemblies as 'fictitious' instead of 'artificial' (*EL* XXI.4).

He adds that, 'in a *Monarchy,* if the *Monarch* makes a decision contrary to the *natural laws,* he is himself at fault, because in him the civil will is the same as the natural' (ibid.). Culpability is 'agent-specific'; it accrues only to the agent who intended the wrongful action. While ownership and liability can be incurred vicariously, culpability cannot be, because intent cannot be transferred from a representative to a representee. For example, if an employee defrauds a customer, her intent to commit fraud is not attributable to her employer. The fact that she represents him does not imply that *he* intended to commit fraud. The employer might be vicariously *liable* for compensating the victim, but he cannot be *culpable* for the fraud unless his own intentions are involved (for instance, if he conspired with the employee). Vicarious culpability is what we commonly call 'guilt by association'. For the same reason, a state cannot be culpable for a murder that one of its soldiers commits. Although the soldier's action can be attributed to the state, his intention cannot be, because intentions are not attributable or transferable. The state can therefore 'own' the act of killing but cannot be culpable for it. If an act of state is a criminal act, then culpability lies with the individual agents who intended the act.

It is true that there are forms of vicarious culpability in some legal systems. Under American federal law, the intentions of employees can be attributed to a corporation, and the corporation itself can therefore be held criminally responsible. But this idea has been subject to intense criticism (e.g., Gallo and Greenfield, 2014; Thomas, 2018), and for good reason. For one thing, vicarious culpability is guilt by association, and guilt by association is widely regarded as unjust (Lewis, 1948). More fundamentally, the assumption that intentions are attributable like actions is mistaken. As Rousseau (2019 [1762]: 59) understood, 'power may very well be transferred, but not will'.[18] There is an asymmetry between actions and intentions. Suppose that I authorize an estate agent to buy a house for me. I am indifferent about the colour of the house. But she happens to like red houses, so she buys me a red house. The act of buying a red house is attributable to me: 'I bought a red house' is true. But the corresponding intention is not attributable to me: it is false that 'I intended to buy a red house', even though it is true that 'the estate agent intended to buy a red house'. The case would be no different if a corporation or a state had authorized the estate agent to buy the house. It is simply false that the intentions of representatives are attributable to the persons that they represent. Vicarious culpability is a conceptually confused aberration.

18. Cf. Edgerton (1927: 841), arguing in favour of corporate criminal responsibility: 'if what his hands do may properly be attributed to the corporation for which he acts, what his brains do may be attributed to it with equal propriety'.

The issue of whether states can be culpable marks an important point of disagreement between proponents of the agential and functional theories.[19] Although states can be held responsible under international law, they cannot be held *criminally* responsible. The Nuremberg Tribunal's (1947: 221) oft-quoted declaration that 'crimes against international law are committed by men, not by abstract entities' remains the rule. As Crawford and Watkins (2010: 285) describe, 'there has been no development of corporate criminal responsibility to parallel the introduction of individual criminal responsibility on the international plane, nor has there been any trend among arbitral tribunals to impose punitive damages on states'. Since the functional theory, like the Hobbesian theory, rejects the idea that states have intentions (see §6), it rules out the possibility that states can be culpable.

The agential theory, on the other hand, implies that states can be culpable. If the state is a 'corporate agent, which in an important sense has a mind of its own', then it can 'exhibit the types of *mens rea* attitudes that are deemed so central to modern criminal culpability—namely, intention, recklessness, negligence, and the like' (Tanguay-Renaud, 2013: 262; see also Lang, 2007, 2011). Note that the agential theory does not *attribute* intentions to states. It does not claim that the intentions of state officials can somehow be transferred to the state as a whole; it claims that states have emergent intentions that are not reducible to the intentions of individuals. I have previously argued that this idea of collective intention does not scale up from small-scale groups, such as committees, to states (§5.1). But the agential theory's argument for holding states criminally responsible is at least plausible and coherent. The idea of vicarious culpability, on the other hand, is entirely baseless.

Even if it were conceptually coherent to assign culpability to states, our attempts to *hold* them culpable, or to punish them, would be in vain. The psychological and material components of culpability are lacking, because states cannot feel guilt or suffer the pain of punishment. Iraq may have been responsible for the 1990 invasion of Kuwait, but it was Iraqis who suffered from the resulting sanctions and reparations. Even the burdens of uniquely corporate 'punishments', such as institutional reform or dissolution, are borne by subjects. When the Allies dismantled and rebuilt the Japanese and German states after the Second World War, the subjects of Japan and Germany paid the price. Forcing these states to reform meant depriving their subjects of political rights. The burdens of punishment are inevitably borne, in some form or another, by the subjects of the target state. It seems implausible to describe these burdens

19. See Fleming (2017b) for a comparison of the agential and functional approaches to the concept of state crime.

as mere 'overspill' or 'misdirected harm' from punishing the state (Erskine, 2010)—analogous to the harm that a criminal's dependents suffer when he is imprisoned—because the harm to subjects is inextricable from the punishment of their state (Alschuler, 2009: 14–15). It is possible to punish a criminal without harming his dependents: he might be given a weekend sentence or a job in prison so that he can earn money for his family, and they might be given ample opportunities to visit him. Even the infliction of physical pain on a criminal does not necessarily harm his dependents. But punishing a state without harming its subjects is almost unimaginable.

Hobbes grappled with the issue of corporate punishment is his discussion of subordinate corporate bodies. Although he did not think corporate entities could be culpable, he did say that a corporate entity 'may be punished, as farreforth as it is capable, as by dissolution, or forfeiture of their Letters, (which is to such artificiall, and fictitious Bodies, capitall,)' (*L* XXII. 352). He added the caveat that 'from corporall penalties Nature hath exempted all Bodies Politique' (ibid.), by which he meant that corporate entities cannot bear the material consequences of punishment. These consequences are inevitably borne by the members of the corporate entity, which is why he insisted that a fine against a corporation should only be levied against 'a Common stock, wherein none of the Innocent Members have propriety' (ibid.). Yet if the material element of punishment (not to mention culpability) cannot be borne by corporate entities, then it is difficult to understand why corporate fines or reform should be considered punitive (cf. Schwenkenbecher, 2010). It seems more appropriate to treat 'fines' as payments of compensation and institutional reform as rehabilitation. Dissolving a corporate entity is more like dismantling a machine than it is like capital punishment: the former members of a dissolved corporation, unlike the executed criminal's cells, can form a new body. Using the language of punishment to describe state responsibility has no obvious benefit, but it does encourage misleading analogies of the kind that Hobbes himself was guilty of using.[20]

The burdens of responsibilities that do not involve wrongdoing are also borne by subjects. Strictly speaking, states cannot be liable any more than they can be culpable. Subjects are ultimately liable for the costs of their state's debts and treaty obligations, usually through taxation or inflation. Although Greece is indebted, Greeks suffer the consequences. I discuss the distribution of liability to subjects in Chapter 5.

---

20. I make several additional arguments against holding states criminally responsible in 'Leviathan on Trial: Should States Be Held Criminally Responsible? (Fleming, forthcoming a). See also Gould (2009) for criticisms of the concept of state crime.

Accountability, like culpability, lies with the state's representatives. The state cannot answer for its actions because it is incapable of speaking on its own. Nor can most of its subjects answer for their state's actions, because most subjects do not have any direct role in their state's actions and do not even know the reasons for them. The task of explaining, justifying, and, if necessary, apologizing for acts of state therefore belongs to the state's representatives. Political representatives usually do not assume personal accountability for acts of state. Instead, as in official apologies (Lind, 2008; Nobles, 2008), they act as artificial persons when they answer for the state. For example, Stephen Harper apologized in the name of Canada for the abuse that indigenous children suffered in 'residential schools'. The people who established and administered these schools are culpable; Canada owes reparations to the victims; the subjects of Canada are liable for the costs; but the current prime minister is accountable. The same division of responsibility occurs in every case: ownership lies with the state, culpability and accountability with its representatives, and liability with its subjects.

State responsibility *qua* ownership is a peculiarly intangible and unstable form of responsibility. It inevitably collapses into the accountability of the state's representatives of the liability of its subjects. When the state does wrong, its representatives are expected to apologize. When the state has obligations, its subjects are expected to bear the costs. One might therefore think that attributing ownership-responsibility to the state is just a figure of speech, or a kind of shorthand. It is tempting to think that the state's responsibilities could, in principle, be expressed in terms of individuals. This would be a mistake.[21] As Carr (1946: 151) recognized, 'the obligation of the state cannot be identified with the obligation of any individual or individuals'. He illustrates this point using the case of 'whether the Belgian Guarantee Treaty of 1839 imposed an obligation on Great Britain to assist Belgium in 1914'.

> The obligation rested neither personally on Palmerston who signed the treaty of 1839, nor personally on Asquith and Grey who had to decide the issue in 1914, neither on all individual Englishmen alive in 1839, nor on all individual Englishmen alive in 1914, but on that fictitious group-person 'Great Britain', which was regarded as capable of moral or immoral behaviour in honouring or dishonouring an obligation (ibid. 150).

Britain's obligation was not equivalent to Palmerston's obligation, since Britain remained bound by the Treaty after he left office, and even after he died. Nor

---

21. See Fleming (2017a) for a semantic argument for why the actions and responsibilities of states cannot be expressed in terms of individuals.

was Britain's obligation equivalent to the sum of Asquith and Grey's obligations, both because the Treaty preceded them and because Britain would still have been bound by it if someone else had been prime minister or foreign secretary. Nor, for a similar reason, can the obligation be identified with the obligations of British subjects. Britain remained bound by the Treaty even though most of the Britons of 1839 had since died and most of the Britons of 1914 had not yet been born when the Treaty was signed. An obligation of a state cannot be identified with the obligations of any set of individuals, past or present.

Although 'moral or immoral behaviour' can be attributed to a state only in a very thin sense, the supposition that states can do good or do wrong is nevertheless a crucial one. The fact that ownership attaches to the state allows responsibilities to be transmitted through time. As Carr (1946: 148–49) recognized, 'personification is the category of thought which expresses the continuity of institutions; and of all institutions the state is the one whose continuity it is most essential to express'. Although the individual subjects and representatives of a state ultimately bear the consequences of its actions, the individuals who bear the consequences are not necessarily the ones who authorized or performed the actions in the first place. I discuss the transmission of responsibilities over time in the next chapter.

§17 Impersonation of the State

Before turning to the Question of Identity, there is one final issue of attribution that must be addressed. Who or what is responsible for the actions of unauthorized representatives and rogue officials? The Hobbesian theory provides an account of *mis*attribution as well as an account of attribution. There are two types of impersonation of the state, each with different consequences: unauthorized representation and misrepresentation.

Unauthorized representation occurs when an agent acts in the name of the state but lacks the authority to do so. Examples include rebels who purport to represent the state but have not been authorized by its subjects (such as the Provisional IRA) and presidents who fail to meet the background conditions for authorization (such as the Supreme Leader of North Korea). Although the actions of these unauthorized representatives are not attributable to the state, they may be attributable to other corporate entities. For example, although members of the Provisional IRA were not authorized representatives of the Republic of Ireland, they were authorized representatives of the Provisional IRA itself. This is why it makes sense to say that the Provisional IRA bombed the Grand Hotel in Brighton but not that Ireland did. The Provisional IRA owns the bombing because its members authorized the bomber. Unauthorized representation of the state can thus generate other kinds of corporate responsibility.

The principle that the actions of governments and government agencies are attributable to the state (see §15.4) does not apply in cases of unauthorized representation. In these cases, state responsibility gives way to 'governmental responsibility'. For example, since the Supreme Leader fails to meet the background conditions for authorization, his actions are not attributable to North Korea. However, he might nevertheless count as an authorized representative of the Workers' Party of Korea or some subgroup thereof. The Workers' Party might therefore be responsible for Kim's nuclear tests even though North Korea is not. Even the most personalized forms of rule are, to some extent, corporate; individuals do not conduct nuclear tests on their own. But the relevant corporate entity for the purpose of responsibility is often the party or the government rather than the state.

Misrepresentation occurs when an authorized representative of the state 'goes rogue', or acts outside of the boundaries of his prescribed role (see §15.3). Such feigned acts of state are attributable only to the agents who perform them. For example, when a soldier extorts money from civilians, his actions are so far outside of his role that his claim to represent the state is no longer plausible. The act of extorting money is his alone, as if he were a criminal. Yet a rogue soldier is not *just* a criminal. The fact that the soldier has been authorized to represent the state means that the state has a (general) duty to prevent him from going rogue in the first place. Although the actions of rogue officials are not acts of state, the state may be responsible for failing to keep its officials under control. For example, France is responsible for failing to prevent its peacekeepers from sexually abusing civilians in the Central African Republic even though these peacekeepers were rogue officials. But when the 'victim' of the act of misrepresentation is the state itself, as in cases of corruption, responsibility lies entirely with the agent who performed the action. To hold a state responsible for failing to prevent its own officials from embezzling public funds would be to 'blame the victim'.

In some cases of misrepresentation, the responsibilities involved are much too large for individuals to bear. This is especially true for sovereign debts. Consider the fourteen billion US dollars that the Mobutu government borrowed in the name of Zaire between 1965 and 1997 (Ndikumana and Boyce, 1998). Even if Mobutu were an authorized representative of Zaire, many of his actions would still have been egregious misrepresentations of the state. Since he embezzled and otherwise misused a large portion of the money that he borrowed in the name of Zaire, and much more besides, the debt ought to have been attributed to him. Mobutu was a rogue official in the highest office. Yet Mobutu obviously could not have paid back the money that he borrowed, especially after he was ousted. Who should bear the costs in cases such as this?

According to current practice, the state is always obligated to repay money that its government borrows, no matter whether the government was authorized or what it did with the money.

> Creditors have the unlimited privilege to lend to whichever sovereign regimes they wish, in whatever amounts they deem fit, and on whatever terms they consider desirable. Their claims against the countries that have borrowed from them are in no way affected by either the nature of the political organization of the country to which they lend, the circumstances that it confronts, or the uses to which it puts the borrowed resources (Barry and Tomitova, 2007: 52).

Given that liability for debt ultimately distributes to the subjects of a state, it is they who ultimately bear the costs. The Hobbesian account of attribution implies that the creditors should instead bear the costs when the state has been impersonated. Since only the actions of authorized representatives can bind the state, those who make agreements with state officials had better make sure (1) that these officials are authorized and (2) that they represent the state in a credible way. As Hobbes says, 'he that maketh a Covenant with the Actor, or Representer, not knowing the Authority he hath, doth it at his own perill' (*L* XVI. 246).

The Hobbesian account of attribution thus lends support to the doctrine of 'odious debt', which says that 'some sovereign debt claims are not binding or enforceable on account of the creditor's awareness of the fact that the proceeds of the loan would be used to oppress the population of the debtor state, or would be used for personal enrichment rather than public purposes' (King, 2016: 2). Creditors have an obligation to ensure that the money they lend will be used for public purposes, such as infrastructure or services. If they fail to verify that the borrowing government credibly represents the state, then the debtor state's obligation to repay the money is void. The Hobbesian account of attribution implies a similar rule for other kinds of responsibilities, such as treaty obligations. A investment treaty that is signed by an unauthorized or rogue president should not bind the state any more than an odious loan. Anyone who makes any kind of agreement with a government 'doth it at his own perill'. I return in Chapter 5 to the issue of when it is legitimate for states to repudiate responsibilities.

———

The aim of this chapter has been to develop a Hobbesian answer to the Question of Ownership. In addition to demonstrating the theoretical plausibility of the Hobbesian account of attribution, I have tried to show that it can guide our practical judgments about state responsibility. The Hobbesian account has both theoretical and practical advantages over the agential and functional alternatives.

One advantage of the Hobbesian account of attribution over the agential account is that it eliminates the need to posit corporate intentions. It explains how states can act using only the basic concepts of authorization and representation. As well as sparing us from ontological commitments and difficult metaphysical issues, the Hobbesian account provides better guidance for our judgments about what counts as an act of state. The vast literature on the agential theory contains very few attempts to develop specific criteria for attribution (Harbour, 2004), in large part because the concepts of corporate agency and intentionality are difficult to operationalize. We might, as Wendt (1999: 222–23) suggests, infer the state's intentions from its laws and policies. For example, the United Kingdom's invasion of Iraq in 2003 could be called 'intentional' because it was approved by an Act of Parliament. But this answer does not always work. For one thing, it is much less plausible to infer corporate intentions from the laws and policies of non-democratic states (see §5.1), because the distinction between the state's intentions and the individual intentions of its leaders is blurred. Did Russia intend to invade Crimea, or was the relevant intention Putin's? Unlike the agential account of attribution, the Hobbesian account applies equally to all kinds of states, from monarchies to democracies.

Further, even in democracies, most actions that state officials perform are not specifically prescribed by laws or policies. This is especially true of wrongful actions, which often violate the state's laws and policies. If a British soldier kills a civilian, or even an enemy soldier, how would we judge whether this act implicates the United Kingdom's intention? Curiously, Wendt (1999: 220–21) resorts to the concept of authorization to account for cases such as this: 'Authorization means that individuals' actions are constituted *as* the actions of a collective. For example, we do not hold the soldier who kills an enemy in war responsible for his actions because he is authorized to kill by his state.' What he fails to realize is that the concept of authorization renders the idea of corporate intention superfluous. The Hobbesian account of attribution uses only the concepts of authorization and representation because these do all of the work.

The functional account of attribution, on the other hand, does propose specific rules of attribution. The conceptual schema of 'organs' and 'functions' has been used to develop an extensive set of legal rules about whether particular actions count as acts of state (Crawford, 2013a; ILC, 2001). But whereas the agential account applies poorly to non-democracies, the functional account makes no distinction between types of governments, which makes the latter far more pernicious. The functional account gives corrupt officials and predatory governments a licence to impersonate the state; Mobutu was no less an 'organ' of Zaire than Bill Clinton was of the United States. The Hobbesian account provides ways of distinguishing attribution from misattribution. Authorization distinguishes legitimate from illegitimate governments, and representation distinguishes plausible from implausible performances of the state's role.

The Hobbesian account of attribution explains how states can act, and hence how they can incur personal responsibilities. But in order for a state to be *held* responsible, it must be the same corporate entity as the one that incurred the responsibility in the first place. Every judgment of state responsibility depends on a judgment of state identity. If the United Kingdom is not the same state as the British Empire, then it is difficult to see how the present-day United Kingdom could be responsible for colonialism or the slave trade. And if the Republic of Turkey is not the same state as the Ottoman Empire, then it is difficult to see how present-day Turkey could be responsible for the Armenian genocide. The next chapter develops a Hobbesian account of corporate identity that explains how states can persist over time despite changes in their populations, territories, governments, and constitutions.

4

Succession

THE QUESTION OF IDENTITY

'As there was order taken for an Artificiall Man, so there be order also taken, for an Artificiall Eternity of life; without which, men that are governed by an Assembly, should return into the condition of Warre in every age; and they that are governed by One man, assoon as their Governour dyeth. This Artificiall Eternity, is that which men call the Right of *Succession*' (*L* XIX. 298).

ON WHAT does the identity of the state depend? The agential account of corporate identity relies on an analogy with personal identity: the identity of the state depends on its self-conception or national narrative, much as the identity of an individual depends on her psychological unity. The functional account relies on an analogy with the identity of a physical object: the identity of the state depends on its matter (territory and population) or its form (constitution). For Hobbes, corporate identity is not closely analogous to personal or physical identity. The identities of states and other corporate entities are peculiar in that they are created and sustained by their representatives. Just as representation transforms a multitude of individuals into one person, representation sustains the identity of this corporate person over time. The criterion for state continuity is 'succession': a state persists as long as it has a continuous series of representatives.[1]

Like his account of attribution, Hobbes' account of succession has many ambiguities and complications. How is it possible to tell whether a new

---

1. International lawyers use 'succession' to refer to 'state succession', or 'the replacement of one State by another in the responsibility for the international relations of territory' (UN, 1978: Art. 2.1b). I follow Hobbes in using 'succession' to refer to the replacement of one *government* with another, which implies the continuity of the state. I use 'discontinuity' and 'non-identity' to denote the replacement of one state with another.

government is a 'successor' to the old government or, instead, the first government of a new state? Does a revolution imply the replacement of one state with another? Can a 'dead' state be 'resurrected', as the Baltic states appeared to be at the end of the Soviet occupation? This chapter reconstructs Hobbes' account of succession and argues that it provides a novel and compelling answer to the Question of Identity.

The chapter has five sections. The first explains the importance of corporate identity for state responsibility. It distinguishes corporate identity from the more common, constructivist idea of social identity; splits the concept of corporate identity into its two components—unity and continuity; and rebuts the argument that the Question of Identity is a pseudo-problem. The second section reconstructs and develops Hobbes' account of corporate identity. For Hobbes, the unity and continuity of the state are both products of representation. The next two sections apply the Hobbesian account of corporate identity to a series of common identity problems. The third section addresses cases of change in a single state, such as territorial changes and revolutions. The fourth section addresses cases of 'relational' change that involve two or more states, such as secession, absorption, and unification. The fifth section develops a Hobbesian account of non-identity, which determines what ought to happen to a state's responsibilities when it ceases to exist.

§18 The Concept of Corporate Identity

'Identity' has many meanings. It is first necessary to distinguish corporate identity from social identity, which is the kind of state identity with which constructivist International Relations scholars are usually concerned. As Wendt (1994: 385) explains, whereas '*social* identities are sets of meanings that an actor attributes to itself while taking the perspectives of others', '*corporate identity* refers to the intrinsic, self-organizing qualities that constitute actor individuality' (emphasis in original). The social identity of a state is its status or role within the society of states. The corporate identity of a state is the bare fact or supposition that it is a unitary and continuous entity.

Whereas the social identities of states are constituted through interaction with other states, their corporate identities are necessarily prior to social interaction (Wendt, 1999: 198). Social interaction presupposes that the interacting entities already have distinct identities. For example, although Canada's social identity as a Western state is a product of its relations with other states, its corporate identity as *this particular state* is necessarily prior. Ascribing Western-ness to Canada presupposes that it is already a single entity that can be distinguished from other states and that persists over time. The corporate identity of a state is the peg on which its social identity hangs. As I explain below, it is also the peg on which the state's responsibilities hang.

Corporate identity has two components. A group has *unity* if it has an identity that is distinct from the identities of its members, and it has *continuity* to the extent that this identity persists over time. Unity is synchronic identity; continuity is diachronic identity. State responsibility presupposes both unity and continuity. First, states must have distinct identities in order to have distinct responsibilities. The distinction between 'the debts of Russia' and 'the debts of Russians' is meaningful only if 'Russia' is something more than shorthand for a list of particular Russians (Fleming, 2017a). Second, states' identities must persist over time in order for their responsibilities to persist.[2] It makes sense to hold present-day European states responsible for colonialism only if these states are continuous with the colonial states of the past. A theory of state responsibility thus requires accounts of both the unity and the continuity of the state.

The Question of Identity is sometimes thought to be a pseudo-problem. The question of whether 'Canada in 2018' is identical to 'Canada in 1900' arises only if we treat Canada as an entity that is distinct from its individual subjects and officials. It might be thought that the problem of corporate identity can be dissolved if we simply refrain from reifying groups, or treating them as entities 'over and above' their members. Derek Parfit makes a version of this argument.

> Suppose that a certain club exists for some time, holding regular meetings. The meetings then cease. Some years later, several people form a club with the same name, and the same rules. We can ask, 'Did these people revive the very same club? Or did they merely start up another club which is exactly similar?' Given certain further details, this would be another empty question. We could know just what happened without answering this question. Suppose that someone said: 'But there must be an answer. The club meeting later must either be, or not be, the very same club.' This would show that this person didn't understand the nature of clubs (Parfit, 2016: 95–96; see also Parfit, 1984: 212–13).

Since a club is nothing 'over and above' its members and rules, the question about its identity is an empty one. If we know all of the facts about the membership and the rules of the Book Club, then we know all there is to know. It does not matter, according to Parfit, whether today's Book Club is identical to or merely similar to the Book Club from years ago. There might not even be a

---

2. I discuss some limited exceptions to this rule in §22.

determinate answer to this question. Parfit (1984: 211–12) makes the same point about 'nations' (by which he means states): 'Though nations exist, a nation is not an entity that exists separately, apart from its citizens and its territory . . . A nation just is these citizens and this territory.'[3] What matters is not whether 'Canada in 2018' is identical to 'Canada in 1900'; there might not even be a determinate answer to this question. What matters are the facts about Canada's subjects, laws, territory, and institutions.

It is not true that questions about the identity of the Book Club or of Canada do not matter, much less that the person who asks them does not understand the nature of clubs or states. If the old Book Club had debts, contractual obligations, or property, then it would matter a great deal whether the 'new' Book Club is the same club. And unless 'Canada in 2018' is identical to 'Canada in 1900', it is difficult to see how present-day Canada could be responsible for the wrongs, debts, or treaty obligations of the Canada of the past. It is true that the answers to questions about the identity of the Book Club or of Canada might sometimes be indeterminate, just as the answers to questions about the identity of a human being or even a table might sometimes be indeterminate (Kripke, 1980: 50–51, note 18). Yet this does not mean that the answers—elusive as they may be—do not matter.

The fundamental problem with Parfit's argument is that it depends on a reductionist view of corporate identity, or the claim that 'the existence of a club is not separate from the existence of its members, acting together in certain ways' (1984: 213). In one sense, this is obviously true: a club is a group of people who act together according to certain rules. But what distinguishes a club from a non-corporate group is precisely that its identity is not reducible to its members and rules. There is a difference between the Book Club and a reading group, just as there is a difference between a corporation and a partnership. The rights and obligations of a reading group or a partnership are nothing more than the rights and obligations of its members. If the reading group owes money, then each member owes a share. But the rights and obligations of a club or a corporation are distinct from the rights and obligations of its members. The fact that the Book Club owes money does not imply that any of its members owe money; the debt attaches to the Book Club *as distinct from* its members. Clubs and companies are corporate groups: 'that form of human association which is not constituted by its component parts—by its members, its officers, its property, its rules—but is separate from all these' (Runciman,

---

3. Kripke (1980: 50) makes a similar argument: 'a description of the world mentioning all facts about persons but omitting those about nations can be a *complete* description of the world, from which the facts about nations follow' (emphasis in original).

2000a: 91). Parfit's mistake is to elide the difference between corporate and non-corporate groups. It might not matter whether today's reading group is the same as or merely similar to yesterday's reading group, but it does matter whether today's Book Club is the same or merely similar.

States are also corporate groups. It is not true that the existence of the state 'just involves the existence of its citizens, living together in certain ways, on its territory' (Parfit, 1984: 211–12). Although a state must have a population, a territory, and a government in order to exist at all, its identity is not the sum of these parts. It might not matter whether today's 'society' or 'nation' is the same as or merely similar to yesterday's, but it matters a great deal whether today's state is the same or merely similar. The continuity of debts, treaty obligations, and reparative obligations—as well as rights and institutional memberships—depends on the continuity of the state. In short, corporate responsibility presupposes corporate identity.

§19 The Conditions for Corporate Identity

Corporate identity is usually taken to be analogous to either personal identity or physical identity. The first view is exemplified by Wendt (1999: 225), who argues that 'what really distinguishes the personal or corporate identity of intentional actors from that of beagles and bicycles is a consciousness and memory of Self as a separate locus of thought and activity'. I have already discussed the problems with the analogy between personal identity and corporate identity (§5.2). One is that the common criterion for personal identity—psychological connectedness—does not apply to the state. Even if states are agents, they do not have anything like subjectivity or consciousness. Another problem is that, unlike human beings, states merge and divide. Even if psychological connectedness did have a corporate analogue, unification and secession would not have human analogues. The analogy between corporate identity and personal identity would be of limited use even if it were conceptually sound.

The second, more common view is that the identity of a state is analogous to the identity of a physical object. This view has two variants. The 'essentialist' variant holds that the identity of the state depends on its core features, particularly the 'nucleus' or 'essential part' of its territory (see §6.2). For example, some international lawyers argue that the Republic of Turkey is the same state as the Ottoman Empire because 'in spite of considerable territorial losses . . . the former capital and the surrounding regions, as well as other zones of historical significance constituting the genuine nucleus of the state, remain untouched' (Öktem, 2011: 575; see also Dumberry, 2012: 248–50). The organic metaphor lurks just beneath the surface: a state retains its identity despite a loss of appendages (colonies and peripheral territories), but it is no longer the same state if it loses its vital organs (the 'capital and the surrounding regions').

Aristotle's account of corporate identity exemplifies the 'formalist' variant of the physical identity view. He argues that the criterion for corporate identity cannot be sameness of population or territory—in whole or in part—because 'it is quite possible to divide both population and territory in two' (1992: III.3, 175). Even the nucleus of a state's population or territory can be divided, as Germany's was at the end of the Second World War. The identity of a state, like the identity of a river, depends on its 'form'—the way in which its constituents are organized—rather than its particular constituents. The identity of a river depends on the source from which it flows rather than the particular water that it contains.[4] The identity of a state depends on its constitution rather than the particular population and territory that it has: 'the main criterion of the continued identity of a state ought to be its constitution' (ibid. III.3, 176). Just as a river retains its identity as different water passes through it, a state retains its identity as its population and territory change. But 'when the constitution changes and becomes different in kind', such as when there is a change from aristocracy to democracy, 'the state also would seem necessarily not to be the same' (ibid.).

Aristotle's analogy between corporate identity and physical identity has set the terms for most subsequent thought about corporate identity. As Tuck (2016: 76) describes, Grotius adopted the idea that the 'people possess identity over time, like a river or the Argonauts' ship'. Contemporary philosophers likewise 'compare the identity of corporations with that of ordinary physical objects' (Welch, 1989: 412). The identity of a corporation 'is no different in principle from the identity of other physical objects. Rocks, rivers, algae, people, hats, bugs, birds—all retain their identities despite changes in composition' (ibid. 413). Aristotle's analogy even appears in legal thought about corporate identity: 'A State, like Heraclitus' river, is in a constant state of flux . . . the criterion of this relative identity cannot be one of substance, but only one of form' (Marek, 1968: 4–5; see also Cheng, 2011: 37).

Hobbes, too, appears to take Aristotle's discussion of corporate identity as his point of departure. He suggests that there is a fundamental similarity between the identities of human beings, rivers, and cities.

> [I]f the name be given for such form as is the beginning of motion, then, as long as that motion remains, it will be the same *individual* thing; as that man will be always the same, whose actions and thoughts proceed all from the

---

4. Aristotle takes the example of the river from Heraclitus.

same beginning of motion, namely, that which was in his generation; and that will be the same river which flows from one and the same fountain, whether the same water, or other water, or something else than water, flow from thence; and that the same city, whose acts proceed continually from the same institution, whether the men be the same or no (*D* XI.7, 137–38).[5]

Hobbes' account of identity might be called 'nominalist', as opposed to Aristotle's formalist account. His key claim is that 'we must consider by what name anything is called, when we inquire concerning the *identity* of it' (*D* XI.7 137; see also *AW* 139).[6] The answer to a question about the identity of an entity depends on how that entity is categorized. As he says, 'it is one thing to ask concerning Socrates, whether he be the same man, and another to ask whether he be the same body' (*D* XI.7, 137). If the relevant category is 'body', then the old Socrates is not identical to the young Socrates, 'for his Body when he is Old, cannot be the same it was when he was an Infant, by reason of the difference of Magnitude' (ibid.). However, if the relevant category is 'man' or 'person', then the old Socrates is identical to the young Socrates, since his 'actions and thoughts proceed all from the same beginning of motion' (ibid.). Whereas the identity of a body depends on its particular matter, the identity of a man depends on his 'generation', or the motion that originally gave him life.

Hobbes also applies his nominalist account of identity to the state: 'When any citizen dies, the material of the state is not the same, i.e. the state is not the same *ens* [or matter]. Yet the uninterrupted degree and motion of government that signalise a state ensure, while they remain as one, that the state is the same in number' (*AW* 141). If the relevant category is 'population' or 'territory', then there is a different state whenever a subject dies or a border changes. But if the relevant category is 'person', then the state persists as long as its 'acts proceed continually from the same institution' (*D* XI.7, 138).

For Hobbes, unlike for Aristotle, the 'institution' on which the identity of the state depends is not its constitution. In his famous discussion of the ship of Theseus, he argues that the form of an entity cannot, by itself, be the basis for its identity.

> [I]f, for example, that ship of Theseus . . . were, after all the planks were changed, the same numerical ship it was at the beginning; and if some man

---

5. I cite *De corpore* (*D*) according to the chapter and paragraph numbers as well as the page numbers from the Molesworth edition.

6. I cite *Thomas White's* De mundo *Examined* (the 'Anti-White', *AW*) according to the page numbers of the 1976 Jones translation.

had kept the old planks as they were taken out, and by putting them afterwards together in the same order, had again made a ship of them, this, without doubt, had also been the same numerical ship with that which was at the beginning; and so there would have been two ships numerically the same, which is absurd (*D* XI.7, 136–37).

If sameness of form were a sufficient condition for identity, then the ship with new planks and the ship made of the old planks would both be identical to the original ship of Theseus. And since identity is a transitive relation, this would have the absurd implication that the two distinct ships are identical to each other. The same line of argument shows that the identity of the state cannot depend entirely on its constitution. Suppose that the subjects of a state gradually emigrate to another territory, where they create a new state that is identical in form. If sameness of constitutional form were a sufficient condition for identity, then both the new state and the old state would be identical to the original state, and hence to each other.

For Hobbes, the 'institution' on which the identity of the state depends is sovereignty. A state retains its identity as long as its actions proceed from 'the same beginning of motion' (*D* XI.7, 137), and the source of the state's motion is sovereignty. As Hobbes says, 'the Soveraign, is the publique Soule, giving Life and Motion to the Common-wealth' (*L* XXIX. 518). Having a sovereign gives a multitude a corporate identity, and this corporate identity persists as long as the sovereignty does. As I explain below, Hobbes uses the ideas of representation and succession to develop this account of corporate identity in his political works.

Although Hobbes compares the identity of a state to both the identity of a human being and the identity of a river, neither analogy can capture the logic of his account of corporate identity. Personal, physical, and corporate identity are similar only in the most general sense: the identities of human beings, rivers, and states all depend the motion that generates them. Hobbes is, after all, a materialist. But corporate identities are also unique. The identity of the state depends neither on its matter nor on its form—neither on its particular population or territory, nor on its constitution—but only on its sovereign. Hobbes thus uses the concept of representation to account for both components of corporate identity. The state has unity because it has a single representative: 'it is the *Unity* of the Representer, not the *Unity* of the Represented, that maketh the Person *One*' (*L* XVI. 248). The state has continuity as long as it has an unbroken series of representatives: 'the uninterrupted degree and motion of government that signalise a state ensure, while they remain as one, that the state is the same in number' (*AW* 141). What follows is not a wholesale endorsement of Hobbes' account of corporate identity, but an attempt to construct a 'Hobbesian' account of corporate identity using the core idea that the identity of the state is a product of representation. The remainder of this section develops Hobbesian accounts of unity and continuity.

§19.1 Unity

In order for a multitude to be united, its members must have a single representative: 'A Multitude of men, are made *One* Person, when they are by one man, or one Person, Represented' (*L* XVI. 248). But having a single representative is not sufficient for unity. An accountant may represent many clients, but this does not make his multitude of clients one person. Since he represents each client as an individual, he is only an agent with many principals. Unity requires that the representative of the multitude act in the name of the group rather than in the name of each individual; he must 'beare their Person' (*L* XVII. 260) instead of their individual persons. There are thus two necessary and jointly sufficient conditions for the unity of a multitude: it must be represented both *by* one person and *as* one person.

Hobbes draws out the implications of his account of unity in *Behemoth*.

> [T]he Scots have their Parliaments, wherein their assent is required to the Laws there made, which is as good. Have not many of the provinces of France their several parliaments and several constitutions? And yet they are all equally natural subjects of the King of France. And therefore for my part I think they were mistaken, both English and Scots, in calling one another foreigners (*B* 34–35A).

Just as the French provinces share an overarching corporate identity—the identity of France—so Scotland and England share the corporate identity of the United Kingdom. It is a mistake for the English and the Scottish to call each other foreigners because they share a sovereign, and hence a corporate identity. But like the provinces, which have distinct corporate identities within France because each has its own provincial representatives, Scotland and England have distinct corporate identities within the United Kingdom. The fact that the English and the Scottish have different *national* identities is entirely beside the point for Hobbes, because corporate identities are constituted by representation rather than by the characteristics of the people who are represented. Even a random collection of individuals would have a corporate identity if it had a common representative. What gives states (as well as provinces, cities, and counties) distinct corporate identities is that they have distinct representatives, not that their inhabitants belong to distinct national or cultural groups.

For Hobbes, unity is a consequence of attribution rather than a precondition for attribution. A multitude is united when it has a representative whose actions are attributed to the whole group; it is not the case that actions can be attributed to the group because it has some preexisting unity. The Hobbesian account of attribution in the previous chapter thus lays the groundwork for the Hobbesian account of corporate identity.

Hobbes stipulated that the representative of the multitude had to be *authorized* in order for the multitude to be united. Yet this stipulation was of little consequence because he set the bar so low for authorization. Being 'represented' by a conqueror who threatens the members of the multitude into 'authorizing' him is sufficient to unite them (*L* XX. 306). But if we set more demanding conditions for authorization, as I have done in the previous chapter (§15), then the conditions for unity also become more demanding. A government that coerces or indoctrinates its subjects into submission does not meet the background conditions for valid authorization, so it cannot give the state unity. Since the North Korean government is not authorized, it cannot give North Koreans a corporate identity, any more than a self-appointed King of Humanity could give humanity a corporate identity. The identity of North Korea is not just fictional, but fraudulent. Only states whose governments pass the minimal conditions for authorization can legitimately have actions and responsibilities attributed to them in the first place (see §17).

Hobbes also stipulated that the unity of a multitude requires a *single* authorized representative—either one man or one assembly. He drew a sharp distinction between the sovereign, who represents the state directly, and public ministers, who represent the state only through the sovereign (see §10). A united multitude can have many public ministers but only one sovereign. For the same reason that a multitude with one sovereign is one person, a multitude with three sovereigns is three persons.

> [I]f the King bear the person of the People, and the generall Assembly bear also the person of the People, and another Assembly bear the person of a Part of the people, they are not one Person, nor one Soveraign, but three Persons, and three Soveraigns (*L* XXIX. 512).

During the English Civil War, when both Parliament and the King purported to represent England, the country was 'two Common-wealths, of one & the same Subjects; which is a Kingdome divided in it selfe, and cannot stand' (*L* XXIX. 510). For Hobbes, the unity of the state depends on the unity of the sovereign.

However, as I have argued in the previous chapter, the modern sovereign is elusive. The distinction between supreme and subordinate representatives, or between the sovereign and the public ministers, is no longer so clear (§14.1). The idea that the identity of the state depends on the identity of a single, sovereign individual or assembly is no longer plausible. Yet we can retain the core idea that the identity of the state depends on its being represented. There need not be a single representative; all that is required for unity is a single 'system of representation'.

Representatives are part of the same system of representation provided that they recognize each other as authorized representatives of the same state. In other words, unity requires *mutual recognition:* each representative must tacitly or explicitly accept the others' claims to act in the name of the state. Recognition between representatives can often be inferred from hierarchies: a soldier and a general both represent the state, but this does not imply disunity because the soldier and the general are part of the same chain of command. The practice of giving and taking orders implies mutual recognition. Where there is no hierarchy among representatives, mutual recognition can be inferred from other tacit signs. Although Congress and the president represent the United States independently of each other, each recognizes that the other is an authorized representative of the United States. The president might veto a bill, but he nevertheless recognizes that Congress has the authority to pass bills. Likewise, Congress might override the president's veto, but it nevertheless recognizes that the president has the authority to exercise his veto. Similarly, the Supreme Court strikes down laws, but it does not deny that Congress has the authority to make laws. There is mutual recognition between the branches of the American government despite the fact that they often act at cross-purposes. Mutual recognition between representatives marks the difference between a state with a separation of powers and 'a Kingdome divided in it selfe' (*L* XXIX. 510).

In sum, there are two conditions for unity, or for the state to have a corporate identity in the first place. The representatives of the state must (1) be authorized and (2) constitute a coherent system of representation. States that fail to meet the 'authorization condition', such as North Korea and Turkmenistan, have only fraudulent unity. States that fail to meet the 'coherence condition', such as Somalia and Syria, do not even have a semblance of unity. Neither have identities that are capable of sustaining responsibilities. Attributing responsibilities to states such as Somalia is largely futile, while attributing responsibilities to states such as North Korea is insidious: it gives the ruling party a corporate veil behind which to hide. When a state fails to meet the conditions for unity, the actions of the factions within it are attributable only to those factions themselves.

§19.2 Continuity

Hobbes' account of continuity is a consequence of his account of unity. Just as having a single representative (or system of representation) gives the multitude unity, having a continuous series of representatives gives the united multitude continuity.

Of all these Formes of Government, the matter being mortall, so that not onely Monarchs, but also whole Assemblies dy, it is necessary for the conservation of the peace of men, that as there was order taken for an Artificiall Man, so there be order also taken, for an Artificiall Eternity of life; without which, men that are governed by an Assembly, should return into the condition of Warre in every age; and they that are governed by One man, as soon as their Governour dyeth. This Artificiall Eternity, is that which men call the Right of *Succession* (*L* XIX. 298).

Hobbes goes on to say a great deal about how disputes about succession can be avoided, but he says nothing further about how exactly the succession of representatives sustains the identity of the state. Yet the logic of the argument is clear: if 'it is the *Unity* of the Representer, not the *Unity* of the Represented, that maketh the Person *One*' (*L* XVI. 248), then it is the continuity of the representer, not the continuity of the represented, that keepeth the person one. The persistence of the state's corporate identity requires an unbroken 'chain of succession', or series of representatives.

The principle that the continuity of a person requires continuity of representation appears elsewhere in Hobbes' thought. In his discussion of the Holy Trinity, he uses the idea of succession to explain how God can 'be said to be three persons' even though he has had more than three representatives over the course of history (*L* XLII. 776). The first person of God was represented by '*Moses*, and his successors the High Priests, and Kings of Judah, in the Old Testament', and the third person of God by 'the *Apostles*, and their successors, from the day of Pentecost (when the *Holy Ghost* descended on them) to this day' (*L* XXXIII. 602). Like the person of the state, each person of God remains the same person as long as it has an unbroken series of representatives. The heretical corollary of this principle is that God ceases to be a person if he ceases to be represented. 'The true God may be Personated' (*L* XVI. 248)— just as, in his previous example, 'An Idol, or meer Figment of the brain, may be Personated'—but this does not mean that he *will* be personated. And if God is not personated, then he is no longer a person. The political implication of the principle of succession is that the identity of the state persists only as long as it is represented. If the chain of succession is broken, such as when a monarch abdicates without a successor, then the multitude ceases to be one person, and the state consequently ceases to exist.

But how is it possible to determine whether a new government is a 'successor' to the old government or, on the contrary, the government of a new state? Hobbes does not provide an answer, and his assumption seems to be that the answer will be obvious. This is often the case: it is obvious that Theresa May's government was the successor to David Cameron's government and hence that May's United Kingdom and Cameron's United Kingdom were the same state. Yet in exceptional cases, such as revolutions and contested elections, it is not obvious whether the new government is the successor to the old. In these cases, Hobbes' rather vague notion of succession is of little help. The remainder of this section develops a more precise notion of succession.

The clearest indication that a new government is the successor to the previous government is *mutual recognition:* the outgoing government recognizes the incoming government as its successor, and the incoming government recognizes the outgoing government as its predecessor. Just as mutual recognition between representatives at a given time implies that they are parts of the same system of representation, mutual recognition between representatives across time implies that they are parts of the same chain of succession. The ritual of 'handing over power', such as when the outgoing American president gives the White House keys to the incoming president, is a sign that each recognizes the other. A coronation ceremony serves a similar function in a monarchy. In addition to encouraging a peaceful transfer of power, mutual recognition between the incoming government and the outgoing government indicates the continuity of the state.

Some forms of recognition are unilateral rather than mutual. *Prospective recognition* occurs when the outgoing government recognizes the incoming government as its successor. The archetypes of prospective recognition in a democracy are concession speeches and congratulatory post-election phone calls; the archetype in a monarchy is a queen's naming of her successor. *Retrospective recognition* occurs when the incoming government recognizes the outgoing government as its predecessor, such as by maintaining its titles and offices or by claiming rights that attach to the antecedent state. For instance, the fact that Trump calls himself the forty-fifth president of the United States (and, despite his earlier objections, admits that Obama was the forty-fourth) implies that Trump recognizes Obama as his predecessor. Similarly, the fact that the first government of the Russian Federation claimed the Soviet Union's seat at the United Nations implies that it recognized the Soviet government as its predecessor. As I discuss in the next section (§20), governments often tacitly recognize their successors and predecessors, and these tacit signs of recognition carry more weight than their explicit statements. Succession is determined more by what representatives do than by what they say.

The claim that identity must be inferred from actions rather than from words may seem to stand in tension with Hobbesian nominalism. Yet the point is thoroughly Hobbesian. In the absence of an authority that fixes the meanings of words, naming and description are inherently unreliable. The identities of business corporations can be determined by words rather than actions because there is a fixed discourse—corporate law—to which we can appeal, as well as a coercive authority that gives this discourse force. But the identities of states cannot be determined in the same way, because there is no 'corporate law' for states, nor any central authority that defines the terms. As a consequence of this 'anarchy of meanings' (Wolin, 2016: 230), there are often several plausible narratives about a state's identity, each of which is advanced by different parties with different interests. When words cannot be trusted, judgments of succession and identity have to be made from actions.

In cases of mutual recognition, it is clear that the new government is the successor to the old and hence that the identity of the state remains the same. 'The United States in 2019' is the same state as 'the United States in 2015' because Trump and Obama recognize each other as successor and predecessor. Complications arise when recognition is not mutual. After losing the 2016 Gambian presidential election, President Yahya Jammeh refused to recognize the result or to give up power to the president-elect, Adama Barrow. It would be odd to conclude that Barrow (if he did manage to obtain power) is not Jammeh's successor, but instead the president of a new state, simply because Jammeh is a sore loser. Prospective recognition is strong evidence of succession, but it is not strictly necessary for succession.

Retrospective recognition, on the other hand, is necessary for succession. A new government is a successor to the former government only if it explicitly or tacitly recognizes the former government as its predecessor. To put it the other way around, a new government that refuses to recognize the previous government is not its successor. For example, after the breakup of the Soviet Union, the governments of Latvia, Lithuania, and Estonia disavowed the Soviet Baltic governments. The new Baltic governments claimed to be the successors to the pre-Soviet Baltic governments, which had been deposed in 1940. What made this claim credible is that the new Baltic governments consistently accepted its consequences: 'The Baltic countries refused . . . to participate in the payment and servicing of the Soviet Union's external debts and did not claim any of its property or assets in foreign countries' (Müllerson, 1993: 483). The Baltic governments also upheld treaties that the pre-Soviet governments had signed: 'the prewar treaties, concluded by the then independent Baltic republics, continue to be in force as long as they have not expressly been terminated' (Van Elsuwege, 2003: 384). If a government consistently refuses to recognize the previous government as its predecessor, then it has a credible claim of non-succession.

Although retrospective recognition is necessary for succession, it is not sufficient. If it were, then governments would be able to hijack the identities of states simply by recognizing former governments as their predecessors. For instance, the Soviet-backed government of Poland, which was 'a classic example of the creation of a puppet entity' (Marek, 1968: 475), 'impersonated'

Poland by claiming to be the successor to the government of the Republic of Poland. The fact that the exiled government of the Republic refused to recognize the Soviet-backed government weakens the latter's claim to be its successor. But since prospective recognition is not necessary for succession, the government of the Republic's non-recognition of the Soviet-backed government is not decisive. Succession sometimes cannot be determined by 'horizontal' forms of recognition—prospective and retrospective recognition between governments—alone.

'Vertical' recognition, or acceptance of the government by its subjects (see §15), is the crucial factor in cases of contested succession. In the absence of prospective recognition, authorization marks the difference between legitimate and illegitimate successor governments. The fact that Barrow won the 2016 Gambian election, and hence had been authorized by the subjects of The Gambia, gave him a credible claim to be Jammeh's successor, despite the fact that Jammeh refused to recognize him. Conversely, the Soviet-backed government of Poland was not the successor to the government of the Polish Republic because it had no credible claim to be authorized by the subjects of Poland. The legitimate successor was the exiled government of the Republic. Vertical recognition determines succession where mutual recognition between the incoming and outgoing governments is absent.

Succession is thus determined by a combination of prospective, retrospective, and vertical recognition. A new government counts as a successor to the previous government if and only if (1) the new government recognizes the previous government as its predecessor; and (a) the previous government recognizes the new government as its successor, or (b) the subjects of the state recognize the new government as legitimate. In other words, succession requires retrospective recognition plus either prospective recognition or vertical recognition.

———

The Hobbesian account of corporate identity has two parts. The first is an account of unity: a multitude is one person, or has one corporate identity, if its representatives meet the minimal conditions for authorization and form a coherent system of representation. The second part is an account of continuity: a corporate entity retains its identity over time as long as it has an unbroken chain of succession. Recognition between representatives at a given time gives the state unity, while recognition between representatives across time gives the state continuity. The next two sections apply the Hobbesian account of corporate identity to a series of common identity problems.

§20 Changes in a Single State

The compositions of states are constantly changing. Elections and coups replace their governments; births, deaths, immigration, and emigration change their populations and demographics; and erosion, tectonic shifts, and boundary changes alter their territory. The forms of states also occasionally change as a result of institutional reforms, constitutional amendments, and revolutions. The Hobbesian account of corporate identity explains how states can persist despite all of these changes. Since the identity of the state depends entirely on its system of representation, changes in its composition and form do not change its identity. Only a break in the chain of succession can extinguish the identity of the state.

The case of the Soviet Union and the Russian Federation illustrates how a state can persist despite changes in both its composition and its form. It also illustrates why succession must be determined by what governments do rather than what they say. On the face of it, the Russian Soviet Federative Socialist Republic (along with each of the other Soviet republics) appeared to secede from the Soviet Union.[7] The Russian Federation claimed only part of the population and territory of the Soviet Union; it had a new government and a new constitution; and, at first, it explicitly stated that the Soviet Union had been dissolved. In the Minsk Declaration of 8 December 1991, the governments of the Russian Federation, Belarus, and Ukraine jointly declared that 'the Union of Soviet Socialist Republics as a subject of international law and a geopolitical reality no longer exists' (UN, 1991a: 3). These three governments, along with the governments of eight other former Soviet republics, later affirmed that, 'with the establishment of the Commonwealth of Independent States, the Union of Soviet Socialist Republics ceases to exist' (UN, 1991b: 5). The Russian Federation both appeared and claimed to be one new state among many.

Contrary to its initial claim to be the government of a new state, the Russian government under Boris Yeltsin tacitly recognized the Soviet government as its predecessor. On 24 December, Yeltsin (1991) informed the Secretary-General that 'the membership of the Union of Soviet Socialist Republics in the United Nations, including the Security Council and all other organs and organizations of the United Nations system, is being continued by the Russian Federation' (see also Blum, 1992). The Russian government even claimed the Soviet Union's representative in the United Nations: 'Yuri M. Vorontsov, the

---

7. 'Secession', or the creation of a new state on part of the territory of an existing state, should not be confused with 'succession', or the replacement of one government with another in the same state. I discuss the consequences of secession for state identity in §21.

former Soviet representative, [was] reaccredited as the representative of the Russian Federation' (NYT, 1991). Institutional memberships are not transferable, nor can they be 'succeeded to' or 'inherited' by a new state (Bühler, 2001: 31).[8] The Yeltsin government's claim to the Soviet Union's membership in the United Nations therefore presupposed that it was the successor to Gorbachev's Soviet government rather than the government of a new state. If the Yeltsin government were not the government of the Soviet Union (or the same state with a different name), then it would not have had a valid claim to the Soviet Union's membership (any more than the government of the Kazakh Republic did). The Russian government thus tacitly recognized the Soviet government as its predecessor.

Yeltsin acknowledged as much when he requested that 'the name "the Russian Federation" should be used in the United Nations in place of the name "the Union of Soviet Socialist Republics"' (Yeltsin, 1991). Consequently, as Yeltsin accepted, the 'Russian Federation maintains full responsibility for all the rights and obligations of the USSR under the Charter of the United Nations, including the financial obligations' (ibid.; see also Ziemele, 2001: 193–202). Despite the appearance that the Russian Federation had seceded from the Soviet Union, which was made plausible by changes in population, territory, and government, it was actually continuous with the Soviet Union. What appeared to be the dissolution of one state and the creation of another was, in terms of identity, just a name change.

The principle behind this analysis of the Soviet case is that certain claims to rights presuppose governmental succession and hence the continuity of the state. If a government claims rights that attach to a particular state, then it presupposes that it is the government of *that state*; this, in turn, entails that it is the successor to the previous government rather than the government of a new state. Claims to institutional memberships, creditors' rights, and treaty rights usually imply succession. For instance, when a new government demands repayment of money that a previous government has lent, the new government tacitly recognizes the previous government as its predecessor, since the new government would not have a valid claim to repayment if it were not the government of the creditor state. To claim the rights of a state is to claim its identity.

8. The United Nations (1947: 2) has clearly stated that new states cannot inherit membership: 'when a new State is created, whatever may be the territory and the populations which it comprises and whether or not they formed part of a State Member of the United Nations, it cannot under the system of the Charter claim the status of a Member of the United Nations unless it has been formally admitted as such in conformity with the provisions of the Charter'.

However, not all claims to rights imply the continuity of the state. Claims to the territory, population, and property of an antecedent state generally do not imply claims to its identity. (But these claims sometimes entail inheritance of some of the antecedent state's responsibilities, as I argue in §22.) The fact that the Russian Federation inherited the bulk of the territory, infrastructure, and weaponry of the Soviet Union does not imply that the former and the latter are the same state, any more than inheriting a relative's property implies that you and the relative are the same person. Only claims to 'personal' or 'identity-specific' rights presuppose continuity.[9] A contract that says 'Jane Smith may use Path A' establishes a personal right; a contract that says 'the owner of Lot B may use Path A' does not, since the right accrues to anyone who owns Lot B. Jane Smith's heir might inherit the latter right, but—not being Jane Smith—could not possibly inherit the former. Likewise, a treaty that says 'the Soviet Union may fish in the Aral Sea' establishes a personal right; a treaty that says 'states that border the Aral Sea may fish there' does not. Claims to the former right presuppose continuity with the Soviet Union, while claims to the latter right do not. One sign of state continuity is thus that the new government claims the personal rights of the antecedent state.

An even clearer sign of state continuity is that the representatives of the state remain the same. Like the breakup of the Soviet Union, the breakup of the Ottoman Empire appeared to be a case of multiple secession, with the Republic of Turkey being one new state among many. There were changes in population and territory; there was a new government and a new constitution; and the new government claimed to be the government of a new state. In the Ottoman Debt Arbitration (UN, 1925), the new Turkish government argued that it should not be solely liable for the debts of the Empire on the grounds that the Republic of Turkey was a new state (alongside the British and French mandates and the new Arab states) rather than the continuing state of the Empire. Yet there was clear evidence that the Turkish government was the successor to the Ottoman government. Although the Republic had a new constitution and a new capital, the Ottoman chain of succession was intact.

> The [R]epublic inherited not only the central territory of the Empire, but also a bureaucratic and military elite who helped to establish a new state. . . . Even the organizational features of the army—ideologically the most republican element of the state apparatus—remained the same, such as military units' numbers (Öktem, 2011: 577–78).

---

9. Personal rights are analogous to what I have called 'personal responsibilities' in the previous chapter (§13).

The decisive factor is that it was not just the 'organizational features' of the state that remained the same, but the representatives themselves: '85 per cent of the Ottoman Empire's civil servants and 93 per cent of its staff officers retained their positions in the new republic' (Poulton, 1997: 88). As in the Soviet case, there was continuity of representation despite many institutional and territorial changes.

So far, the Hobbesian account of corporate identity is in line with the international legal doctrine of state continuity: changes in the populations, territories, governments, and even constitutions of states do not affect their identities (see §6.2). In the Russian/Soviet and Turkish/Ottoman cases, the Hobbesian account merely provides an alternative justification for the judgments of identity that international lawyers have already made. The legal basis for Russian/Soviet and Turkish/Ottoman continuity is that there is continuity of the 'nucleus' of each state's territory (Crawford, 2007: 676–77; Dumberry, 2012: 248–50; Öktem, 2011: 575–76). According to the Hobbesian account, the basis for continuity in these cases in that there is succession, or continuity of representation. Yet the two accounts differ about many other cases. In particular, the Hobbesian account of corporate identity provides a better analysis of cases in which states undergo complete losses or changes of territory.

Annexation is one such kind of case. The three Baltic states were annexed by the Soviet Union in 1940 and did not regain their independence until 1991. According to the 'nucleus account', the Baltic states' complete losses of their territories should have resulted in their extinction. However, international lawyers have established a rule that 'annexation of the territory of a State as a result of the illegal use of force', provided that it is temporary, 'does not bring about the extinction of the State' (Crawford, 2007: 690). Present-day Latvia, Lithuania, and Estonia are therefore considered to be continuous with the pre-annexation Baltic states, not with the Baltic Soviet Republics (Van Elsuwege, 2003). The principle behind this rule is *ex iniuria jus non oritur*—illegal acts cannot make law. However, if the annexation persists, *ex iniuria* gives way to *ex factis jus oritur*—the principle that the law must recognize the facts (Marek, 1968: 328–30, 566). For instance, although the American annexation of Hawaii was illegal (Craven, 2002), the Kingdom of Hawaii has nevertheless ceased to exist, and Hawaii is now part of the United States. But what determines whether or not an illegal annexation is a done deal? The rule about illegal annexation is an awkward exception to the nucleus account of corporate identity, which is subject to a further exception: the state persists as long as it retains the nucleus of its territory, except in cases of illegal annexation, except when the illegal annexation persists for so long that it appears to be irreversible.

The Hobbesian account of corporate identity provides a much simpler account of illegal annexation: the annexed state persists as long as its chain of succession is unbroken. The chain of succession can be kept alive by a government-in-exile, such as the many exiled governments in London during the Second World War. These governments maintained the continuity of their states despite the fact that their territories had been annexed or occupied. What determines whether annexation is a done deal is whether the annexed state continues to be represented. The difference between the Baltic states and the Kingdom of Hawaii is that the former continued to be represented despite the annexation.

A government-in-exile is not the only possible vehicle for keeping the chain of succession alive. Of the three Baltic states, only Estonia had a government-in-exile, and the authority of that government was questionable. Estonia at one point 'had two governments in exile at one time', and, even when it had only one, 'its reputation and authority among Estonian refugees was not very high' (Mälksoo, 2000: 298–99). Lithuania and Latvia failed to establish governments-in-exile, in large part because most members of their governments had been killed or deported to the Soviet Union. The task of representing the Baltic states fell to their diplomatic and consular missions, which were financed by gold deposits in Western banks (Misiunas, 1991: 141; Marek, 1968: 399–410). In addition to their normal functions, the Baltic legations 'functioned *de facto* as quasi-governments':

> The Estonian general consulate in New York, led by Johannes Kaiv and later by Ernst Jaakson, continued its uninterrupted functioning throughout the entire period of Soviet rule in Estonia. It continued to issue new passports to the citizens of the Republic of Estonia (so-called Jaakson passports), and symbolized the continued *de iure* existence of its state (Mälksoo, 2000: 312).

Similarly, 'the Latvian Minister in London had been granted, by the [pre-annexation] Latvian Government, emergency powers', which 'conferred on him a status similar to that of an actual Foreign Minister' (Marek, 1968: 410). The post-Soviet Baltic states are continuous with the pre-Soviet Baltic states because the Baltic legations maintained their chains of succession during the occupation. The important factor is not that the Soviet annexations were illegal; it is that, despite the annexations, the Baltic states still had representatives who kept their chains of succession alive.

A conspicuous feature of the Baltic case is that many other states continued to recognize the Baltic states throughout the Soviet period. The Baltic legations probably would not have been able to exist without external, and particularly American, recognition. Further, the continuity of treaty relations between the Baltic states and other states would not have been possible if those other states ceased to recognized the Baltic states. One might therefore think that the continuity of external recognition, not the continuity of representation, is what sustains the identity of the state.

Other cases suggest that state continuity is possible in the absence of external recognition. The Polish government-in-exile during the Second World War 'represented the immediate continuation of the Government which had functioned in Poland itself prior to, and during, the invasion' (Marek, 1968: 439, note 3). But in 1945, most states—including its host state, the United Kingdom—withdrew recognition from the government-in-exile. However, 'the Polish Government did not go into liquidation and has, on the contrary, remained in existence in London, although such existence is of necessity precarious' (ibid. 535). The exiled Polish government continued to exist until the Polish Republic was restored, and, crucially, the new government of the Republic recognized the exiled government as its predecessor.

> On 22 December 1990, in Warsaw's Royal Castle, as the last President of the government-in-exile, [Kaczorowski] handed over to President Lech Wałęsa the presidential insignia: the flag of the Republic, presidential seals (one each for ink, wax and dry embossing) and the original of the Constitution of April 1935 (Rojek, 2004: 45).

This mutual recognition between the new Polish government and the government-in-exile implies the continuity of the Polish Republic, despite the fact that most states had withdrawn recognition from the Republic several decades before. What matters for the continuity of the state is not whether other governments recognize the government-in-exile, but whether, at the end of the occupation, the restored government recognizes the government-in-exile as its predecessor.

The case of Italy's annexation of Ethiopia in 1936 even more clearly illustrates the irrelevance of external recognition to the continuity of the state. By 1938, almost all states had recognized the annexation, and there were few vestiges of the Ethiopian state left: 'There remained not even a government in exile, or recognized legations which could have been instrumental in carrying on Ethiopia's continuity through the critical period' (Marek, 1968: 278). Yet the identity of Ethiopia was sustained by 'the Emperor [Haile Selassie], as the exiled claimant to his throne and country' (ibid. 278). Other states assumed as much when they 'reestablished' diplomatic relations with Ethiopia after the end of the Italian occupation (ibid. 275). But this fickle re-recognition of independent Ethiopia counts for just as little as the fickle withdrawal of recognition in the first place. External recognition carries no independent weight. If it is not based on actual evidence of state continuity—a continuous chain of succession, or at least continuity of some other feature—then it is simply arbitrary.[10]

---

10. The Hobbesian account of corporate identity thus supports the declaratory theory of recognition, which holds that 'recognition of new States is a political act which is in principle

The Ethiopian case marks the outer limit of state continuity. There was hardly a system of representation left; the identity of the state was sustained solely by its exiled emperor. Although Ethiopia's chain of succession was precarious, it was nevertheless unbroken. Ethiopia, the Baltic states, and Poland stand in contrast to the Kingdom of Hawaii, Czechoslovakia, and the many other states that have ceased to be represented at all. Annexed states survive as long as they have representatives who carry on their chains of succession, but no state can survive a total loss of representation.

Interregnums present a difficult problem for any account of state identity, and perhaps especially for the Hobbesian account. What if Ethiopia did not have an emperor-in-exile, but some descendant of Haile Selassie assumed the throne and 'reconstituted' the kingdom a few years later? Following Hobbesian logic, this reconstituted kingdom would be a new state. A total loss of representation—even for a day—would break the chain of succession, regardless of whether the royal bloodline continues. However, interregnums do not necessarily break the chain of succession. Ethiopia would have been able to persist without an emperor if it still had other representatives, such as diplomats and civil servants, who carried on its chain of succession during the interregnum. But in a state with only one representative, the loss of that representative spells the demise of the state. Any later 'reconstitution' of the state would instead be the creation of a new state.

For these reasons, Israel is a new state. There is no chain of succession that connects present-day Israel to the Kingdoms of Samaria or Judah. Israel officially came into being when David Ben-Gurion declared the existence of the State of Israel on 14 May 1948. This could be considered the first act of the new Israeli state: the declaration united the multitude of Jewish settlers into one person. The first act of representation was also an act of unification.[11] Alternatively, Israel's chain of succession might have been created slightly earlier by the People's Council, chaired by Ben-Gurion, which was transformed into the Provisional State Council by the declaration of Israeli statehood (Sager 1978). The chain of succession might even be traced back to an earlier Zionist organization in the Mandate

---

independent of the existence of the new State' (Crawford, 1977: 93). See Marek (1968: 130–39) on the conceptual problems with the constitutive theory of recognition, or the view that statehood depends on external recognition.

11. Israel is not a counterexample to the argument that states are created by representation. It is true that the creation of Israel would not have been possible without external forces, just as the continuity of the Baltic states would not have been possible without external forces. But these external forces were not sufficient for the creation of Israel, just as external forces were not sufficient for the continuity of the Baltic states. Representation was a necessary and decisive factor in each case.

of Palestine. But the fact that Jews have lived in the Levant since the destruction of the ancient kingdoms of Israel is irrelevant to the question of continuity, as is the fact that there is considerable territorial overlap between those kingdoms and present-day Israel. The continuity of the state depends not on the continuity of population or territory, but on the continuity of representation.

Cases of relocation demonstrate the irrelevance of territory. Some island states, such as the Maldives and Kiribati, could lose all of their territory to sea-level rises by the end of the next century. The former president of the Maldives proposed 'a plan that would use tourism revenues from the present to establish a sovereign wealth fund with which he could buy a new country—or at least part of one—in the future' (Schmidle, 2009). The territorial nucleus account of identity has the implausible implication that relocation of the Maldives would literally make it 'a new country', free of all of its current debts and obligations. Relocation would be, strictly speaking, impossible. If the territorial nucleus of a state is essential to its identity, then a loss of this territorial nucleus necessarily implies the extinction of the state. The Hobbesian account, on the other hand, implies that relocation of the Maldives would leave its identity intact. The post-relocation state would be continuous with the pre-relocation state provided that the post-relocation government were the successor to the pre-relocation government.

The Hobbesian account of corporate identity thus explains how states can persist despite changes in their populations, territories, governments, constitutions, and names. Even revolutions, annexations, and relocations do not affect the identity of the state, provided that its chain of succession remains unbroken. Apparent discontinuity is common, as in the Russian/Soviet and Turkish/Ottoman cases, but actual discontinuity is rare. New governments almost always tacitly recognize previous governments as their predecessors. I discuss cases of discontinuity, such as dissolutions and absorptions, in the next section.

§21 Relational Changes

The previous section applied the Hobbesian account of corporate identity to cases of change in individual states. This section addresses 'relational' changes, or those that involve multiple states. There are five logically distinct kinds of cases: (1) cession, in which one state transfers territory to another; (2) secession, in which part of a state separates to form a new state; (3) absorption, in which one state becomes part of another; (4) unification, in which two or more states merge to form a new state; and (5) dissolution, in which a state ceases to exist.[12] Some of the specific cases are the same as those in the last

---

12. These five types overlap with the six types in international law: 'Unification of states, dissolution of states, incorporation [or absorption] of states, secession, "newly independent

section, because changes in the form or composition of one state are often accompanied by relational changes. For instance, the breakup of the Soviet Union was simultaneously a case of continuity (of the Soviet Union/the Russian Federation) and of secession (of the other Republics). Yet the individual and relational aspects of these cases must be separated because they involve different conceptual issues. The individual aspects involve a single chain of succession; the question is simply whether or not the chain remains unbroken. The relational aspects involve the merging and branching of chains of succession; the question is not just which chains remain unbroken, but also how many chains there are.

The simplest kind of case is cession of territory from one state to another, such as the Russian Empire's sale of Alaska to the United States in 1867. Cession has no consequences for the identity of the ceding state or the receiving state. This follows from what has been said before. Since the identity of a state depends on its system of representation, not on its territory, a gain or loss of territory does not affect its identity.

Secession is more complicated. It is clear that secession does not affect the identity of the original state, because a loss of territory or population does not affect the identity of the state in general. The question is what happens to the seceding part. In some cases, such as the secession of Bangladesh from Pakistan, secession involves the creation of a new chain of succession and hence a new corporate entity. Bangladesh was created 'from scratch' during the War of Independence—the Provisional Government of the People's Republic of Bangladesh was the first link in its new chain of succession. In other cases, such as the secession from the Soviet Union of its constituent Republics, secession involves a change in the status of an existing corporate entity. Each of the Republics had its own chain of succession and its own corporate identity within the Soviet Union. When Kazakhstan seceded from the Soviet Union, it became a new state, but it was nevertheless continuous with the Kazakh Soviet Socialist Republic. There was succession despite secession: the chairman of the Supreme Soviet of Kazakhstan became the president of the Republic of Kazakhstan. It follows that any obligations of the Kazakh Soviet Socialist Republic became obligations of the Republic of Kazakhstan. Secession can entail either the creation of a new corporate entity or a change in the status of an existing corporate entity.

Absorption of one state by another is the obverse of secession. In some cases, absorption involves the dissolution of the absorbed corporate entity.

---

states" and cession/transfer of territory' (Dumberry, 2012: 240, note 13). I treat decolonization, or the emergence of 'newly independent states', as a type of secession.

There is no continuity between the Kingdom of Hawaii and the American State (or Territory) of Hawaii, since the Kingdom's chain of succession was broken when the monarchy was overthrown. The State of Hawaii is therefore a new corporate entity. In other cases, absorption involves a loss of statehood but continuity of the absorbed corporate entity. When Newfoundland joined the Canadian federation in 1949, it did not cease to exist; it simply went from being a state to being a province. Absorption can entail either the dissolution of the absorbed entity or a change in its status.

Unification occurs when two or more states combine to form a new state. It is logically distinct from absorption because it involves the creation of a new chain of succession. But as with absorption, unification can involve either the continuity or the dissolution of the uniting entities. When four of the colonies of British North America united in 1867, they created a new, federal chain of succession and a new corporate entity called Canada. The colonies retained their own chains of succession and therefore did not cease to exist; they simply became provinces. But when North Yemen and South Yemen united in 1990, they simultaneously created a new chain of succession and broke their previous chains of succession. The *Agreement on the Establishment of the Republic of Yemen* (1991: Art. 1) established a 'full and complete union' between the two states, 'in which the international personality of each of them shall be integrated in a single international person called "the Republic of Yemen"', with 'one legislative, executive and judicial power' (see also Crawford, 2013a: 448). Unification entails the creation of a new corporate entity and either the dissolution of the uniting entities or a change in their status.

Dissolution occurs when a state ceases to exist, typically as a result of absorption or multiple secessions. The breakup of Czechoslovakia, unlike the breakup of the Soviet Union, was a true case of dissolution because neither the Czech Republic nor the Slovak Republic claimed the identity of Czechoslovakia.

> In view of the fact that the Czech and Slovak Federal Republic [CSFR] ceased to exist as of December 31, 1992, and there was no continuing international person which could claim the original UN seat of the former CSFR, both the Czech Republic and the Slovak Republic . . . had to apply anew for UN membership and were, subsequently, on January 19, 1993, admitted to the United Nations (Bühler, 2001: 275; see also Crawford, 2007: 402).

The dissolution of Czechoslovakia was a case of secession without remainder: the two parts of the state seceded to form two new states. However, it is possible for a state to be dissolved without being absorbed or replaced. Unless the Maldives and Kiribati either find new territory or fortify their existing territory, they might be 'dissolved' by the ocean. This implies that dissolution is not necessarily relational, though it almost always is.

There is often uncertainty about whether a particular case is a case of unification or absorption, secession or dissolution. Although our intuitive understandings of these distinctions suffice in simple cases, they tend to fail us in more complicated cases. The Russian/Soviet and Turkish/Ottoman cases were not, as they appeared to be, cases of dissolution. They were actually cases of continuity (of the Soviet Union/Russia and the Ottoman Empire/Turkey) combined with multiple secessions (of the other Soviet Republics and the Arab territories). The Hobbesian account of corporate identity helps us to analyse complicated cases by defining the types of relational cases more precisely, according to what happens to the relevant chains of succession.

One potentially deceptive case is that of the 'unification' of the Federal Republic of Germany (FRG) and the German Democratic Republic (GDR) in 1990. The *Treaty on the Final Settlement with Respect to Germany* (1991) seems to suggest that the FRG and the GDR merged to form a new state, 'the united Germany'. For instance, in Article 3, 'the Governments of the Federal Republic of Germany and the German Democratic Republic reaffirm their renunciation of the manufacture and possession of and control over nuclear, biological and chemical weapons'. In addition, 'they declare that the united Germany, too, will abide by these commitments', including 'the Treaty on the Non-Proliferation of Nuclear Weapons'. If the united Germany were continuous with either the FRG or the GDR, then the latter declaration would have been unnecessary. The united Germany would have automatically been bound by all agreements of a state with which it were continuous. The declaration would have been necessary only if the united Germany were, as 'unification' suggests, a new state.

The *Treaty on the Establishment of German Unity* (1991), on the other hand, suggests that the 'unification' was really a case of absorption.

> Upon the accession of the German Democratic Republic to the Federal Republic of Germany in accordance with Article 23 of the Basic Law taking effect on 3 October 1990 the *Länder* of Brandenburg, Mecklenburg-Western Pomerania, Saxony, Saxony-Anhalt and Thuringia shall become *Länder* of the Federal Republic of Germany (Art. 1.1).

The FRG's chain of succession continued, while the GDR's came to an end. This is confirmed by Article 42, which says that the GDR's Volkskammer shall 'elect 144 Members of Parliament to be delegated to the [FRG's] 11th Bundestag' before the Volkskammer is abolished. Another sign that the FRG absorbed the GDR is that 'the FRG's membership in the United Nations now covered former GDR territory as well, substituting for the latter's membership as of October 3, 1990' (von der Dunk and Kooijmans, 1991: 552). If the united Germany were a new state, then it would have had to apply for a new membership.[13]

A more complicated and contested case is that of the 'two Chinas'. At the end of the Chinese Civil War (1946–1950), two governments claimed to represent the whole of China: the government of the People's Republic of China (PRC) in Beijing and the government of the Republic of China (ROC) in Taipei. The Beijing government had gained control of almost all of the territory of pre-war China, and the Taipei government—which had been the government of pre-war China—had fled to Taiwan from the mainland. According to the Beijing government, the result of the war was 'a successor government situation' in which 'the ROC government was "replaced" as the government of all of China' (Li, 1979: 136; see also Bush, 2011). This implies that the PRC was continuous with pre-war China. There was a new government, not a new state. But according to the Taipei government, there was no succession, nor any such state as the PRC. The pre-war government had been exiled from the mainland, but it remained the only legitimate government of China. In the beginning, the Taipei government won the day: 'For nearly twenty-two years, the [Taipei government's] delegation to the United Nations represented China in both the United Nations General Assembly and the Security Council' (Chen, 1998: 234). But in 1971, the Beijing government took over China's seat at the United Nations, and the Taipei government eventually gave up its claim to be the government of the whole of China. The Beijing government's claim that the PRC is continuous with pre-war China is now widely accepted (Vidmar, 2013: 158–59).

However, the Beijing government's claim that it simply replaced the pre-war government is not quite right. The result of the civil war could not have been just a change in government, since there was only one state before the civil war but two states in its immediate aftermath. Although the PRC and the ROC claimed the same territory, they in fact had distinct territories, populations, and, most importantly, chains of succession. The question, then, is which state (if either) was continuous with pre-war China.[14] The case of the 'two Chinas' must be a case of either secession or dissolution. There are three

13. Another important question is whether the FRG was, as it claimed to be, continuous with the German *Reich*. This issue is too complicated to adequately address here. See Hailbronner (1991: 27–34), von der Dunk and Kooijmans (1991: 521–22), and Crawford (2007: 453–66, 519–23).

14. Whether the ROC or Taiwan is *still* a state is a separate question (see Crawford, 2007: 206–21).

possibilities: the ROC seceded from pre-war China; the PRC seceded from pre-war China; or pre-war China was dissolved and two new states were created.

According to the nucleus account of corporate identity, the PRC is continuous with pre-war China because the PRC has the same territorial nucleus. This implies that Taiwan seceded from the PRC. But if we apply the nucleus account in this case, then we should also apply it in other cases in which governments relocate (see §20). If we accept that Taiwan must have seceded from the PRC because it lacks the territorial nucleus of pre-war China, then we should also say that the Maldives and Kiribati would be dissolved if they relocated to escape the rising sea. A consistent application of the nucleus account is difficult to justify.

According to the Hobbesian account of corporate identity, the PRC seceded from pre-war China, and Taiwan is continuous with the ROC. Although the Beijing government controls almost all of the territory of pre-war China, the Taipei government has a much stronger claim to be the successor to the pre-war government. In fact, the first Taipei government was more than the successor; it *was* the pre-war government. Taiwan inherited pre-war China's system of representation: 'the KMT [Chinese Nationalist Party] imposed its governmental structure (imported from China) to replace the Japanese law ... the bureaucrats from China, who were forced into exile in Taiwan by Mao's troops, were able to retain power' (Chen, 1998: 232). In terms of identity, what happened in 1949 was not a change in the government of China; it was the secession of the PRC from pre-war China.

One might doubt that Taiwan is continuous with the ROC on the grounds that Taiwan is no longer a state, if it ever was. But as I have previously argued, a state can be continuous with a non-state corporate entity. The Republic of Kazakhstan is continuous with the Kazakh Soviet Socialist Republic; the Canadian province of Newfoundland is continuous with the Dominion of Newfoundland; and the State of Virginia is continuous with the Virginia Colony, and possibly even with the Virginia Company. A corporate entity persists despite changes in its status, provided that its chain of succession remains unbroken. It is obvious that, whatever Taiwan is, its government is the extension of pre-war China's chain of succession.

In sum, the Hobbesian account of corporate identity categorizes relational cases of change in states according to what happens to the relevant chains of succession. (1) Cession is a transfer of territory without any change in the chain of succession of either the ceding state or the receiving state (as in the sale of Alaska). (2) Secession is a split in a state's chain of succession in which the original chain of succession remains intact; the seceding state's chain of succession is either the continuation of a provincial chain of succession (as in the Republic of Kazakhstan) or is altogether new (as in Bangladesh). (3) Absorption is a merger of two or more states' chains of succession in which one of the original chains remains intact; the absorbed state's chain of succession either becomes a provincial chain of succession (as in Newfoundland) or is broken (as in the Kingdom of Hawaii). (4) Unification is a merger of two or more states' chains of succession in which a new chain of succession is created; the unifying states' chains of succession either become provincial chains of succession (as in the Canadian provinces) or are broken (as in North and South Yemen). (5) Dissolution is a break in a state's chain of succession, either with continuity of its provincial chains of succession (as in Czechoslovakia) or without any continuity (as in the hypothetical submersion of the Maldives).

§22 Non-Identity

Continuity of the state implies continuity of its responsibilities.[15] But does discontinuity of the state imply the negation of its responsibilities? For instance, does the dissolution of Czechoslovakia extinguish its debts, or should they be divided among the Czech Republic and Slovakia? This section examines what ought to happen to states' responsibilities in cases of secession, absorption, unification, and dissolution.

International lawyers have attempted to develop rules for dividing responsibility in cases of discontinuity. Two *Vienna Conventions* propose rules for dividing debts and treaty obligations (UN, 1978, 1983), and the International Law Commission is currently developing rules for dividing responsibility for wrongdoing (Šturma, 2017). The general principle is that a new state ought to assume 'an equitable proportion' of its antecedent state's responsibilities, except if the new state is a post-colonial state. 'Newly independent states' do not have to assume a share of their former colonizers' responsibilities. One problem with the *Vienna Conventions* is that they do not specify what counts as an equitable proportion (Blum, 1997: 272). Another is that they have had limited uptake: 'The 1983 Convention lacks the requisite number of state parties and never entered into force ... The 1978 Convention did enter into force, but to date it has only twenty-two parties' (Cheng, 2011: 11–12). The legal rules regarding state responsibility in cases of discontinuity are contested and uncertain, in large part because cases of discontinuity are so varied that 'it is difficult to reach any conclusions of general application' (Crawford, 2013a: 455).

---

15. There are some limited exceptions to this principle, which I discuss in §26.

Although it is not possible to develop universal rules for cases of discontinuity, it is possible to sketch some general principles. There ought to be a presumption against accession to responsibility in cases of discontinuity: a state does not automatically accede to the responsibilities of an antecedent state with which it shares population or territory.[16] As a new corporate entity, a new state is presumably free of responsibilities. It is not bound by treaties that it did not sign, does not owe money that it did not borrow, and has no reparative obligations for wrongs that it did not commit. However, there are at least two circumstances in which the 'clean slate presumption' should be overturned: (1) when a state agrees to assume the responsibilities of an antecedent state and (2) when a state adopts or perpetuates the actions of an antecedent state.[17]

'Accession by agreement' occurs when a state agrees to assume the responsibilities of an antecedent state. In many cases of discontinuity, the division of responsibility is settled by agreement. The Czech Republic and Slovakia agreed to divide Czechoslovakia's debt on a per capita basis (Blum, 1997: 293), and the Federal Republic of Germany agreed to assume all of the German Democratic Republic's debt (*Treaty*, 1991: Art. 23). The Republic of Turkey and the former Ottoman territories agreed to divide the Ottoman debt according to their respective annual revenues:

> The Treaty of Lausanne . . . enunciated the principle that the share in the Turkish [i.e., Ottoman] Debt apportioned to each state should bear the same proportion to the total amount as the average total revenue of the territory attributed to each state bore, in typical financial years, to the average total revenue of the Ottoman Empire (Brown, 1926: 137).

The only condition for accession by agreement is that the agreement must be made by an authorized government. The agreement to divide Czechoslovakia's debt was valid because the governments of the Czech Republic and Slovakia were authorized. But some of the post-Soviet states, such as Turkmenistan, could not have made a valid agreement to assume a share of the Soviet Union's debt because their governments failed to meet the conditions for authorization. A government cannot agree to assume responsibilities in the name of

---

16. To 'accede to' a responsibility is to assume a responsibility that originally belonged to another state. I use 'accession to responsibility' rather than the legal term, 'succession to responsibility', to distinguish my account from the legal account, and because I have already given a precise meaning to 'succession'.

17. The 'clean slate' of a new state is never totally blank; it comes inscribed with the general responsibilities of customary international law. Accession pertains to personal responsibilities (§13).

the state unless it has a credible claim to be an authorized representative of the state.

'Accession by implication' occurs when a state adopts or perpetuates the actions of an antecedent state, and hence assumes the responsibilities that follow from these actions. Suppose (contrary to what has been established in §20) that the Republic of Turkey was, as it claimed to be, discontinuous with the Ottoman Empire. This would entail a presumption that the Republic is not responsible for the Ottoman Empire's genocide against its Armenian population. But this presumption would be overturned by the fact that the Turkish National Movement—the first link in the 'new' Republic's embryonic chain of succession—continued the Empire's genocide during the Turkish-Armenian War (Akçam, 2006: Chapter 8).[18] Even if the Republic were not continuous with the Empire, and even though the Republic has refused to take responsibility for the genocide, it would have acceded to this responsibility by implication. The Republic incurred responsibility for the Empire's genocide by perpetuating it.

Accession by agreement and by implication decisively overturn the clean slate presumption. If a state agrees to assume an antecedent state's responsibilities, or it adopts or perpetuates the actions from which these responsibilities follow, then it accedes to the antecedent state's responsibilities. There is also a third but less decisive way in which the clean slate presumption could be overturned. 'Accession by inheritance' occurs when a state claims the assets of an antecedent state. Just as the heir to an estate inherits some of the liabilities of the deceased person along with her property, a new state inherits some of the liabilities of an antecedent state along with its property (Pasternak, forthcoming). Like other analogies between states and human beings, the inheritance analogy is imprecise and potentially misleading, so it is doubtful that any firm conclusions can be drawn from it (Crawford, 2013a: 440; Öktem, 2011: 563–64). Interpersonal inheritance is triggered only when a person dies, but interstate inheritance can be triggered without the 'death' of a state, as in cases of secession. With this caveat in mind, there are two questions that must be answered in order for the inheritance analogy to be applied: (1) what is included in the state's 'estate'?; (2) which responsibilities does a state's 'heir' accede to?

The state's estate comprises its property, or the things that it owns. It includes military equipment, embassies and consulates, state-owned companies, sovereign wealth funds, and public infrastructure. It does not include the

18. See Dumberry (2012, 2014) on Turkish/Ottoman identity and the Armenian genocide.

state's personal rights, such as institutional memberships. States do not 'own' their memberships in the United Nations; these memberships are non-transferable, so they cannot be inherited (see §20 above). Nor does the state's estate include its population or territory. The state *has* a population and a territory, but it does not own them, any more than a human being owns her appendages. In other words, population and territory are not parts of the state's estate; they are simply parts of the state. The fact that a state claims part of the territory or population of an antecedent state therefore does not imply inheritance of the antecedent state's responsibilities. For instance, the fact that Ukraine claimed part of the territory of the Soviet Union did not, by itself, make Ukraine liable for a share of the Soviet debt. Nor would the Maldives accede to a share of another state's debt simply by acquiring part of that state's territory. The state's estate includes only the things that it can be said to own.

The next question is what kinds of responsibilities states can inherit. Debts and other financial obligations are inheritable. As in most legal systems, the heir to an estate has to pay off the debts of the deceased as a condition of inheriting her property. If you inherit a house, then you also inherit the mortgage. Similarly, if a state inherits infrastructure or military equipment, then it inherits a share of the antecedent state's debt. Since Ukraine inherited about 18 per cent of the Soviet Union's Black Sea Fleet, it should have inherited a proportionate share of the Soviet debt. Ukraine's fair share of the Soviet debt is equal to the total share of Soviet assets that it inherited. Reparative obligations are also inheritable. Although torts were once considered to be personal, meaning that the liability died with the tortfeasor, 'both civil and common law jurisdictions now generally provide for the survivability of actions against deceased tortfeasors' (Crawford, 2013a: 441). Like other financial obligations, torts must be paid out of the deceased person's estate. States can inherit reparative obligations just as they inherit debts. However, many treaty obligations are non-transferable, just as many contracts are non-transferable. Treaties and contracts are often personal, like institutional memberships. For instance, an independent Quebec would not automatically accede to the North American Free Trade Agreement, for the same reason that it would not automatically accede to membership in the United Nations. In general, only financial obligations are inheritable.

The inheritance analogy suggests the following rule: when a state inherits the property of an antecedent state, it accedes to a proportionate share of that state's financial obligations. However, the analogy also suggests that there is a limit to the amount of debt to which the heir state can accede. In most modern legal systems, an heir assumes liabilities only up to the value of the estate: 'successors are not liable to contribute resources that they own independently of the inheritance' (Miller, 2007: 150).[19] If a son inherits a 500,000-dollar house from his mother, then he has to assume the 480,000-dollar mortgage and possibly her 20,000-dollar credit-card debt. But if the mother's debts exceed the value of her estate, then her son has no obligation to pay the excess. Her estate would then be insolvent, so the creditors would have to absorb the loss. Similarly, if a state inherits 500 million dollars worth of infrastructure, then it should assume a proportionate share of the antecedent state's financial obligations, but only up to 500 million dollars. The heir state is not obligated to assume debt in excess of the value of the property that it claims. This limit marks the crucial difference between inherited and non-inherited financial obligations. Whereas a state's inherited obligations are limited by the value of the property that it inherits, its non-inherited obligations persist in full as long as the state does.

———

The identity of the state is, as Carr (1946: 146) described it, 'a necessary fiction'. What sustains this fiction is the practice of representing the state. The state has a corporate identity only because it has representatives who speak and act in its name, and this identity persists only as long as the state has a continuous chain of succession. Without representation, the state is 'but a word, without substance, and cannot stand' (*L* XXXI. 554). Yet the fiction of corporate identity is as indispensable as it is ephemeral. The very idea that states can have responsibilities depends on it, as does the continuity of these responsibilities over time and through generations. As Maitland (2003: 69) said about the personality of the state, 'a fiction that we needs must feign is somehow or another very like the simple truth'.

Although corporate identity is fictional, it is not infinitely malleable. Political fictions, unlike mere nonsense, are bound by the constraints of logical consistency. Corporate identity is not closely analogous to personal identity or physical identity, but it is nevertheless subject to the logical constraints of identity in general. The Hobbesian account of corporate identity begins with the principle that claims about state identity are credible only insofar as they are consistent.

The Hobbesian account is, in a general sense, 'constructivist': the identity of the state depends on the political processes of authorization and

---

19. See Miller's (2007: 147–151) discussion of the ethics and the law of inheritance. He notes that, in Roman law, inheritance of liability was not limited to the value of the estate, but the heir-apparent could choose whether to assume the role of heir.

representation rather than on material factors such as territory and population. But it is not constructivist in the sense that International Relations scholars commonly use the term. The corporate identity of the state is not *externally* constituted by the recognition of other states; it is *internally* constituted by the state's representatives and by the subjects who authorize them. The identity of the state depends on what its authorized representatives do, not on what they (or the representatives of other states) say. Assertions of identity are cheap, and external recognition is often fickle and arbitrary. However, the actions of governments entail presuppositions of state identity, and these provide the most reliable basis for judgments of state identity.

Taken together, this chapter and the previous chapter explain how subjects constitute the identity of the state via their authorized representatives. Subjects authorize representatives; those representatives act in the name of the state; and the practice of representing the state as a whole *makes* the state a whole (gives it unity) and keeps it whole (gives it continuity). Being parts of this whole, in turn, makes individuals subjects. This Hobbesian logic is not quite circular, because a 'multitude' of individuals who are not yet subjects can initiate the whole process, and hence become subjects, by authorizing representatives (see §10). But once the process of political representation has been set in motion, something like constructivist 'co-constitution' takes over: subjects constitute representatives, representatives constitute the state, and the state constitutes subjects.

So far, I have focused on the role of subjects in authorizing the representatives of the state. However, as I explain in the next chapter, not all subjects are authors of the state's actions. Some subjects refuse to authorize the government, and others, such as young children, cannot authorize anyone. If subjects have a *defining* characteristic, it is that they are 'subjected' to the consequences of the state's actions. They are the people who bear the costs and burdens of debts, treaty obligations, and reparations. I now turn to the question of when it is legitimate for states to distribute these costs and burdens to their subjects.

5

Distribution

THE QUESTION OF FULFILMENT

'And because the Multitude naturally is not *One*, but *Many*; they cannot be understood for one; but many Authors, of every thing their Representative saith, or doth in their name' (*L* XVI. 250).

UNDER WHAT conditions should the costs and burdens of the state's responsibilities be distributed to its subjects? There are two common answers to this question (see §5.3). According to the authorization account of distribution, subjects should bear the costs if they have authorized the state, such as by accepting its protection. According to the participation account, subjects should bear the costs if they have participated in the state, such as by voting or using public services. The problem with both of these accounts is that they cannot justify distributing liability across generations. Even if the state's identity persists for centuries, its subjects do not. Since subjects cannot possibly have authorized or participated in a state before they were born, neither authorization nor participation can explain why they should bear the costs of intergenerational debts, treaty obligations, or reparative obligations.

This chapter develops a Hobbesian account of distribution that explains why subjects who are neither authors nor participants should nevertheless be liable for acts of state. The central idea is 'authorization by fiction', which is based on Hobbes' idea of 'representation by fiction' (see §10). Much as guardians authorize representatives for wards, subjects authorize representatives for the people among them and after them—children and future subjects—who are incapable of authorizing representatives on their own. Authorization by fiction gives the young and the unborn a vicarious 'presence' in the state's actions, which renders them liable for the costs of discharging the state's responsibilities. I qualify this overly simplified argument throughout the chapter.

The chapter has four sections. The first section examines the problem of distributing liability to subjects and the previous attempts to address it. I identify two normatively relevant aspects of distribution—whether the costs that subjects bear are diffuse or burdensome, and whether the costs are distributed within a generation or across generations—and I show that neither the authorization account nor the participation account can provide a justification for intergenerational distribution. The second section uses the idea of authorization by fiction to develop a Hobbesian account of distribution. I argue that there is a 'presumption of legitimate distribution' as long as the government of the state is authorized, but that the strength of this presumption depends on how intergenerational and how burdensome the distribution is. The third section examines how, when the distribution is legitimate, liability ought to be divided up among subjects. The fourth section examines how the presumption of legitimate distribution can be overturned, and when a state can legitimately repudiate its responsibilities.

§23 The Problem of Distribution

States are incapable of acting on their own, so their responsibilities must be distributed to individuals in order to be fulfilled (see §5.3). The core of an answer to the Question of Fulfilment must therefore be an account of distribution. There are two classes of people to whom the state's responsibilities can be distributed: its representatives and its subjects. Distribution to representatives is relatively unproblematic. The representatives of a state are obligated to uphold its agreements, honour its debts, and apologize for its wrongs simply because that is what their jobs require. Like corporate executives and employees, political representatives and state officials typically assume their roles voluntarily, and these roles require that they do their parts to ensure that the state fulfils its responsibilities.

Distributing the state's responsibilities to its subjects is more difficult to justify. The role of subject, unlike the role of representative, is typically involuntary (see §1). When a state pays reparations or repays a loan, the costs inevitably fall on its subjects, usually in the form of taxation, inflation, or a reduction in public services. When sanctions are imposed on a state, its subjects suffer from the interruption of economic activity. An account of distribution has to explain why subjects ought to bear these costs, despite the fact that most subjects of most states have not chosen to be subjects and cannot easily leave. It is not necessary to show that subjects are *culpable* for what their state does—that they are guilty or blameworthy. Liability and culpability can and do come apart (see §16). However, it is necessary to show that subjects are implicated in acts of state somehow.

Cases of distribution vary in two normatively relevant ways. The first important factor is the size of the burden that subjects bear. In some cases, the distribution of liability is *diffuse,* which means that the cost to any individual subject is materially insignificant. The cost of repaying a single one-million-dollar Treasury Bill is so small compared to the budget of the United States that the cost to any particular American is negligible. In other cases, the distribution is *burdensome,* which means that individual subjects bear significant costs. Iraqis suffered greatly from the sanctions and reparations against Iraq after the 1990 invasion of Kuwait, and Greeks suffered greatly as a result of the Greek Debt Crisis that began in 2009. Whereas diffuse distributions show up in the state's budget and in economic data, burdensome distributions are apparent to an observer on the ground.

The second normatively relevant factor is how much time has elapsed between attribution and distribution of the responsibility. If the majority of the state's subjects at the time of distribution were subjects at the time of attribution, then the distribution is *intragenerational.* For instance, most of the subjects who bear the cost of repaying a one-year Treasury Bill were subjects of the United States when the Treasury Bill was issued. Births, deaths, immigration, and emigration result in only a modest change in the composition of the population over the course of a year. But if the majority of the subjects at the time of distribution were *not* subjects at the time of attribution, then the distribution is *intergenerational.*[1] In 2014, the United Kingdom repaid a series of 'consolidated annuities', or perpetual bonds, that were issued between 1752 and 1927 (Kollewe and Farrell, 2014). The distribution was intergenerational because most of the repayment costs, as well as many of the interest costs, were distributed to subjects who were born after the money was borrowed.

The distinctions between diffuse or burdensome and intra- or intergenerational distribution are graded rather than binary. Although some distributions are purely of one type—for instance, reparations for 'historic' wrongs, such as slavery, are purely intergenerational—most distributions fall somewhere in between. In addition, some distributions become more intergenerational and more or less burdensome over time. Germany's reparations for the Holocaust

---

1. Strictly speaking, it is possible for the distribution of liability to be *intra*generational even when the majority of the subjects at the time of distribution were not subjects at the time of attribution. The population might 'turn over' within a generation because of a large wave of immigration. In Lebanon, where about one in four subjects is now a Syrian refugee, the population has turned over much faster than it would have through births and deaths alone. Although 'intra/intercohort' would be more precise, I use 'intra/intergenerational' because the language of generations is more familiar and intuitive, and because the turnover in a state's population is usually driven by births and deaths.

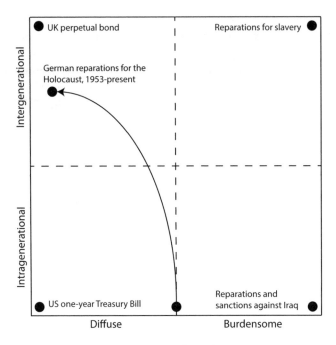

FIGURE 3. Types of Distribution

became less burdensome as the compensation was paid but more intergenerational as the Germans of the Second World War died out. Combining the two distinctions gives us four broad types of distribution. I return to the types of distribution in the next section. I turn now to the difficulty that intergenerational distribution poses for existing accounts of distribution.

There are two common accounts of distribution (see §5.3). According to the authorization account, subjects ought to share liability for acts of state if they have tacitly authorized the state, such as by accepting its protection (Parrish, 2009; Stilz, 2011). According to the participation account, subjects ought to share liability for acts of state if they have 'intentionally participated' in the collective project of the state, such as by paying taxes, voting, claiming benefits, or taking pride in their citizenship (Jubb, 2014; Pasternak, 2013; Vernon, 2011). Whereas the authorization account focuses on the structure of the state, the participation account focuses on subjects' attitudes and actions toward the state. I leave aside the fine details and the relative merits of the two accounts here. The important point is that neither can justify intergenerational distribution.

The problem with the authorization account is that subjects who have not yet been born cannot grant authority. Authorization, tacit or explicit, has to be inferred from actions or attitudes. But people who do not exist cannot act and do not have attitudes. Although you might be an author of a debt that your state incurs today, you cannot possibly be an author of a debt that your state incurred before you were born. It is difficult to see how authorization could be retroactive. Authorization follows from the will (see §15.1), and it is not possible to 'will' something that has already happened. I may approve of the destruction of the Berlin Wall, but I was not around to 'will' it. Similarly, I may admire the government of Mackenzie King, which led Canada during the Second World War, but I was not around to authorize it. Retrospective approval and admiration are possible; retroactive authorization is not. The fact that the current subjects of the United Kingdom are authors of the bonds that the state issues today does not imply that they are authors of the bonds that the state issued a century or more ago. When subjects authorize a government, they become liable for what that government does in the near future, but not for what the government (or its predecessors) did in the past.

The participation account suffers from the same kind of problem. While participating in the state might make you liable for what the state does, it is difficult to see how it could make you liable for what the state did before you were born. Thompson (2006: 160) makes this point in a discussion of historic injustice.

> Accounts of shared or collective responsibility that make it depend on individuals contributing to the achievement of a common objective or participating together in a joint action . . . do not encompass cases where individuals cannot have contributed or participated. Not being born when an injustice took place seems a very good reason for denying any responsibility.

Most Americans in 1850 may have been complicit in slavery, either directly by owning slaves or indirectly by participating in the state that made the institution of slavery possible. But present-day Americans could not possibly have participated in slavery, either directly or indirectly, because they did not exist during the time of slavery. Thompson's point is not that there is no justification for distributing the costs of reparations across generations, but that the participation account cannot provide one.

The authorization and participation accounts thus suffer from the same problem. Neither can justify intergenerational distribution, for the simple reason that it is not possible to authorize or to participate before you were born. Any other account that attempts to justify distribution according to the wills or actions of subjects is bound to fail for the same reason. An adequate account of distribution has to face the fact that intergenerational debts, treaty obligations, and reparations impose costs on subjects that they could not possibly have brought on themselves. The justification for intergenerational distribution has to be sought elsewhere.

There are two other arguments that are sometimes invoked to justify intergenerational distribution. One is that subjects are liable for acts of state insofar as they benefit from them (Butt, 2007). For example, subjects of the former colonial powers should bear the costs of reparations to former colonies because colonialism has unjustly enriched them (e.g., Beckles, 2013). But as Thompson (2006: 158) points out, this argument has a crucial limitation: 'If an injustice produces no benefits for existing people, then on this account they have no responsibility.' Moreover, the 'benefiting from injustice' argument is not really an account of distribution at all. It implies that people who benefit from a wrongful act should bear the costs of compensating the victims, regardless of whether they are subjects of the state that committed the wrongful act. If Switzerland's subjects were enriched by the Holocaust but (counterfactually) Germany's subjects were not, then the Swiss, not the Germans, should bear the costs of reparations. Whatever its merits, the benefiting from injustice argument does not explain specifically why *subjects* ought to bear the costs of fulfilling their state's responsibilities.

The idea of 'national responsibility' is also invoked to justify intergenerational distribution of liability (Abdel-Nour, 2003; Miller, 2007). One could argue that present-day Germans ought to bear the costs of reparations for the Holocaust because they are members of the German nation, which, via the German state, carried out the Holocaust. The limitation of this argument is that the set of subjects is not coextensive with the set of nationals. As Miller (2007: 111–12) argues, national responsibility is distinct from—and, in his view, 'more basic than'—state responsibility: 'national responsibility and state responsibility may coincide, [but] in other cases this may not happen'. Not all subjects of Germany are members of the German nation, and not all members of the German nation are subjects of Germany. If the costs of Germany's reparations for the Holocaust were distributed to Germans, then some subjects of Germany would escape liability, and some non-subjects would be liable. Like the 'benefiting from injustice' argument, the national responsibility argument is not really an account of distribution. National responsibility is an account of why people should share liability for what their co-nationals do, not an account of why subjects should share liability for what their states do. The next section develops a Hobbesian account of distribution, which explains why *subjects in particular* ought to bear the costs of their state's responsibilities, even if the state incurred those responsibilities before they were born.

§24 The Conditions for Distribution

The starting point for the Hobbesian account of distribution is the Hobbesian account of authorization. Recall from Chapter 3 that two conditions must be met in order for a government to count as an authorized representative of the state: (1) the government must satisfy the background conditions for valid authorization (i.e., it must not systematically indoctrinate or coerce its subjects); and (2) a substantial number of subjects must accept that the government is legitimate (as demonstrated by elections or by some other means). The argument of this section is that if the government of a state is authorized at the time of attribution, then there is a presumption that it is legitimate to distribute the costs of fulfilling the state's responsibilities to its subjects.

§24.1 Intragenerational Distribution

The simplest distribution of liability is one that is both diffuse and intragenerational. The archetype is the repayment of a small short-term bond, such as a one-year United States Treasury Bill (issued in denominations of one thousand to five million dollars). Most subjects of the United States can legitimately be made to bear the costs of repayment because they are authors of the debt, both at the time of attribution and at the time of distribution. They have authorized both the government that issued the bond and the government that will repay the money when the bond matures.

Even in the simplest case, there are some subjects who cannot be counted as authors of the state's responsibilities (see §15.2). Pasternak (2013: 371) argues that these non-authorizing subjects include those 'who genuinely reject their citizenship status—who would like to give it up had they the real opportunity to do so'. Subjects who credibly, consistently, and publicly disavow the state, such as radical separatists and pacifists, cannot plausibly be counted as authors of its responsibilities. In addition, there are some subjects who cannot *possibly* be authors of the state's responsibilities. As Hobbes says,

> naturall fooles, children, or mad-men . . . had never power to make any covenant, or to understand the consequences thereof; and consequently never took upon them to authorise the actions of any Soveraign, as they must do that make to themselves a Common-wealth (*L* XXVI. 422).

'Incapable' subjects cannot authorize a government any more than 'brute beasts' can (ibid.). Nor can prisoners authorize a government, regardless of whether the laws of the state actually disenfranchise them. Even by Hobbes' meagre standards for authorization, people who are 'kept in prison, or bonds' are rendered incapable granting valid authority (*L* XX. 312; §15.1 above). There are always some subjects who cannot be counted as authors of the state's responsibilities, either because they refuse to authorize the government ('dissenting subjects') or because they are incapable of doing so ('incapable subjects'). I call them all 'non-authorizing subjects'.

Distributing liability to non-authorizing subjects is relatively unproblematic when the distribution is diffuse. The fact that most subjects have authorized the government is sufficient to justify distributing the costs of the state's responsibilities to all subjects, since the costs that the non-authors bear is negligible. The state's obligations to compensate victims of its wrongs, repay its creditors, and uphold its agreements far outweigh any claims that non-authorizing subjects might have to be exempt from costs that are materially insignificant. If the government is authorized and the distribution is diffuse, then there is a strong presumption that it is legitimate to distribute liability to all subjects.

Difficulties arise when the distribution is burdensome. The costs of repaying a single bond or of compensating one injured person are negligible, but the costs of repaying thousands of bonds or compensating millions of people can be enormous. Many diffuse distributions can add up to a burdensome distribution. The archetype of a burdensome distribution is the combination of sanctions and reparations against Iraq after its invasion of Kuwait in 1990. The United Nations Security Council imposed an almost total embargo against Iraq. The state was permitted to sell a limited amount of oil in order to buy food and medicine, but the United Nations withheld 30 per cent of the revenue (later reduced to 25 per cent) to compensate the victims of the invasion and occupation. The United Nations Compensation Commission (2018) ultimately held Iraq liable for 52.4 billion US dollars in reparations, 78 per cent of which was awarded to Kuwait and its citizens (see also Van Houtte, Das, and Delmartino, 2006). A report commissioned by the UN Security Council (1999: 35–38) describes the toll that the sanctions and reparations took on Iraqis.

> Per capita income fell from 3,416 US dollars in 1985 to 1,500 in 1991 and has decreased to less than 1,036 in 1998. Other sources estimate a decrease in per capita GDP to as low as 450 US dollars in 1995. . . . The dietary energy supply had fallen from 3,120 to 1,093 kilo calories per capita/per day by 1994–95. The prevalence of malnutrition in Iraqi children under five almost doubled from 1991 to 1996 (from 12% to 23%).

The report concludes that 'the gravity of the humanitarian situation of the Iraqi people is indisputable and cannot be overstated' (ibid. 46).[2] The

---

2. A recent study suggests that the Iraqi government manipulated child mortality statistics to exaggerate the severity of the humanitarian situation (Dyson and Cetorelli, 2017; cf.

question is when, if ever, it is legitimate to distribute costs and burdens of this magnitude to the subjects of a state.

Burdensome distributions are always regrettable and often tragic. The people who bear the burdens of large-scale sanctions and reparations are often 'guilty' of nothing more than being born in the wrong country at the wrong time (see §1). Even if they have authorized the government, the costs that they bear as a result of its actions are often grossly disproportionate to the contributions that they have made to those actions. Subjects usually do not morally deserve the burdens that they bear. Burdensome distributions of liability can be justified only in the sense that waging war can be justified: they may be necessary or obligatory despite the evils that they entail.

A burdensome distribution is easiest to justify when the subjects who bear the burdens are the authors of the state's responsibilities. Subjects, like private individuals, sometimes have to bear large costs as a result of actions done under their authority. If an employee injures someone in the course of his duties, then his employer is partly liable for compensating the victim, even if the compensation payments cause her financial hardship. The employer ought to bear the costs because, having hired the employee, she is the author of the harm that he has caused. Similarly, if an authorized government wages an aggressive war, then the state owes reparations to the victims, even if the reparations payments are burdensome to its subjects. The subjects are liable because, having authorized the government, they are the authors of the war. This analogy is a weak one, because employers typically have far more control over their employees than subjects have over their governments. Yet the logic still holds: authorization entails liability. The government of Iraq probably did not meet the conditions for authorization at the time of the invasion of Kuwait. But if the government were authorized, then distributing liability to the subjects who authorized it would have been presumptively legitimate, even though the distribution was very burdensome.

Burdensome distributions are much more difficult to justify in relation to subjects who do not or cannot authorize the government. A minority of non-authorizing subjects can be ignored when the distribution is diffuse, but not when the distribution is burdensome. The costs that these subjects bear become normatively significant as soon as they become materially significant.

Non-authorizing subjects tend to suffer greatly from burdensome distributions, such as large debts and reparations. Children and other 'incapable'

Alnasrawi, 2001: 214). Yet there was little need to exaggerate, because there is plenty of other evidence that the subjects of Iraq, and children in particular, did suffer greatly as a result of the sanctions and reparations.

subjects bear little of the tax burden but often suffer the most from reductions in public services. Although incapable subjects cannot truly be authors, I argue that they can be authors 'by fiction'. When subjects authorize political representatives, they grant authority not only for themselves, but also for the people among them who cannot grant authority on their own. So if most subjects are authors of the state's responsibilities, then the incapable subjects among them can be understood as 'fictive authors' of the state's responsibilities.

The idea of authorization by fiction follows from Hobbes' idea of 'representation by fiction' (see §10). Just as 'Children, Fooles, and Mad-men that have no use of Reason, may be Personated by Guardians' (L XVI. 248), those guardians may grant authority on behalf of the wards whom they personate. If guardians can act in the names of wards, and authorization is simply a type of action, then guardians can authorize in the names of wards. For instance, the guardians of children can authorize lawyers, accountants, and estate agents to represent them. The logic of guardianship extends to the political domain. Guardians can authorize political representatives for wards, much as they authorize legal representatives for wards.

True authorization must be voluntary, which means that it must proceed from the author's will (see §15.1). But fictive authorization is not voluntary in relation to the fictive author because it proceeds from the will of a third party. The authority of a child's lawyer is derived from the will of her guardian rather than the will of the child herself. What gives the child a 'presence' in the actions of her lawyer is that there is a third party—her guardian, or in some cases a judge—who is capable of representing the interests of the child and of objecting to what the lawyer does if he fails to act in her interests. As Runciman (2007: 99) argues, 'incapable persons and things can have a presence in the actions of their representatives, so long as that presence is capable of being asserted by someone. It does not have to be asserted by the person being represented themselves'. Incapable persons can thus be represented 'so long as a mechanism exists for objecting to what is being done in their name' (ibid. 98). Whereas true authority derives from the author's will, fictive authority derives from a third party's representation of the fictive author's interests.

There are three kinds of objection mechanisms that make fictive authorization possible. *Internal* mechanisms operate within the representative relationship, such as when the guardian who has authorized a child's lawyer objects to what the lawyer does in the child's name. *External* mechanisms register objections from outside the representative relationship, such as when a judge objects to what the child's guardian or lawyer does in her name. *Retrospective* mechanisms register objections after the representative relationship has ended, such as when a child grows up and objects to what her guardian or lawyer has done in her name. Retrospective mechanisms are not strictly necessary for fictive authorization, and in some cases are not possible. For instance, a person in a coma cannot object to what his lawyer did if he never wakes up, but his guardian-appointed lawyer may nevertheless have a legitimate claim to represent him. Internal and external objection mechanisms are necessary. The guardian who authorizes the ward's lawyer must be able to withdraw this authority, at least periodically, and there must be someone, such as a judge, who can 'guard the guardian'. The internal and external objection mechanisms together ensure that the incapable person has a genuine presence in the actions of her representative. Objection mechanisms thus distinguish fictive authorization from fraudulent authorization.

In order for subjects to authorize a government on behalf of the incapable subjects among them, there must be mechanisms for objecting to the government on behalf of those incapable subjects. The internal objection mechanism is the normal authorization procedure. Subjects can withdraw authority from a government that fails to represent the interests of incapable subjects (for instance, by voting it out of office), just as a guardian can withdraw authority from a lawyer who fails to represent the interests of a ward. The external objection mechanism operates through civil society. A children's advocate or an interest group can object to a government that fails to represent the interests of children, much as a social worker can object to a guardian who fails to represent the interests of a particular child. The retrospective objection mechanism becomes possible when incapable subjects come of age or regain their faculties. Subjects can retrospectively object to a past government that failed to protect them when they were children (for instance, by electing a government that condemns the actions of the past government), much as an adult can object to what a guardian did in her name when she was a child.[3] The internal, external, and retrospective objection mechanisms together ensure that incapable subjects have a presence in the state's actions.

Fictive authorization creates a presumption of legitimate distribution for incapable subjects. Although the government's actions do not derive from the wills of incapable subjects, these actions may nevertheless derive from a credible representation of their interests. This is sufficient to justify distributing the costs of the state's responsibilities to them, even when the distribution is burdensome. The fact that a state's debt imposes significant costs on children does not, by itself, make that debt odious. The debt might have been incurred

---

3. Like all state/human analogies, these three analogies should be used with caution. The objection mechanisms do not work exactly the same way in the individual and political cases. In particular, while the objection of a single guardian, judge, or grown-up ward can be decisive, the objection of a single subject is never decisive.

with their interests in mind, even though they could not have truly authorized the government that incurred it. Children can have a genuine presence in the actions of the government, provided that the necessary objection mechanisms are in place. However, the presumption of legitimate distribution is weaker for fictive authors than it is for true authors. For this reason, as I argue in §25, it is desirable to divide liability among subjects in a way that minimizes the burdens that incapable subjects bear.

'Dissenting subjects', or subjects who refuse to authorize the government, also bear the costs of its responsibilities. For example, pacifists bear the costs of war debts and reparations through the tax system, and these costs may well be burdensome. But authorization by fiction, like representation by fiction, is possible only for people who are incapable of speaking and acting on their own. 'Guardianship' of competent adults is essentially slavery. A parent can authorize a representative for a young child, but not for a competent grown-up child, and certainly not against that grown-up child's will. Similarly, while subjects can authorize political representatives on behalf of the incapable subjects among them, they cannot authorize representatives on behalf of the subjects among them who simply refuse to authorize. One might argue, as Stilz (2011) does, that all subjects ought to share liability for the state's responsibilities because they all require the state to protect their rights. But this argument has no force against the most radical pacifists and separatists, who would, if they had the option, take their chances without a state rather than accept the protection of the one that they have. Nor does this argument have any force against indigenous people who reject modern forms of political organization. An account of distribution has to contend with the fact that some subjects are not authors of the state's actions.

The burdens that dissenting subjects bear are best understood as a kind of collateral damage. State responsibility would not be possible if the costs of fulfilling the state's responsibilities could not be distributed to its subjects. Debts and reparations could not be paid, treaties could not be upheld, and sanctions could not be imposed. Yet it may be difficult to confine the costs to the subjects who are authors or fictive authors of the state's actions. So if most subjects have a presence in the state's actions, then some 'overspill' of liability to the dissenting subjects among them is permissible, though always regrettable. As with other kinds of collateral damage, the distribution of liability to non-authorizing subjects ought to be mitigated, and it requires proportionality. The more dissenting subjects there are, and the less important the responsibility is, the more difficult it is to justify distributing the costs to the dissenters.

In sum, it is presumptively legitimate to distribute liability to subjects intragenerationally provided that the government of the state meets the conditions for authorization. Most subjects can legitimately be made to bear the costs because they are authors of the state's responsibilities. When the distribution is diffuse, the costs to non-authorizing subjects are negligible and can therefore be ignored. But when the distribution is burdensome, the presumption of legitimate distribution becomes weaker. Distributing liability to incapable subjects is justified insofar as there are mechanisms by which others can represent their interests and object to the government on their behalf, and distributing liability to dissenting subjects is sometimes permissible as a kind of collateral damage.

§24.2 Intergenerational Distribution

Liberal political philosophers have long worried that there is something unjust about distributing responsibility across generations. Thomas Jefferson (1999 [1789]: 594) argued that 'no generation can contract debts greater than may be paid during the course of it's [sic] own existence'. Since 'one generation is to another as one independant nation to another' (ibid.), intergenerational distribution of debt is equivalent to distributing the debts of an empire to a colony. Thomas Paine (2012 [1791]) argued, on similar grounds, that 'governing beyond the grave, is the most ridiculous and insolent of all tyrannies'. John Stuart Mill (1870) later argued that states 'should conclude their treaties, as commercial treaties are usually concluded, only for terms of years', and that sanctions and reparations against states 'ought not ... to exceed the length of a generation; or, more properly, the period at the end of which a majority of the adult population will have grown up from childhood subsequently to the offence'. More recently, Waldron (2006) and Dworkin (2013) have questioned whether treaties should be binding in perpetuity: 'It seems unfair that people should suffer serious disadvantage only because politicians chosen by entirely different people under entirely different constitutions signed a document many generations ago' (Dworkin, 2013: 8).

The problem with intergenerational distributions of liability is, in Hobbesian terms, that authority dies with the authors. If the justification for distributing liability to subjects is that they are authors of the state's responsibilities, then intergenerational distribution is unjustifiable, because subjects cannot possibly be authors of responsibilities that their state incurred before they were born (see §23). Consider the United Kingdom's perpetual bonds from 1853. The justification for distributing the repayment costs to the subjects of the United Kingdom in 2014 cannot possibly be that they are authors of the debt, because none of the subjects of the United Kingdom in 2014 were alive when the bonds were issued. In this case, the repayment costs are so diffuse that they might be normatively insignificant. But a justification for more burdensome intergenerational distributions has to answer 'Jefferson's challenge': why should one generation be liable for the actions of a government that was authorized by another generation?

Thompson (2009: 62) argues that intergenerational distribution can be justified on grounds of intergenerational equity.

> We ought to do for our predecessors what we think we are entitled to claim from our survivors. If I think that my survivors ought to fulfil certain demands (were I to make them), then I have to accept a duty to fulfil relevantly similar demands that were made, or could be made, by those whom I survive.

If the current generation expects future generations to bear the costs of debts that it incurs, then the current generation must bear the costs of debts that past generations have incurred. A generation cannot make commitments that bind future generations unless it is willing to honour the commitments that past generations have made.

There are two problems with this line of argument. First, as Miller (2007: 144) points out, it provides only a conditional justification for intergenerational distribution. If the current generation did *not* incur any intergenerational responsibilities, then it could, without any inconsistency, repudiate the intergenerational responsibilities of past generations. Yet this objection is of no real consequence, since every generation actually does make intergenerational commitments.

The second, more fundamental problem with Thompson's argument is that it establishes a necessary condition for intergenerational distribution but not a sufficient condition. What the argument shows is that the current generation *cannot* legitimately expect future generations to bear the costs of its debts if it does not honour the debts of previous generations. This follows from the principle of intergenerational equity. But it does not follow that the current generation *can* legitimately expect future generations to bear the costs of its debts as long as it honours the debts of previous generations. Consider another example with the same form. The current generation cannot legitimately expect future generations to bear the costs of its pollution if it does not accept that it was legitimate for previous generations to pollute. But it does not follow that the current generation can legitimately pollute as long as it accepts that it was legitimate for previous generations to do so. Honouring the debts of the previous generation does not give the current generation the right to incur debts that the next generation will have to pay, any more than accepting the costs of the previous generation's pollution gives the current generation the right to pollute.

What needs to be explained is why it was legitimate for some generation to initiate the practice of making intergenerational commitments in the first place. A retrospective justification will not work: the fact that the current generation honours the commitments of past generations does not, by itself, give it the right to make commitments that bind future generations. An adequate justification has to be prospective: it has to explain why a generation that did not inherit any intergenerational commitments—such as the first generation of subjects in a new state—would have the right to make commitments that bind subsequent generations. A prospective justification for intergenerational distribution of liability has to refer to future subjects. And since future subjects do not yet exist, the justification has to refer to their interests rather than their wills. The question, then, is how the interests of future generations can have a genuine presence in the current generation's decisions.

The idea of authorization by fiction explains how it is possible to give future subjects a presence in acts of state, just as it is possible to give a presence to incapable subjects. If children and corporate entities can be represented, despite the fact that they are incapable of authorizing their own representatives, then so can the subjects of the future (Brito Vieira and Runciman, 2008: 182–92). And if it is possible to represent future subjects, then it is possible to grant fictive authority on their behalf. The logic of guardianship extends from subjects who cannot (yet) speak for themselves to subjects who do not yet exist.

What is required is a set of internal and external mechanisms by which third parties can register objections on behalf of future subjects. First, through the normal authorization procedure, subjects can periodically withdraw authority from the government if it fails to represent the interests of future subjects. Second, through protests and petitions, interest groups and advocates can object on behalf of future subjects to what the government does. These objection mechanisms can give future subjects a genuine presence in acts of state. Future subjects count as fictive authors of the state's responsibilities, and intergenerational distribution is therefore presumptively legitimate, provided that the state had internal and external objection mechanisms at the time of attribution. For the same reason that subjects ought to bear the costs of debts that their state incurred when they were children, they ought to bear the costs of debts that their state incurred before they were born.

The obvious problem with fictive authorization in the case of future subjects is that people tend to discount the future—especially the future in which they no longer expect to be alive. Limited time-horizons also pose a problem for fictive authorization in the case of children, but the problem is much more severe in the case of future subjects. As Brito Vieira and Runciman (2008: 187) point out, the interests of children are effectively given a presence by 'all those representatives, and all those voters, who have children and take children's interests into account when they decide how to act'. But subjects and representatives give much less weight to the interests of their more distant descendants. Many authorized governments have run up large debts that future subjects will have to pay and made environmental messes that future subjects will have to clean up. There may well have been internal and external objection mechanisms, and many subjects and interest groups have objected to policies that were detrimental to the interests of future subjects, but the interests of the present won the day. Future subjects often have some presence in acts of state, but they rarely have a sufficient presence. The longer the timespan, the more the future tends to be discounted, and the less effective the internal and external objection mechanisms become. So although it is presumptively legitimate to distribute the costs of the state's responsibilities to its future subjects, this presumption is far weaker than it is for incapable subjects.

Since the internal and external objection mechanisms are less effective in the case of future subjects, the retrospective objection mechanism is accordingly more important. Future subjects will eventually become current subjects; they will retrospectively judge whether past governments have adequately represented their interests. I explore in §26 when retrospective objections are sufficient to overturn the presumption of legitimate distribution.

There is one final kind of distribution that remains to be justified. The argument so far is that it is presumptively legitimate for the state to distribute liability to its subjects as long as the government meets the conditions for authorization. But what if the government was authorized at the time of attribution but not at the time of distribution? Suppose that an authorized government incurred debt but was later deposed in a coup and replaced by an unauthorized government. Although debts incurred by the unauthorized government cannot legitimately be distributed to subjects, since those debts are not attributable to the state in the first place, the debts of the authorized government can legitimately be distributed. The fact that the authorized government has been deposed does not change the fact that the subjects of the state are authors (or fictive authors) of the debt that this government incurred. What matters is whether the government at the time of attribution was authorized, not whether the government at the time of distribution is authorized. However, as I argue in the next section, *divisions* of liability that are determined by unauthorized governments have to be held to a higher standard.

———

The strength of the presumption of legitimate distribution depends on two factors: whether the distribution is diffuse or burdensome, and whether it is intragenerational or intergenerational. The presumption is strongest in diffuse intragenerational cases, such as when the state incurs a small short-term debt. Most subjects ought to bear the costs because they are authors of the debt, and the costs to the non-authors are normatively insignificant because they are negligible. The presumption is weaker in burdensome intragenerational cases, such as when the state incurs a large short-term debt. Again, most subjects ought to bear the costs because they are authors of the debt. The costs to incapable subjects are justifiable provided that there are mechanisms for representing their interests, and the costs to dissenting subjects are permissible as a kind of collateral damage. The presumption is weaker still in diffuse intergenerational cases, such as when the state incurs a small long-term debt. Future subjects ought to bear the costs provided that, at the time of attribution, the state had internal and external objection mechanisms that gave their interests a genuine presence in acts of state. Yet because subjects and governments tend to discount the interests of future subjects, the presumption of legitimate distribution is weaker for them than it is for incapable subjects. The presumption is even weaker in burdensome intergenerational cases, such as when a state incurs a large long-term debt, because the tension between the interests of current and future subjects is even more acute. In short, the more intergenerational and the more burdensome the distribution is, the weaker the presumption of legitimate distribution becomes.

§25 The Division of Liability

The previous two sections addressed the question of when it is legitimate to distribute the costs of the state's responsibilities to its subjects. But when it has been established that distributing liability to subjects is legitimate, there is a further question of how the costs ought to be divided up among them. This section draws on Collins' (2016) idea of 'source-tracking' to determine what a legitimate division of liability would look like. I argue that, in practice, authorized governments should have a more or less free hand to divide liability, but that divisions of liability by unauthorized governments and third parties should be held to a higher standard.

Pasternak (2011: 220–28) identifies three ideal-typical rules for dividing liability among subjects. Although her focus is on the costs of sanctions, her three rules apply to any kind of liability. The first rule is equal division, which apportions an equal share of liability to each subject. Equal division can be construed in absolute terms, meaning that each subject bears the same cost, or in relative terms, meaning that each subject bears the same burden. An absolutely equal division of debt would mean that each subject pays the same amount; a relatively equal division would mean that each subject pays the same proportion of his or her income. The justification for an equal division rule follows from the idea that 'citizenship is a common destiny' (Walzer, 1977: 297). Since subjects are political equals, they 'should see themselves as having equal shares in their joint political activities and as equal bearers of responsibility for them' (Pasternak, 2011: 226).

The second division rule is proportional, which means that the costs of fulfilling a responsibility are apportioned to subjects according to their personal connections to it. For example, a proportional division of reparations would assign liability to subjects in proportion to their contributions to the wrong to be repaired. Subjects who helped to perpetrate the wrong would bear the greatest share of the costs; those who tried to prevent the wrong would bear the least (if any); and passive subjects would fall somewhere in between. The justification for a proportional division rule appeals to the idea of fairness (ibid. 224). It seems unfair that subjects who protested against an aggressive war should bear the same share of the reparations burden as subjects who participated in or supported the war. If certain subjects have a stronger or weaker connection to the actions that generated a responsibility, then considerations of fairness suggest that they should bear more or less of the cost of fulfilling it.

The third possible division rule is random, which means that liability is apportioned according to 'luck or chance, rather than by a systematic principle' (ibid. 222). Economic sanctions often produce divisions of liability that are random in this sense. Subjects do not bear the costs equally or in proportion to their contributions to the actions that brought about the sanctions. The subjects who bear the costs of an embargo are usually just unlucky that they work in an export-driven industry. A random division might be justified on utilitarian grounds: 'if there are good reasons to think that sanctioning the group would stop it from perpetrating greater wrongs, then the fact that this measure would have an impact on group members on a random basis should perhaps be ignored' (ibid. 224).

Of the three rules, proportional division has the strongest justification. Random division is, as Pasternak (2011: 224) argues, justifiable merely as 'a moral compromise, permissible not because it is supported by some underlying normative principle but by virtue of the fact that it produces an overall desired outcome'. An embargo that imposes costs on subjects randomly is normatively suboptimal, even if it achieves a desirable objective. Equal division is also suboptimal. Even if we think citizenship is a common destiny, considerations of fairness provide a compelling reason to take the connections between individual subjects and acts of state into account. The political equality of subjects does not justify an equal division of liability any more than it justifies a flat tax. If the ideally just tax system is one that divides the tax burden among subjects proportionally (according to wealth, need, or other criteria), then the ideally just liability-division system is also one that divides costs pro-portionally. This parallel is not coincidental, since the major part of the liability-division system *is* the tax system. The ideal division rule is proportional—the question is, in proportion to what?

Collins' (2016) idea of 'source-tracking' provides a precise account of pro-portional division. She proposes a two-step process.

> First, the costs [of fulfilling the state's responsibility] are divided among duty sources, in accordance with those sources' strength. Second, the costs earmarked to each source are divided amongst members in proportion to members' individual instantiations of that source (ibid. 350–51).

A 'duty source' is a principle (such as causation or capacity) that gives a duty normative force. Individuals 'instantiate' a duty source when their actions or cir-cumstances correspond to that source. For example, consider Canada's duty to reduce carbon emissions. Suppose that the sources of this duty are in equal parts causally contributing to climate change (as an oil-producing state) and having the capacity to help mitigate it (as a wealthy state). According to source-tracking, the costs of reducing Canada's carbon emissions should be divided equally between subjects who instantiate causation (those who profit from carbon-emitting indus-tries) and subjects who instantiate capacity (those who are wealthy enough to bear the costs of mitigating climate change). The ideal division mechanism would therefore be a combination of carbon taxation and progressive taxation. The core idea of source-tracking is that the division of liability should track subjects' per-sonal connections to the responsibility in question.

One problem with source-tracking, as Collins recognizes, is that some sources of states' responsibilities are not instantiated by any of their subjects.

> Suppose the state . . . incurs a wrongdoing-based duty to compensate these present-day people, although no present-day individuals contributed to the wrong. The source-tracking model is silent on how the state should pass the cost of its duty onto its members. It seems the state bears a duty, but no individual should bear costs through its fulfilment. The duty is thus 'short-fallen' (Collins, 2016: 335).

Collins argues that the costs of shortfallen responsibilities should not be dis-tributed unless there is some secondary source that is instantiated by the sub-jects of the state. If the state's wrongdoing is not instantiated by any of its members, then its reparative obligation might still be distributed, but only if there is some other source—such as 'association, benefit, capacity, or some combination of these'—that is instantiated (ibid. 357). However, relying on secondary sources will not always work. In particular, it is difficult to see why the costs of debts and treaty obligations should be distributed at all. The source of a debt or a treaty obligation is an agreement. The state owes money because it borrowed the money, and it is bound by a treaty because it signed the treaty. Yet it is not even clear what it would mean for an agreement to be instantiated by individuals. If it means that those individuals have agreed, then debts and treaty obligations will only ever be instantiated by a few representatives of the state. Source-tracking provides a plausible account of how the costs of reparative obligations should be divided among subjects, but it struggles to explain why treaty obligations or debts should be distributed in the first place.

The problem with Collins' source-tracking proposal is that it elides an important difference between small, participatory groups and large, non-participatory groups. She first develops the idea of source-tracking 'with regard to small-scale groups', such as 'a team of mountaineers' or 'five teenage friends who earn pocket money on weekends' (ibid. 345–47). She then 'applies the source-tracking proposal to states' (ibid.), with the assumption that dividing liability in states differs only in scale. As I have previously argued (§1, §5.1), it is often a mistake to make inferences about states and corporations from examples of small groups. There are conceptual differences as well as differences in scale. The members of a team of mountaineers participate directly in its collective actions. For the team to do wrong (e.g., to loot a cabin) is for the individual mountaineers to act in ways that bring about the wrong (such as by picking the lock or acting as a lookout). Source-tracking the team's wrong is straightforward because its members instantiate the wrong by directly participating in it. But in a state or a corporation, the relation between the corporate entity's actions and its members is mediated by authorization. For the state to do wrong (e.g., to violate another state's sovereignty) is for the authorized representatives of the state to act in ways that bring about the wrong (such as by planning and executing an invasion). Source-tracking does not work the same way because most subjects do not participate in the state's wrongdoing and therefore do not directly instantiate it. Subjects are one step removed: they authorize representatives, and these representatives instantiate the state's wrongdoing. Liability-division in the state must therefore take the relations of authority between its subjects and its representatives into account.

Authorization is the ultimate source of many of the state's responsibilities. Although the 'proximate' source of a treaty obligation is an agreement, its 'ultimate' source, which makes the agreement valid, is authorization. Similarly, although the proximate source of a reparative obligation is wrongdoing, its ultimate source, which makes the wrongdoing attributable to the state, is authorization. The division of liability for treaty obligations, reparative obligations, and debts should track authorization rather than direct instantiation of responsibility-sources. Subjects are liable for the costs of upholding a treaty not because they instantiate the agreement, whatever that might mean, but because they are authors of it (whether truly or by fiction). Likewise, subjects are liable for the costs of the state's reparative obligations not because they are among the wrongdoers, nor because they are beneficiaries of the wrongdoing—they need not be either—but simply because they are authors of the wrongdoing. Obviously, the individual wrongdoers ought to be held personally liable (and culpable), but their liability is concurrent with, not derived from, the state's reparative obligations. Authorization, not instantiation, should thus be the primary basis for dividing liability among subjects.

A perfect system of liability-division would use both source-tracking and 'author-tracking'. There is a natural division of labour between the two. For 'personal responsibilities', which follow from the actions of the state's authorized representatives (see §13), the division of liability should track authorization. Since authorization is the ultimate source of debts, reparative obligations, and treaty obligations, liability should be divided among the authors. I say more below about precisely what this division should look like. But for 'general responsibilities', which follow from the state's characteristics or capacities, the division of liability should be source-tracked. It does not make sense to 'author-track' purely capacity-based duties, such as duties to provide humanitarian aid. Subjects can be authors of a debt, but they could not be authors of a humanitarian duty (unless it were codified in a treaty). General responsibilities have to be source-tracked because direct source-instantiation is the only possible connection that subjects have to them. The costs of fulfilling a capacity-based humanitarian duty therefore ought to be divided among subjects according to capacity, such as through progressive taxation. The perfect liability-division system would source-track the state's general responsibilities and author-track its personal responsibilities.

If the state's personal responsibilities are to be divided among their authors, then there is a further question about what this division should look like. The baseline ought to be an equal division of costs to each author. Since authorization is binary in relation to each subject—each subject either is or is not an author—there is no reason to assign more liability to some authors than to others. Of course, subjects who participate in acts of state or protest against them should bear more or less *individual* responsibility for them, but their shares of liability for the state's responsibility should nevertheless be equal. An author-tracked division of liability thus seems to look a lot like Pasternak's equal division.

However, as I have argued in the previous section, not all subjects are authors of the state's responsibilities. Incapable subjects and future subjects can, at most, be considered fictive authors, and dissenting subjects cannot be considered authors at all. Even though it is justifiable to distribute liability to all subjects provided that the government meets the conditions for authorization, liability should be divided in a way that mitigates the burdens that these fictive authors and non-authors bear. The ideal rule is a 'trickle-down' division. First, the full amount of liability should be divided among the authorizing subjects such that each bears an equal burden. Then, if there is any liability left over— for instance, if the authors are no longer alive or are unable to bear the costs in full—the remaining liability should be divided among incapable subjects, then future subjects, and finally dissenting subjects in that order of priority.

To use a stylized example, suppose that State A owes 100 million dollars in reparations to State B for an aggressive war. State A has a million subjects: 900,000 authorizing subjects, 50,000 children, 30,000 subjects who were not yet born when the war was waged, and 20,000 radical pacifists who disavow the state and minimize their contact with it. In the first instance, the full 100 million dollars ought to be divided among the authorizing subjects such that each bears a relatively equal share of the cost. If a subject who has an annual income of 100,000 dollars pays 1,000 dollars, then a subject who has an annual income of 200,000 dollars should pay 2,000 dollars. The distribution is complete if the full 100 million dollars can be recovered from the authorizing subjects. But if there is a shortfall—say, of 10 million dollars—then the remaining costs ought to be divided equally among the incapable subjects. State A might have to cut funding for healthcare and education to make up the shortfall. Since fictive authorization creates a weaker presumption of legitimate distribution than does true authorization, incapable subjects ought to be included in the division of liability *only if* the full amount cannot be divided among the authorizing subjects.

Suppose that fifty years have passed, and most of the subjects from the time of the war have since died. The full amount of the remaining liability—say, 5 million dollars—ought to be paid by the authors of the war who are still alive. Only when there is a shortfall should liability be divided among the incapable subjects, and only when there is *still* a shortfall should liability be divided among the subjects who were not yet born when the state waged the war. Fictive authorization is weaker for future subjects than it is for incapable subjects, since the tendency to discount the future means that future subjects tend to have less of a presence in acts of state. The division of liability therefore ought to cross generational boundaries only if liability cannot be confined to the generations that include the authors.

Dissenting subjects, such as radical pacifists, ought to be included in the division of liability only as a last resort. The presumption of legitimate distribution is even weaker for them than it is for subjects who were not yet born at the time of the war. Whereas the unborn might have had some presence in the decision to wage the war—the government at the time might have waged it with their interests in mind—a radical pacifist who consistently and credibly disavows the state demonstrates that she is 'absent' from the state's actions. The division of liability should not include dissenting subjects unless it is impossible to exclude them.

The trickle-down model provides a standard by which to judge actual divisions of liability. But in practice, the division rarely tracks responsibility-sources or authorization; it is determined primarily by the preexisting laws and institutions of the state, and particularly by the tax system. Debts and reparations are typically paid out of general revenue. Even when they are not, as in the case of Iraq's reparations for the invasion of Kuwait, the division of liability tends to be based on practical rather than normative considerations. The reason for garnishing Iraq's oil revenue to pay the reparations was not that Iraqis in the oil industry instantiated the source of the reparative obligation, nor that they were the authors of the war. Garnishing oil revenue was simply the easiest way to extract reparations payments from Iraq. The question, then, is how large the gap between the ideal division and the actual division can get before the distribution of liability is rendered illegitimate.[4]

One important consideration is whether the division is determined 'internally' by the government of the state or 'externally' by a third party. Internal divisions of liability are presumptively legitimate as long as they are determined by an authorized government. The division of liability has to be determined by someone, and an authorized government has the strongest claim to be able to determine it, since most subjects have a genuine presence in its decisions. This presumption can be overturned only when the division of liability is severely unjust or exploitative. Consider a state, such as the pre–Civil War United States, that has an elected government but also permits slavery. Although the state is unjust, its government nevertheless meets the minimal conditions for authorization, because a substantial proportion of the subjects actually accept the government as legitimate (see §15.2). The actions of the government are therefore attributable to the state. But suppose that the state uses the proceeds of slavery or human trafficking to pay its debts. The fact that the government is authorized implies that it is legitimate for the state to distribute liability to its subjects. Yet the *division* of liability is illegitimate because it is severely exploitative. Internal divisions of liability that deviate from the ideal ought to be tolerated in all but the most extreme cases.

External divisions of liability, or divisions that are imposed by other states or by international organizations, ought to be held to a higher standard. Third parties might sometimes have legitimate claims to determine the division of liability, but these claims are much weaker than those of authorized governments. External divisions must therefore be held to a standard that is closer to the ideal. The third party must ensure not only that the division of liability is

---

4. I use 'ideal' loosely, because it is always 'non-ideal' to divide the costs of wrongdoing among innocent parties.

not exploitative, but also that the burdens that non-authorizing subjects bear are mitigated as much as possible. Consider the division of liability for Iraq's invasion of Kuwait. The UN Security Council largely dictated the division: it decided how much oil Iraq would be allowed to export, what the revenue could be used for, and how much revenue would be withheld for reparations payments. Since the subjects of Iraq did not authorize the Security Council, the division of liability has to be held to a high standard.[5] The fact that the sanctions and reparations imposed costs on the population 'randomly' (in Pasternak's sense) calls the legitimacy of the division into question. The Security Council did not do enough to mitigate the burdens on children, the disabled, or political dissidents, as is clear from the UN Security Council's (1999: 36–37) report: 'The most vulnerable groups have been the hardest hit, especially children under five years of age . . . hospitals and health centers have remained without repair and maintenance . . . School enrollment for all ages (6–23) has declined to 53%'. An external division of liability is legitimate only if the third party takes pains to mitigate the burdens that non-authorizing subjects bear.

The case is similar for divisions that are determined by unauthorized governments. As I have previously argued (§24), although an unauthorized government cannot legitimately distribute the costs of responsibilities that it incurred, it might nevertheless be legitimate for the unauthorized government to distribute the costs of responsibilities that a previous, authorized government incurred. Even if the authorized government has been deposed, subjects are still authors of its debts and reparative obligations. But if the current government is unauthorized, then it has hardly any right to determine the division. The Iraqi government had an even less credible claim to determine the division of liability for the reparations than did the Security Council. An unauthorized division has to approximate the ideal division in order to be legitimate.

————

In sum, the applicable rule for dividing liability depends on whether the responsibility in question is general or personal. While general responsibilities (such as humanitarian duties) ought to be source-tracked, personal responsibilities (such as debts and reparations) ought to be author-tracked. In practice,

5. Subjects indirectly authorize international organizations when their authorized governments apply for membership. But this form of indirect authorization is very weak because it is a one-off. The fact that a long-gone Hashemite monarch of Iraq signed the United Nations Charter in 1943 does not mean that Iraqis in the 1990s were authors of the Security Council's actions.

the standard for a legitimate division depends on who determines the division. Internal divisions are legitimate as long as they are not severely exploitative. Authorized governments should have a more or less free hand to divide liability, since most subjects have a genuine presence in their actions. External divisions are legitimate only if the third party that determines the division takes steps to mitigate the burdens that non-authorizing subjects bear. Although third parties, and especially international organizations, might have some right to determine the division of liability, they have much less standing than authorized governments, and their divisions should therefore be held to a higher standard. Unauthorized divisions should be held to the highest standard. Since unauthorized governments have hardly any right to determine the division, their divisions of liability are legitimate only if they approximate the ideal division.

§26 Non-Fulfilment

What has been established so far is that the distribution (and division) of liability is presumptively legitimate provided that the government of the state meets the conditions for authorization. Yet there are some circumstances in which the presumption of legitimate distribution can be overturned. This section develops an account of 'non-fulfilment', which determines when states can justifiably refuse to fulfil their responsibilities.

Two fundamental principles come into conflict in cases of non-fulfilment. On one side is the principle of sovereignty. If we take seriously the idea that Parliament (or some other person or assembly) is the supreme authority, which can amend or abrogate any law, then it seems that Parliament can also nullify or repudiate any obligation that is created by law. It is difficult to see how a sovereign could bind itself with a treaty if it cannot bind itself with legislation. On the other side is the principle of rational consistency. Persons— individual and corporate—have to stand by their words and actions in order to avoid self-contradiction. As Hobbes says,

> [T]here is in every breach of covenant a contradiction properly so called; for he that covenanteth, willeth to do, or omit, in the time to come; and he that doth any action, willeth it in that present, which is part of the future time, contained in the covenant: and therefore he that violateth a covenant, willeth the doing and the not doing of the same thing, at the same time; which is a plain contradiction (*EL* XVI.2).

A state that signs a treaty and then repudiates it contradicts itself and therefore fails to perform as a competent person (Pettit, 2012: 133). The principle of *pacta sunt servanda* is thus derived from the more basic principle of rational consistency. Whereas sovereignty implies the right to nullify or repudiate responsibilities, the requirement of consistency over time implies that states should own the consequences of their words and actions.

Both principles have intolerable implications if they are taken to be absolute. If we take sovereignty to be absolute, as Hobbes does, then 'state responsibility' is an empty phrase (see §12). States can never truly be bound by their words or actions because they can release themselves from their obligations whenever it is expedient. But if we take rational consistency to be absolute, then state responsibility becomes 'the tyranny of past governments'. An absolutist interpretation of *pacta sunt servanda* would give governments (which inevitably have limited time-horizons) the right to bind future governments indefinitely, and contrary to the interests of future subjects. Intuitively, there is something unjust about an agreement (such as a perpetual lease or bond) that confers benefits on the subjects of the present at the expense of subjects far into the future. This is the concern that animated Jefferson's and Mill's objections to intergenerational debts and treaties. An account of non-fulfilment has to try to reconcile the tension between sovereignty and rational consistency.

Runciman (2007) argues that sovereignty ought to take priority. Although 'no national government can repudiate all the commitments of its predecessors and expect to be taken seriously . . . it is the objections or otherwise of the active public, and not the expectation of consistency over time on the part of an inactive "people", that is the final arbiter of political representation' (ibid. 106). The active public is the body of subjects *qua* authors of the government, while the inactive 'people' is the state, as it is for Hobbes (see §14). Runciman argues that the responsibilities of the state cannot stand in the face of overwhelming objections from subjects.

> Public opinion may turn decisively against a government seeking to uphold earlier commitments undertaken in the name of the people—for example, many democratic governments have been forced to repudiate their public debts because of the objections of large sections of their populations to the privations honouring those debts would entail. In these circumstances, the non-objection criterion trumps the claims of rational consistency (ibid.).

However, only certain kinds of objections on the part of subjects count. Objections that individual subjects make in their own names—'I disavow this debt'—have no force. Only objections made in the name of the state—'we declare that Greece disavows this debt'—can have any force. When a substantial number of subjects do object in the name of the state, Runciman argues, rational consistency must give way to sovereignty, and the obligation to pay the debt must give way to the will to repudiate it.

Runciman's example suggests that non-fulfilment must take the form of an internal objection: the subjects must authorize a new government with a mandate to repudiate the debt. But non-fulfilment could conceivably take the form of an external or retrospective objection. A third party, such as an international organization, could object to the debt. External objections carry less weight than internal objections, since third parties do not normally have the authority to represent the state, but these objections become important when subjects do not have the opportunity to object. An objection from the United Nations could even be decisive if the legitimacy of the government that incurred the debt were questionable. Alternatively, if the debt is intergenerational, the objection could be retrospective. The current subjects of the state could authorize a government with a mandate to repudiate debts that its predecessors incurred. In any case, as Runciman argues, a credible objection must be made in the name of the state rather than in the names of individual subjects.

The question that Runciman leaves unanswered is what constitutes a legitimate *reason* to repudiate responsibilities. His account of repudiation is purely formal. It tells us what form non-fulfilment must take—namely, a competing representation of the state—but it says nothing about what the content of a legitimate claim must be. Consistency must sometimes bend to sovereignty, but this cannot mean that it is legitimate for the state to repudiate responsibilities arbitrarily, or whenever it is expedient. Non-fulfilment requires reasons, albeit reasons that correspond to the structure of representative politics. I argue that there are four legitimate reasons for non-fulfilment: impossibility, misattribution, non-identity, and misdistribution. While the first is a factual reason, the other three are normative reasons that correspond to the three Fundamental Questions.

The first legitimate reason for non-fulfilment is that the responsibility is impossible to fulfil. A responsibility that is unfulfillable must be suspended, or temporarily set aside, as long as there is a possibility that a change in circumstances will make it possible for the state to fulfil it in the future. The responsibility becomes null if it becomes overwhelmingly probable that the responsibility will remain unfulfillable. As Article 61(1) of the *Vienna Convention on the Law of Treaties* says,

> A party may invoke the impossibility of performing a treaty as a ground for terminating or withdrawing from it if the impossibility results from the permanent disappearance or destruction of an object indispensable for the execution of the treaty. If the impossibility is temporary, it may be invoked only as a ground for suspending the operation of the treaty (UN, 1969).

If a state (say, Ethiopia) signed a treaty that obligates it to patrol its coastline for pirates, but it no longer has a coastline, then the state can suspend the treaty on grounds of impossibility. Whether the state can justifiably withdraw from the treaty will depend on whether there is a possibility that it will get its coastline back. There is no real conflict between sovereignty and rational consistency in cases of impossibility. The principle of *pacta sunt servanda* presupposes the possibility of fulfilment; agreements must be kept only if they can be kept. The principle here can be generalized: responsibilities must be fulfilled only if they can be fulfilled.

The second legitimate reason for non-fulfilment is that the responsibility is misattributed—that the actions that generated the responsibility were not valid acts of state (see §17). Either the actions were misrepresentations of the state (as in corruption), or the agents who performed the actions were not authorized representatives of the state (such as members of an unauthorized government). For instance, Mobutu's debts might be misattributed to Zaire either because he used the money for personal enrichment or because he was not an authorized representative of Zaire. Generalizing from the idea of 'odious debt', misattributed responsibilities can be called 'odious responsibilities'. The conflict between sovereignty and rational consistency is only apparent in cases of misattribution. States do not contradict themselves when they refuse to stand by words or actions that were not theirs to begin with.

The third legitimate reason for non-fulfilment is non-identity—that the allegedly responsible state is not the same state as the one to which the responsibility was attributed. Responsibilities that are based on mistaken identity might be called 'existentially odious'. Yet non-identity does not justify non-fulfilment unless it is accompanied by non-accession. It has to be shown *both* that the state in question is not identical to the responsible state *and* that the state in question did not accede to the other state's responsibilities by agreement, implication, or inheritance (see §22). For example, if the Russian Federation were (counterfactually) discontinuous with the Soviet Union, this would not necessarily mean that the Russian Federation can justifiably repudiate all of the Soviet Union's debt. Total repudiation would be justified only if the Russian Federation did not explicitly or tacitly agree to assume the Soviet Union's debts and did not claim any of its property. In cases of non-identity, as in cases of misattribution, the conflict between sovereignty and rational consistency is only apparent. Responsibility presupposes identity; a state is not bound to fulfil some other state's responsibilities.

The fourth legitimate reason for non-fulfilment is misdistribution—that it is unjustifiable to distribute the costs of fulfilling the responsibility to the state's subjects. This is the kind of reason that Runciman's (2007: 106) example suggests: the debt is attributable to the state, and the state in question is the same state as the one that borrowed the money, but the subjects of the state overwhelmingly object to the debt. It is in cases such as this that sovereignty and rational consistency truly collide. Either the objections prevail over the debt, or the debt prevails over the objections.

The requirement of rational consistency is more or less absolute for voluntary associations, such as corporations and universities, but less stringent for states. When people choose to become members of a university, they accept a 'membership bargain' (Stilz, 2011: 196). They benefit from being members, so they should also bear the burdens of membership. These burdens include the costs of discharging the university's contractual and reparative obligations. If the burdens of the university's obligations become onerous, the members of the university have no right to complain, both because they chose to join and because they can leave fairly easily. But this line of argument does not apply to the subjects of a state, many of whom did not choose to join and cannot easily leave. Debts, reparations, treaty obligations, and sanctions impose burdens on subjects that they can opt out of only with great difficulty, if at all. Since states are involuntary associations (see §1), subjects' objections to the distribution of liability carry significant normative weight. The objection mechanisms of representative politics are often the only modes of recourse that subjects have against 'misdistribution'.[6]

Subjects' objections to the distribution of liability ought to prevail only if two conditions are met. First, the distribution must be burdensome. Objections to fulfilling an otherwise valid responsibility are normatively significant only if the costs to subjects of fulfilling that responsibility are materially significant. The state's imperative to fulfil its responsibilities outweighs subjects' objections when the costs to those subjects would be negligible. A burdensome debt might be misdistributed, but a diffuse debt cannot be.

Second, the subjects who object must lack a genuine presence in the actions that generated the responsibility. The claim of 'absence' is easiest to make for intergenerational responsibilities. If the state incurred a debt a hundred years ago, then the current subjects might claim that the government that borrowed the money discounted their interests in favour of the interests of the subjects of the time. The plausibility of this claim will depend on what the money was used for and whether the state had effective internal and external objection mechanisms at the time of attribution. But the retrospective objection

6. I make a more detailed version of this argument elsewhere (Fleming, 2020). There I focus specifically on treaties, and, for the sake of argument, I take the agential theory as my starting point. I argue that, *even if* states are understood as rational agents, overwhelming popular objections to a treaty should take priority over the requirement of rational consistency.

mechanism is ultimately the decisive one; it is up to current subjects to judge whether past governments have adequately represented their interests.

The claim of absence is more difficult to make when the responsibility in question is intragenerational. Although there is a strong presumption that most subjects have a presence in the actions of an authorized government, claims of absence are still possible. Subjects might object to the debt on the grounds that it served the government's interests but not theirs. In any case, for non-fulfilment to be justified on grounds of misdistribution, the responsibility in question must be burdensome, and the subjects who object to it must make a credible claim of 'absence'.

There is one final legitimate reason for non-fulfilment: forgiveness. A creditor or an injured party can release a state from its debts or reparative obligations, even if the responsible state does not have a cop-out. This might be done in order to bring about peace, reconciliation, or economic development. Forgiveness is unlike the previous four reasons in that it is a matter of charity rather than a matter of right. States have a right to repudiate responsibilities in cases of impossibility, misattribution, non-identity, and misdistribution, but forgiveness depends entirely on the good will of the party to which the responsibility is owed.

————

Distribution is essentially the flipside of attribution. Just as authorization determines whose actions are attributable to the state, it determines to whom the costs of fulfilling the consequent responsibilities ought to be distributed. The Hobbesian account of distribution thus uses the same vocabulary as the authorization account of distribution (Parrish, 2009; Stilz, 2011). The crucial difference is that the Hobbesian account takes seriously the fact that there are many subjects who cannot plausibly, or even possibly, count as authors of the state's responsibilities. The idea of authorization by fiction fills the gap. The logic of fictive authorization is similar to the logic of guardianship: people who cannot authorize their own representatives can have representatives authorized for them by third parties. Although incapable subjects and future subjects cannot truly be authors of the state's responsibilities, they can be fictive authors, provided that there are mechanisms that give their interests a presence in the state's actions.

This chapter has focused squarely on distributing liability from the state to its subjects. It is worth mentioning that there are other ways of apportioning the costs of reparations and debts. May (2012: 194) proposes 'a worldwide no-fault insurance scheme' in which 'every State of the world would have to pay into a fund that would be used to pay *all* restitution and reparations at the end of war or mass atrocity' (emphasis in original). There is already something like a global insurance scheme for sovereign debt, though it leaves a lot to be desired. Creditors can buy insurance to protect themselves against the risk of default, and the International Monetary Fund serves as a 'lender of last resort'. As it stands, there is no global insurance scheme for reparations, and the creation of one seems a long way off. State responsibility will remain the primary mechanism of cost-allocation in international affairs for the foreseeable future. I turn next to the question of what that future is likely to hold.

Conclusion

The Future of State Responsibility

WHAT MAKES the Hobbesian theory of state responsibility a 'political' theory is that it is built from the basic concepts of representative politics. Unlike the agential theory, which requires the metaphysics of corporate agency, the Hobbesian theory requires only the concepts of authority and representation. There are no corporate wills or intentions; there are only authors, representatives, and the fiction of state personality. But unlike the functional theory, which elides issues of legitimacy, the Hobbesian theory puts them at the forefront. To act in the name of the state is not just to perform a governmental function; it is to provide a plausible representation of the state, and to do so with authority. The central claim of the Hobbesian theory is that states are responsible for the actions of their *authorized representatives*. The best vocabulary with which to talk about state responsibility is that of authorization and representation, not that of agency and intentionality, nor that of organs and functions. This conclusion summarizes the advantages of the Hobbesian theory and then looks to the future of state responsibility.

One advantage of the Hobbesian theory is that it accords well with the ways that we commonly think about state responsibility. If there were a dispute about whether a state owes money, we would not ask, 'did the official who borrowed the money act according to the state's will?' Although we might ask, 'did the official who borrowed the money perform a governmental function?', only a lawyer would stop there. We would also ask whether the official was authorized—politically, not just legally—whether he acted within his authority, and whether borrowing the money was a plausible representation of the state. The idea of 'odious debt' has such broad resonance outside the legal domain precisely because we tend think in these terms. The Mobutu government's debt is intuitively different from the American government's debt because Mobutu's claims of authorization and representation were far less credible. The Hobbesian theory of state responsibility refines and organizes our intuitive ways of making normative judgments about acts of state.

The more fundamental advantage of the Hobbesian theory is that it corresponds to the conceptual structure that is implicit in the practice of state responsibility. The agential and functional theories rely on analogies that fail to adequately capture this structure. The analogy between states and human beings, which underpins the agential theory, is sometimes a helpful heuristic. Thinking of treaties as interpersonal contracts and of reparations as torts may indeed be useful at times (see §7). Yet the analogy becomes misleading if we put too much stock in it. Unlike individuals, states act only vicariously; they merge and divide; and the process of distributing the state's responsibilities to its subjects has no individual-level analogue (see §5). The analogy of a principal–agent relation, which underpins the functional theory, is to some extent a helpful corrective, but it comes with blind spots of its own. Unlike principals, states cannot authorize their own representatives. Their representatives are authorized by their subjects, who are ultimately liable for what those representatives do. The principal–agent analogy illuminates the relation between the state and its representatives but obscures the equally important relation between its representatives and its subjects (see §6). State responsibility has a conceptual structure that neither analogy fully captures: subjects authorize representatives; these representatives act in the name of the state; responsibility for their actions attaches to the state; the state persists over time as long as it continues to be represented; and the costs of fulfilling the state's responsibilities are distributed to its subjects.

An important implication of the Hobbesian theory is that state responsibility should be reparative rather than punitive. Since states do not have wills or intentions, they cannot truly be culpable or guilty (see §16). 'Blaming' a state is metaphorical if it is meaningful at all. The purpose of holding states responsible for wrongdoing is to repair harms and to prevent future wrongdoing. Reparations should be understood as compensation, not as punitive damages. Sanctions should be understood as means of changing behaviour, not of punishing 'criminal' states. If an outlet for retribution is necessary in the international order, then it should be found in criminal trials of individuals (for the time being).

The functional theory also implies that retributive understandings of state responsibility should be abandoned, and for precisely the same reason. But whereas the functional theory provides only an instrumental justification for holding states responsible, the Hobbesian theory provides a genuinely normative justification. Proponents of the functional theory typically see state responsibility as a crude, albeit useful, mechanism for allocating costs. As Cassese (2005: 241) says, 'the international community is so primitive that the archaic concept of collective responsibility still prevails'. The implication is that, in a more developed international community, state responsibility should be replaced with 'a feasible alternative to the current system . . . that does more good, overall' (Murphy, 2010: 311), such as a global insurance scheme. There are good reasons to develop alternative mechanisms for allocating the costs of reparations and sovereign defaults, because there are some cases in which the costs cannot or should not be allocated to the subjects of the wrong-doer or debtor state. It may be that the costs are too large for them to bear, or that subjects have a good reason to refuse to bear them (see §26). But even if there were alternative cost-allocation mechanisms, there would still be com-pelling normative reasons to hold states responsible. Wars and debts are not acts of God, like floods and earthquakes, which do not implicate anyone. Nor are they 'acts of humanity', like climate change or pollution, which implicate just about everyone. Wars and debts implicate particular states and particular subjects. When the authorized representatives of the United Kingdom borrow money, that act has a normative connection to the United Kingdom *qua* owner and to the subjects of the United Kingdom *qua* authors. The authors of a war or a debt ought to bear the costs in the first instance, even if the costs could be pooled or shifted. The Hobbesian theory thus provides a non-retributive con-ception of state responsibility that is genuinely normative. The agential theory is a moral theory, the functional theory is an instrumental theory, and the Hobbesian theory is a political theory.

Along the way, I have had to address many issues that reach far beyond state responsibility: the nature of authorization, representation, and legitimacy; the ontology and identity of the state; the meanings of responsibility, liability, accountability, and culpability; and what it means to be a subject of a state. Many of these apparently disparate issues turn out to be too interrelated to address in isolation. For instance, the identity of the state cannot be under-stood apart from representation, because representation gives the state unity and continuity. Representation cannot be understood apart from authoriza-tion, which determines whether representatives are legitimate, and legitimacy cannot be understood apart from the subjects to whom claims of representa-tion must be legitimated. As Gould (2009: 702) suggests, the most fundamen-tal questions in political theory are best addressed 'not in the abstract, but guided by cognate questions'. State responsibility is important not only in its own right, but also as a 'cognate question' through which to address more fundamental issues of authorization, representation, responsibility, and statehood.

Understanding state responsibility might even give us a better understand-ing of individual responsibility. Throughout the book, I have criticized the analogy between states and human beings. More specifically, I have criticized the practice of drawing inferences about state responsibility from individual responsibility. But it could be fruitful to turn the analogy on its head and to draw inferences in the opposite direction. As Jackson (2004) argues, it makes just as much sense to say that 'people are states too' as it does to say that 'states are people too'.

The Hobbesian answers to the Three Fundamental Questions apply surprisingly well to individuals. How do individuals act?—through their authorized representatives. The difference between states and individuals is only that individuals can represent themselves. How can an individual persist over time despite changes in her body?—by representing herself as the same person. Every word you utter and every action you take is a representation of yourself. The 'succession' of these representations sustains the continuity of your person, much as the succession of the state's representatives sustains the continuity of its person. The succession of 'selves' is akin to the succession of governments. Who should be liable for individuals' actions?—the authors of these actions. The difference between states and individuals is that individuals can be authors of their own actions, whereas acts of state are always authored by individual subjects. The Hobbesian theory thus applies to natural persons as well as corporate persons. Inverting the state–human analogy could help us to see individual responsibility in a new light. 'Statomorphizing' individuals is far more likely to generate novel insights than anthropomorphizing states, if only because of the rarity of statomorphism. At this point, it goes without saying that analogies between states and human beings should be used with caution. But the inverted analogy—people are states too—is less likely to mislead because it is obvious that it is only a crude analogy.

I conclude with some speculative remarks about three ongoing developments that are likely to alter the practice of state responsibility as we know it: the development of international criminal law; the proliferation of treaties; and the development of new technologies, such as autonomous vehicles and weapons.

§27 International Criminal Law

Since the end of the Second World War, there has been a trend toward holding individuals responsible for acts of state. International criminal law has many earlier antecedents (Crootof, 2016: 1358–60; Van Schaack and Slye, 2007), but it became well established with the Nuremberg and Tokyo Trials. The International Criminal Tribunals for Rwanda and the Former Yugoslavia reinforced the norm that state officials are individually responsible for their actions, and this norm has become firmly entrenched with the creation of the International Criminal Court. Although there has been some notable opposition to the Court itself, especially from the United States and the African Union (BBC, 2017a; Ralph, 2007), the *idea* of international criminal responsibility is still widely accepted. One might have expected the rise of international criminal law to bring about the decline of state responsibility, since holding individuals responsible for acts of state seems to render state responsibility redundant. Yet nothing of the sort has happened.

There are two reasons that international criminal law has not displaced state responsibility. The first is that the two forms of responsibility are 'non-exclusive': the responsibility of an individual neither entails or precludes the responsibility of her state (Bonafè, 2009: 5; Nollkaemper, 2003). State responsibility and individual responsibility can even coincide. For instance, a state and its officials can be held concurrently responsible for the very same act of genocide. There is a 'division of labour' between the two forms of responsibility: 'the principal distinction between individual and state responsibility . . . is the difference between criminal liability and "civil" liability' (Reid, 2005: 798). Whereas state responsibility is concerned with repairing harm and providing compensation, international criminal law is concerned with punishing wrong-doers. The two forms of responsibility can coexist without redundancy because they serve different purposes.

The deeper reason that the rise of individual responsibility has not led to the decline of state responsibility is that neither form of responsibility is *capable* of serving the purpose of the other. There is no other rational way to draw up the division of labour. On one side, as I have argued, it is a mistake to try to 'criminalize' state responsibility because states cannot truly be culpable. On the other side, trying to extract compensation from individuals would often be futile. State officials rarely have enough resources to pay reparations for large-scale wrongs, so compensation has to be sought from the states that they represent. Further, even if individual responsibility could replace state responsibility *for wrongdoing*, it could not replace state responsibility in general. States would continue to be the primary bearers of debts and treaty obligations even if they no longer bore reparative obligations. There is thus no reason to expect the development of international criminal law to spell the decline of state responsibility, or even a reduction in its domain. On the contrary, as I argue in §29, technological developments may soon expand the domain of state responsibility and send international criminal law into decline.

§28 The Proliferation of Treaties

Another important development since the end of the Second World War is the enormous expansion in both the number and the scope of international treaties. There are over 560 multilateral treaties registered with the United Nations, which cover everything from navigation to trade to drug control (UNTC, 2018). In addition, there are thousands of bilateral treaties. The proliferation of bilateral investment treaties (BITs) is especially striking. From 1989 to 2017, the number of BITs in force has ballooned from 385 to nearly 3,000 (UNCTAD, 2000: 1; UNCTAD, 2017: 111). These treaties are designed to protect the interests of foreign investors, typically by preventing expropriation of their assets and by allowing them to use international arbitration instead of the host state's courts to resolve disputes. As treaties proliferate, states are saddled with more and more obligations.

The proliferation of treaties increases the tension between sovereignty and rational consistency, as domestic policy goals frequently come into conflict with treaty obligations. A sovereigntist backlash has already begun, especially among developing states: 'Between 1 January 2016 and 1 April 2017, terminations became effective for at least 19 IIAs [international investment agreements], with more scheduled to take effect later the year . . . 16 were unilaterally denounced' (UNCTAD, 2017: 112). South Africa has replaced most of its BITs with investor protection legislation (Schlemmer, 2016), and Ecuador has terminated all of its BITs (Olivet, 2017). Some developed states are also taking the sovereigntist path, though for different reasons. The United States has ordered 'performance reviews of, inter alia, all bilateral, plurilateral and multilateral investment agreements to which the United States is a party' (UNCTAD, 2017: 112). Investment treaties usually have renegotiation and withdrawal provisions (Gordon and Pohl, 2015), which tends to mitigate the tension between sovereignty and rational consistency, but a significant minority of treaties do not (Koremenos, 2005). It remains to be seen whether the post-war project of a treaty-bound world will be able to withstand the sovereigntist backlash.

The recent flurry of treaty terminations underscores the importance of an account of non-fulfilment, or repudiation.[1] The risk of legitimating the practice of treaty repudiation is that it would undermine the binding force of treaties. Yet a stubborn insistence that agreements must always be kept would also undermine the project of a treaty-bound world. There is an important difference between repudiating a treaty because it is expedient to do so and repudiating it on grounds of misattribution, non-identity, or misdistribution (see §26). If we refuse to make a distinction between legitimate and illegitimate repudiation, then every repudiation becomes a direct affront to the principle that agreements must be kept. But if we do make this distinction, and we carefully specify the conditions under which agreements must be kept, then we have some hope of mitigating the damage that the sovereigntist backlash causes. The best way to preserve *pacta sunt servanda* is to admit that there are some limited exceptions to it.

---

1. See Fleming (2020) for an account of treaty repudiation.

§29 Cyborg States and Robotic Representatives

I have so far assumed that the subjects and representatives of states are all either human beings or corporate entities (the members of which are ultimately human beings). As Hobbes says, the 'matter' and the 'artificer' of the artificial man are both man: the state is both composed of and created by human beings (*L* Intro. 18). New technologies will force us to revise this assumption. The most important challenge for state responsibility will come from the 'internal mechanization' of the state.[2] As states rely more and more on algorithms to make decisions and on machines to implement them, our understanding of state responsibility will have to adapt.

Most existing theories of responsibility, and all theories of state responsibility, implicitly rely on the 'tool model' of technology, which treats technological artefacts as extensions of human agency. Hammers, rifles, vehicles, and drones merely augment the capacities of the human agents who use them. A soldier who kills a civilian with a projectile is therefore no less responsible than if he had killed that civilian with his bare hands. But the development of systems with sophisticated capacities for learning and decision-making has called the tool model into question (Sullins 2011: 152–53). In its 2017 Resolution on artificial intelligence and robots, the European Parliament suggests that the tool model will no longer suffice in a world with 'autonomous robots', such as self-driving vehicles: 'the more autonomous robots are, the less they can be considered to be simple tools in the hands of other actors (such as the manufacturer, the operator, the owner, the user, etc.)' (European Parliament, 2017: 6–7). As the learning and decision-making capacities of robots become increasingly sophisticated, they become 'more and more similar to agents that interact with their environment' (ibid. 6). At some point, it will no longer be the case that the behaviour of the robot 'can be traced back to a specific human agent' (ibid. 7).

In legal systems and ethical frameworks based on the tool model of technology, autonomous robots will create 'responsibility gaps' (Matthias, 2004). As the European Parliament's Resolution explains,

> The existing rules on liability [only] cover cases where the cause of the robot's act or omission can be traced back to a specific human agent such as the manufacturer, the operator, the owner or the user and where that agent could have foreseen and avoided the robot's harmful behaviour (2017: 7).

2. I take this phrase from Matwyshyn (2010), who analyses the implications of the internal mechanization of corporations.

Under 'the traditional rules', people are held liable only for the *foreseeable* consequences of their actions. Liability typically requires recklessness, negligence, or some other foresight-related failure. But harms caused by autonomous robots might not be foreseeable from the perspective of any individual. Some algorithms are 'opaque': it is not possible to retrace their steps and explain how they made their decisions (Castelvecchi, 2016). If retrospective explanation is not possible, then foreseeability is hopeless, and liability is out of the question.

Suppose that a soldier deploys an autonomous vehicle to deliver a load of supplies. All he does is set the destination; the vehicle then uses a combination of data, software, and sensors to navigate its way there. Who should be held responsible if the vehicle swerves onto a sidewalk and runs over a pedestrian? The soldier has a good excuse, since all he did was program the destination. He could not have foreseen the accident, let alone averted it. It is tempting to say that the manufacturer (or programmer) of the vehicle is responsible. But unless the manufacturer was negligent, or there was a defect in the vehicle, the manufacturer also has a good excuse. Autonomous vehicles learn from data that they (or a larger network of vehicles) collect along the way, so the accident might have been an unfortunate consequence of a combination of data, software, and hardware that the manufacturer could not have foreseen. This is just a simplified illustration of a responsibility gap that autonomous robots might create. Autonomous weapons pose more complicated problems (Beard, 2014; Crootof, 2016), as do cases in which robots operate in networks instead of in isolation.

Autonomous robots create a particular kind of responsibility gap for state responsibility, which might be called an 'attribution gap'. As it stands, an act of state requires an act of an individual; the state cannot act unless the actions of one or more individuals are attributed to it (see §6). If the behaviour of a robot cannot be traced back to specific individuals, then it seems that it cannot be attributed to the state either.

The responsibility gaps that autonomous robots create are analogous to the responsibility gaps that collective action creates. Just as autonomous robots can behave in ways that their users and manufacturers cannot foresee, many individuals acting together can produce outcomes that none of them can foresee.

On November 28, 1979, a flight operated by Air New Zealand crashed directly into the side of Mount Erebus, a 12,000 foot volcano, killing all 257 people aboard. An inquiry determined that the primary cause of the crash was an inadequate company organization that led to the filing of a faulty computer flight plan. In this case, various employees' actions combined to create a disaster that no one employee could have reasonably foreseen (Stilz, 2011: 193).

The result is a responsibility gap—or, as Stilz calls it, a 'responsibility shortfall'. Since the 'total harm' is 'more than the employees' intentional contributions', the families of the victims would be left without adequate compensation if they could seek compensation only from individual employees (ibid.). Similarly, people who are injured by autonomous robots might be left without adequate compensation if they could seek compensation only from the users or manufacturers. In the robot case, as in the corporate case, many (or even all) of the individuals involved have good reasons to deny responsibility for the outcome. An autonomous robot can be understood as collective action congealed in an object: many individuals have created a system whose behaviour cannot be traced back to any of them.

The usual way of filling a responsibility gap created by collective action is to hold the whole group responsible. Air New Zealand could be held responsible for the Mount Erebus disaster even though none of its employees could have foreseen the disaster. Since the sum of the employees' actions produced the disaster, and since the employees' actions are all attributable to the corporation, the corporation is responsible for the disaster. The European Parliament's Resolution suggests that the responsibility gaps created by autonomous robots can be filled in a similar way, by 'incorporating' robots. Just as corporations are treated as persons that can be held responsible, autonomous robots could be granted 'the status of electronic persons responsible for making good any damage they may cause' (European Parliament, 2017: 18).[3] People who are injured by autonomous robots could then seek compensation from the robots themselves. It would no longer be necessary to prove that the user or manufacturer of the robot was negligent or reckless; injured parties would only have to prove that the robot caused the injury. Since robots, unlike corporations, do not have bank accounts, their users and manufacturers (including states) would have to pay into an insurance fund to cover the damage that their robots cause (ibid. 17–18). Nominal responsibility, or what I have called 'ownership' (§16), would attach to the robots, while compensation would be provided by an insurance system. Treating robots as corporate-like persons rather than as tools could thus eliminate the responsibility gaps that autonomous robots create.

There is a much simpler way of filling these responsibility gaps, which is parasitic on corporate responsibility rather than analogous to it. The European

3. See Solum (1992) for an early exploration of electronic personhood and Bayern (2016) on how existing corporate law could be used to give legal personhood to autonomous systems.

Parliament's Resolution maps the agential theory onto robots: it treats them as agents that can bear responsibility in their own right. Analogizing between robots and corporations, which are themselves understood by analogy with human beings, comes with all of the drawbacks of the agential theory and more.[4] Instead, robots could be treated as agents in a different sense—as representatives. An autonomous robot could, in Hobbesian terms, be understood as a peculiar kind of representative artificial person (see §10). It can represent other persons, but it cannot represent itself. It can perform actions, but it cannot take responsibility for them. This 'representative' model of autonomous robots is somewhere between the tool model and the electronic personhood model. It recognizes that autonomous robots differ from simple tools, but it stops short of treating them as responsibility-bearing entities in their own right. The representative model would suffice to close the attribution gap, because it would eliminate the need to trace the actions of robots back to specific human beings. The actions of autonomous robots could be attributed to the state directly, rather than indirectly via human 'users'. The question in each case would be whether the *robot* was authorized to act in the name of the state.

If the actions of autonomous robots were attributable directly to the state, then state responsibility itself could become a way to fill responsibility gaps. The state could be held responsible for harms caused by its autonomous vehicles or weapons when the people who manufactured or deployed those systems have good excuses, or when it is simply too complicated to trace the actions of the systems back to particular individuals. Similarly, corporations could be held responsible for their autonomous robots. The development of new technologies will probably lead to an expansion in the domain of state responsibility, and of corporate responsibility more generally, because individual forms of responsibility will become impossible or impractical.

In the long run, the mechanization of the state will significantly narrow the domain of international criminal law. Criminal responsibility is bound up with culpability, and culpability (unlike ownership, accountability, or liability) requires intent (see §16). As states rely more and more on machines, and as machines become increasingly autonomous, it will become increasingly difficult to connect criminal actions to individuals' intentions. As Crootof (2016: 1375) argues, 'autonomous weapon systems will inevitably commit a serious violation of international humanitarian law without any human being acting intentionally or recklessly. Absent such willful human action, no one can—or should—be

---

4. Critics have argued that an 'electronic person' could be a 'legal black hole, an entity that absorbs a human actor's legal responsibilities and from which no glint of accountability is seen' (Bryson, Diamantis, and Grant, 2017: 289).

held criminally liable [i.e., culpable]'. For example, suppose that a fleet of fully autonomous drones has attacked a convoy of refugees after misidentifying it as a convoy of enemy forces. The military personnel who deployed the drones and the company that manufactured the drones had taken all reasonable precautions to ensure that the drones adhered to the Geneva Convention. They had extensively tested the drones and found them to be better at distinguishing combatants from civilians and less likely than human-operated drones or aircraft to cause collateral damage. Alas, the fleet of drones attacked the convoy of refugees, contrary to the intentions of everyone involved. Further, there were thousands of people involved in the deployment, and not one of them had the 'global' intention to deploy the drones. The decision to deploy was made by an algorithm. Although the act of attacking the refugees looks to be criminal, no one had the corresponding *mens rea*. Atrocities committed by autonomous robots will often be so far removed from the intentions of individuals that it will be impossible—in practice, if not in principle—to assign culpability to anyone.

If the drones are understood as robotic representatives, then it is still possible to assign individual *liability* for their actions. The 'deployers' of autonomous robots could be held liable for the actions of the robots, much as employers are held liable for the actions of their (even more autonomous) employees. Although the deployers did not control the drones, and although they could not have foreseen that the drones would attack the convoy of refugees, the deployers could be held vicariously liable as authors of the drones' actions. To deploy the drones is to authorize them, and hence to make oneself liable for the damage that they cause. However, *culpability* cannot be vicarious, because intentions cannot be transferred from one person to another (see §16). The deployers, like the employers, can be vicariously liable but not vicariously culpable. Since none of the deployers intended for the drones to attack the convoy—on the contrary, they all intended to prevent a catastrophe such as this—none of them could be culpable for the attack.

The decline of criminal responsibility will undoubtedly cause problems. Although it will often be impossible to identify culpable individuals, human beings will still *want* to assign culpability. Retributive impulses will have to be redirected somewhere or sublimated somehow. Holding autonomous robots criminally responsible would be mistaken for some of the same reasons that holding corporate entities criminally responsible is mistaken. For the foreseeable future, even the most 'intelligent' machines will not be able to feel guilt or suffer the pain of punishment (see §16). But in order to provide an outlet for the reactive attitudes of the public, it will be necessary to publicly acknowledge the role that robots play in wrongdoing. One possibility is to resurrect and reconfigure the old idea of 'deodand'—the 'practice of forfeiting the offending animal or object to the Crown and then using the proceeds for charitable purposes'

(Alschuler, 2009: 4, note 2). For instance, a self-driving car that killed a pedestrian would have to be forfeited and sold. Deodand need not imply that the 'offending' object is culpable, and for that reason would avoid the absurdities of holding robots criminally responsible. But it would provide an outlet for our reactive attitudes when machines cause harm but no one is to blame. Identifying the machine that caused the harm and requiring the owner to forfeit it would create the appearance that someone has 'paid the price'. If a fleet of autonomous drones attacks a convoy of refugees, then the drones should be forfeited to an international organization, which can then sell them or scrap them. Deodand would not provide the same kind of closure or satisfaction as punishing war criminals, but it might be the best way of appeasing demands for retribution when there are no culpable individuals.

Even individual *liability* will come under pressure from the forces of mechanization. Most autonomous systems will be made and deployed by corporate entities, not by individuals. Car companies will manufacture autonomous vehicles, and, for the most part, transportation companies will deploy them. States will manufacture and deploy autonomous weapons. The most powerful algorithms will be possessed by large states and corporations. Responsibility for the use of these systems will have to be assigned to corporate entities: first, because it will be difficult or impossible to attribute the operations of these systems to individual human beings; second, because only corporate entities will have pockets deep enough to provide compensation when these systems cause large-scale harm. A theory of state responsibility is more necessary than ever, because individual responsibility will soon be in decline.

––––––––

The greatest virtue of the Hobbesian theory of state responsibility is that it is flexible, like the theory of the state that underpins it. The concepts of authorization and representation apply to monarchies as well as democracies, corporations as well as states, and robots as well as human beings. The vocabulary of political representation has been in use for centuries, and it has so far been able to adapt to great technological and societal changes. This is not to say that the Hobbesian theory is timeless. Representative politics will eventually become obsolete, just as feudal politics became obsolete. But while our politics are representative, as they will be for the foreseeable future, thinking about state responsibility in Hobbesian terms remains our best bet.

Abdel-Nour, Farid. 2003. 'National Responsibility.' *Political Theory* 31 (5): 693–719.

Abizadeh, Arash. 2012. 'The Representation of Hobbesian Sovereignty.' In *Hobbes Today: Insights for the 21st Century,* ed. S. A. Lloyd. Cambridge: Cambridge University Press, 113–52.

———. 2017. 'Hobbes's Conventionalist Theology, the Trinity, and God as an Artificial Person by Fiction.' *The Historical Journal* 60 (4): 915–40.

Agreement on the Establishment of the Republic of Yemen. 1991 [1990]. Trans. Nassib G. Ziadé. 22 April. Reproduced in *International Legal Materials* 30 (3): 820–23.

Akçam, Taner. 2006. *A Shameful Act: The Armenian Genocide and the Question of Turkish Responsibility.* New York: Metropolitan Books.

Alnasrawi, Abbas. 2001. 'Iraq: Economic Sanctions and Consequences, 1990–2000.' *Third World Quarterly* 22 (2): 205–18.

Alschuler, Albert. 2009. 'Two Ways to Think about the Punishment of Corporations.' Northwestern University School of Law, *Faculty Working Papers* 192.

Aristotle. 1992. *The Politics,* trans. T. A. Sinclair. London: Penguin.

Barry, Christian, and Lydia Tomitova. 2007. 'Fairness in Sovereign Debt.' *Ethics & International Affairs* 21 (s1): 41–79.

Bartelson, Jens. 1998. 'Second Natures: Is the State Identical with Itself?' *European Journal of International Relations* 4 (3): 295–326.

Bayern, Shawn. 2016. 'The Implications of Modern Business-Entity Law for the Regulation of Autonomous Systems.' *European Journal of Risk Regulation* 7 (2): 297–309.

Baumgold, Deborah. 1988. *Hobbes's Political Theory.* Cambridge: Cambridge University Press.

BBC (British Broadcasting Corporation). 2017a. 'African Union Backs Mass Withdrawal from ICC.' *BBC News,* 1 February.

BBC (British Broadcasting Corporation). 2017b. 'New Zealand River First in the World to be Given Legal Human Status.' *BBC News,* 15 March.

Beard, Jack M. 2015. 'Autonomous Weapons and Human Responsibilities.' *Georgetown Journal of International Law* 45 (3): 617–81.

Beckles, Hilary M. 2013. *Britain's Black Debt: Reparations for Caribbean Slavery and Native Genocide.* Kingston: University of West Indies Press.

Bell, Duncan. 2003. 'Mythscapes: Memory, Mythology, and National Identity.' *British Journal of Sociology* 54 (1): 63–81.

Bewley-Taylor, David R. 2012. *International Drug Control: Consensus Fractured.* Cambridge: Cambridge University Press.

Blum, Daniel S. 1997. 'The Apportionment of Public Debt and Assets During State Secession.' *Case Western Reserve Journal of International Law* 29 (2): 263–98.

Blum, Yehuda Z. 1992. 'Russia Takes Over the Soviet Union's Seat at the United Nations.' *European Journal of International Law* 3 (2): 354–61.

Bonafè, Beatrice I. 2009. *The Relationship between State and Individual Responsibility for International Crimes.* Leiden: Martinus Nijhoff.

Bostrom, Nick, and Eliezer Yudkowsky. 2014. 'The Ethics of Artificial Intelligence.' In *The Cambridge Handbook of Artificial Intelligence,* eds. Keith Frankish and William M. Ramsay. Cambridge: Cambridge University Press.

Boucher, David. 2001. 'Resurrecting Pufendorf and Capturing the Westphalian Moment.' *Review of International Studies* 27 (4): 557–77.

Bratman, Michael E. 1999. *Faces of Intention: Selected Essays on Intention and Agency.* Cambridge: Cambridge University Press.

Brito Vieira, Mónica. 2009. *The Elements of Representation in Hobbes: Aesthetics, Theatre, Law, and Theology in the Construction of Hobbes's Theory of the State.* Leiden: Brill.

Brito Vieira, Mónica, and David Runciman. 2008. *Representation.* Cambridge: Polity.

Brown, Chris. 2004. 'Do Great Powers Have Great Responsibilities?: Great Powers and Moral Agency.' *Global Society* 18 (1): 5–19.

Brown, Philip M. 1926. 'Ottoman Public Debt Arbitration.' *American Journal of International Law* 20 (1): 135–39.

Brownlie, Ian. 1983. *System of the Law of Nations: State Responsibility (Part I).* Oxford: Oxford University Press.

Bryson, Joanna J., Mihailis E. Diamantis, and Thomas D. Grant. 2017. 'Of, For, and By the People: The Legal Lacuna of Synthetic Persons.' *Artificial Intelligence and Law* 25 (3): 273–91.

Bühler, Konrad G. 2001. *State Succession and Membership in International Organizations: Legal Theories versus Political Pragmatism.* The Hague: Kluwer.

Bush, Richard C. 2011. 'The Significance of the Republic of China for Cross-Strait Relations.' Brookings Institution, 20 May.

Butt, Daniel. 2006. 'Nations, Overlapping Generations, and Historic Injustice.' *American Philosophical Quarterly* 43 (4): 357–67.

———. 2007. 'On Benefiting from Injustice.' *Canadian Journal of Philosophy* 37 (1): 129–52.

Carr, E. H. 1946. *The Twenty Years' Crisis 1919–1939: An Introduction to the Study of International Relations.* London: Macmillan.

Cassese, Antonio. 2005. *International Law,* 2nd edn. Oxford: Oxford University Press.

———. 2007. 'The *Nicaragua* and *Tadić* Tests Revisited in Light of the ICJ Judgment on Genocide in Bosnia.' *European Journal of International Law* 18 (4): 649–68.

Castelvecchi, Davide. 2016. 'Can We Open the Black Box of AI?' *Nature* 538: 20–23.

Chen, Angeline G. 1998. 'Taiwan's International Personality: Crossing the River by Feeling the Stones.' *Loyola of Los Angeles International and Comparative Law Review* 20 (2): 223–55.

Cheng, Tai-Heng. 2011. 'Why New States Accept Old Obligations.' *University of Illinois Law Review* 2011 (1): 1–51.

Ciepley, David. 2013. 'Beyond Public and Private: Toward a Political Theory of the Corporation.' *American Political Science Review* 107 (1): 139–58.

Collins, Stephanie. 2016. 'Distributing States' Duties.' *The Journal of Political Philosophy* 24 (3): 344–66.

Collins, Stephanie, and Holly Lawford-Smith. 2016. 'The Transfer of Duties: From Individuals to States and Back Again.' In *The Epistemic Life of Groups: Essays in the Epistemology of Collectives*, eds. Michael S. Brady and Miranda Fricker. Oxford: Oxford University Press, 150–72.

Condorelli, Luigi, and Claus Kress. 2010. 'The Rules of Attribution: General Considerations.' In *The Law of International Responsibility*, eds. James Crawford, Alain Pellett, Simon Olleson, and Kate Parlett. Oxford: Oxford University Press, 221–36.

Cooper, David E. 1968. 'Collective Responsibility.' *Philosophy* 43 (165): 258–68.

Copp, David. 1980. 'Hobbes on Artificial Persons and Collective Actions.' *The Philosophical Review* 89 (4): 579–606.

Craven, Matthew C. R. 1998. 'The Problem of State Succession and the Identity of States under International Law.' *European Journal of International Law* 9 (1): 142–62.

———. 2002. 'Continuity of the Hawaiian Kingdom.' Legal Brief for the acting Council of Regency, 12 July.

Crawford, James. 1977. 'The Criteria for Statehood in International Law.' *British Yearbook of International Law* 48 (1): 93–182.

———. 2007. *The Creation of States in International Law*, 2nd edn. New York: Oxford University Press.

———. 2013a. *State Responsibility: The General Part*. New York: Cambridge University Press.

Crawford, James, and Jeremy Watkins. 2010. 'International Responsibility.' In *The Philosophy of International Law*, eds. Samantha Besson and John Tasioulas. Oxford: Oxford University Press, 283–98.

Crawford, Neta C. 2013b. *Accountability for Killing: Moral Responsibility for Collateral Damage in America's Post-9/11 Wars*. New York: Oxford University Press.

Crootof, Rebecca. 2016. 'War Torts: Accountability for Autonomous Weapons.' *University of Pennsylvania Law Review* 164 (6): 1347–1402.

Derathé, Robert. 1995. *Jean-Jacques Rousseau et la science politique de son temps*. Paris: Librairie Philosophique J. Vrin.

Dewey, John. 1926. 'The Historic Background of Corporate Legal Personality.' *Yale Law Journal* 35 (6): 655–73.

Douglass, Robin. 2014. 'The Body Politic "is a fictitious body": Hobbes on Imagination and Fiction.' *Hobbes Studies* 27 (2): 126–47.

———. 2018. 'Authorisation and Representation before *Leviathan*.' *Hobbes Studies* 31 (1): 30–47.

Dumberry, Patrick. 2012. 'Is Turkey the "Continuing" State of the Ottoman Empire Under International Law?' *Netherlands International Law Review* 59 (2): 235–62.

———. 2014. 'The Consequences of Turkey Being the "Continuing" State of the Ottoman Empire in Terms of International Responsibility for Internationally Wrongful Acts.' *International Criminal Law Review* 14 (2): 261–73.

Dunne, Tim. 2008. 'Good Citizen Europe.' *International Affairs* 84 (1): 13–28.

Dworkin, Ronald. 2013. 'A New Philosophy for International Law.' *Philosophy & Public Affairs* 41 (1): 2–30.

Dyson, Tim, and Valeria Cetorelli. 2017. 'Changing Views on Child Mortality and Economic Sanctions in Iraq: A History of Lies, Damned Lies and Statistics.' *BMJ Global Health* 2017 (2): 1–5.

Easton, David. 1981. 'The Political System Besieged by the State.' *Political Theory* 9 (3): 303–25.

Eckert, Amy E. 2009. 'National Defense and State Personality.' *Journal of International Political Theory* 5 (2): 161–76.

Edgerton, Henry W. 'Corporate Criminal Responsibility.' *Yale Law Journal* 36 (4): 827–44.

Erskine, Toni. 2001. 'Assigning Responsibilities to Institutional Moral Agents: The Case of States and "Quasi-States."' *Ethics & International Affairs* 15 (2): 67–85.

———. 2003. 'Introduction: Making Sense of "Responsibility" in International Relations—Key Questions and Concepts.' In *Can Institutions Have Responsibilities? Collective Moral Agency and International Relations*, ed. Toni Erskine. New York: Palgrave Macmillan, 1–16.

———. 2004. '"Blood on the UN's Hands"?: Assigning Duties and Apportioning Blame to an Intergovernmental Organisation.' *Global Society* 18 (1): 21–42.

———. 2008. 'How Should We Respond to Delinquent Institutions?' *Journal of International Political Theory* 4 (1): 1–8.

———. 2010. 'Kicking Bodies and Damning Souls: The Danger of Harming "Innocent" Individuals while Punishing "Delinquent" States.' *Ethics & International Affairs* 24 (3): 261–85.

———. 2014. 'Coalitions of the Willing and Responsibilities to Protect: Informal Associations, Enhanced Capacities, and Shared Moral Burdens.' *Ethics & International Affairs* 28 (1): 115–45.

Estlund, David. 2007. 'On Following Orders in an Unjust War.' *The Journal of Political Philosophy* 15 (2): 213–34.

———. 2011. 'Human Nature and the Limits (If Any) of Political Philosophy.' *Philosophy & Public Affairs* 39 (3): 207–37.

Ethics & International Affairs (editors). 2007. 'Excessive Indebtedness as an Ethical Problem.' *Ethics & International Affairs* 21 (s1): 1–7.

European Parliament. 2017. *Motion for a European Parliament Resolution, with Recommendations to the Commission on Civil Law Rules on Robotics.* Committee on Legal Affairs, 24 February.

Feinberg, Joel. 1968. 'Collective Responsibility.' *The Journal of Philosophy* 65 (21): 674–88.

Finkelstein, Claire. 2005. 'Responsibility for Unintended Consequences.' *Ohio State Journal of Criminal Law* 2 (2): 579–99.

Floridi, Luciano, and J. W. Sanders. 2004. 'On the Morality of Artificial Agents.' *Minds and Machines* 14 (3): 349–79.

Fleming, Sean. 2017a. 'Artificial Persons and Attributed Actions: How to Interpret Action-Sentences about States.' *European Journal of International Relations* 24 (4): 930–50.

———. 2017b. 'Moral Agents and Legal Persons: The Ethics and the Law of State Responsibility.' *International Theory* 9 (3): 466–89.

———. 2020. 'A Political Theory of Treaty Repudiation.' *The Journal of Political Philosophy* 28 (1): 3–26.

———. Forthcoming a. 'Leviathan on Trial: Should States Be Held Criminally Responsible? *International Theory*.

———. Forthcoming b. 'The Two Faces of Personhood: Hobbes, Corporate Agency and the Personality of the State.' *European Journal of Political Theory*. DOI: 10.1177/1474885117731941.

Forsyth, Murray. 1981. 'Thomas Hobbes and the Constituent Power of the People.' *Political Studies* 29 (2): 191–203.

French, Peter A. 1979. 'The Corporation as a Moral Person.' *American Philosophical Quarterly* 16 (3): 207–15.

———. 1984. *Collective and Corporate Responsibility*. New York: Columbia University Press.

———. 1995. *Corporate Ethics*. Fort Worth, TX: Harcourt Brace.

———. 1998. 'Types of Collectivities.' In *Individual and Collective Responsibility*, 2nd edn. ed. Peter French. Rochester, VT: Schenkman, 33–50.

Gallo, John N., and Daniel M. Greenfield. 2014. 'The Corporate Criminal Defendant's Illusory Right to Trial: A Proposal for Reform.' *Notre Dame Journal of Law, Ethics & Public Policy* 28 (2): 525–47.

Galston, William. 2010. 'Realism in Political Theory.' *European Journal of Political Theory* 9 (4): 385–411.

Garrett, Brian. 1998. *Personal Identity and Self-Consciousness*. New York: Routledge.

Garsten, Bryan. 2010. 'Religion and Representation in Hobbes.' In *Leviathan,* ed. Ian Shapiro. New Haven: Yale University Press, 519–46.

Gibney, Mark. 2015. 'The Downing of MH17: Russian Responsibility?' *Human Rights Law Review* 15 (1): 169–78.

Gilabert, Pablo, and Holly Lawford-Smith. 2012. 'Political Feasibility: A Conceptual Exploration.' *Political Studies* 60 (4): 809–25.

Gilbert, Margaret P. 1990. 'Walking Together: A Paradigmatic Social Phenomenon.' *Midwest Studies in Philosophy* 15 (1): 1–14.

———. 2000. *Sociality and Responsibility*. Lanham, MD: Rowman and Littlefield.

———. 2006. 'Who's to Blame?: Collective Moral Responsibility and Its Implications for Group Members.' *Midwest Studies in Philosophy* 30 (1): 94–114.

Gilpin, Robert G. 1984. 'The Richness of the Tradition of Political Realism.' *International Organization* 38 (2): 287–304.

Glannon, Walter. 1998. 'Moral Responsibility and Personal Identity.' *American Philosophical Quarterly* 35 (3): 231–49.

Gold, Matea, Mark Berman, and Renae Merle. 2016. '"Not My President": Thousands Protest Trump in Rallies Across the U.S.' *The Washington Post,* 11 November.

Goodin, Robert E. 1995. *Utilitarianism as a Public Philosophy*. Cambridge: Cambridge University Press.

Gordon, Kathryn, and Joachim Pohl. 2015. 'Investment Treaties Over Time: Treaty Practice and Interpretation in a Changing World.' *OECD Working Papers.*

Gould, Harry D. 2009. 'International Criminal Bodies.' *Review of International Studies* 35 (3): 701–21.

Green, Michael J. 2015. 'Authorization and Political Authority in Hobbes.' *Journal of the History of Philosophy* 53 (1): 25–47.

Hailbronner, Kay. 1991. 'Legal Aspects of the Unification of the Two German States.' *European Journal of International Law* 2 (1): 18–41.

Hall, Edward. 2015. 'Bernard Williams and the Basic Legitimation Demand: A Defence.' *Political Studies* 63 (2): 466–80.

———. 2017. 'How to do Realistic Political Theory (and Why You Might Want To).' *European Journal of Political Theory* 16 (3): 283–303.

Harbour, Frances. 2004. 'Moral Agency and Moral Responsibility in Humanitarian Intervention.' *Global Society* 18 (1): 61–75.

Harris, Sam. 2012. *Free Will*. New York: Free Press.

Held, Virginia. 1970. 'Can a Random Collection of Individuals Be Morally Responsible?' *The Journal of Philosophy* 67 (14): 471–81.

Hobbes, Thomas. 1839 [1655]. *De corpore* [*D*]. In *The English Works of Thomas Hobbes of Malmesbury Volume I*, ed. William Molesworth. London: John Bohn.

———. 1976 [1642–43]. *Thomas White's* De Mundo *Examined* [*AW*], trans. Harold W. Jones. London: Bradford University Press.

———. 1990 [1681]. *Behemoth, or The Long Parliament* [*B*]. Chicago: University of Chicago Press.

———. 1991 [1658]. *On Man* [*De homine, DH*], trans. Charles T. Wood, T.S.K. Scott-Craig, and Bernard Gert. In *Man and Citizen,* ed. Bernard Gert. Indianapolis: Hackett, 34–85.

———. 1994 [1640]. *Human Nature and De Corpore Politico* [*The Elements of Law, Natural and Politic, EL*]. Oxford: Oxford University Press.

———. 1998 [1642/1647]. *On the Citizen* [*De cive, DC*], trans. Richard Tuck and Michael Silverthorne. New York: Cambridge University Press.

———. 2011 [1682]. 'An Answer to a Book Published by Dr. Bramhall, late Bishop of Derry; called "The Catching of Leviathan [*AB*]."' In *Leviathan Parts I and II,* revised edition, eds. A. P. Martinich and Brian Battiste. Peterborough, ON: Broadview, 386–403.

———. 2012 [1651 and 1668]. *Leviathan: The English and Latin Texts* [*L* and *LL*], ed. Noel Malcolm. Oxford: Clarendon Press.

Holland, Ben. 2011. 'The Moral Person of the State: Emer de Vattel and the Foundations of International Legal Order.' *History of European Ideas* 37 (4): 438–45.

———. 2017. *The Moral Person of the State: Pufendorf, Sovereignty and Composite Polities.* Cambridge: Cambridge University Press.

Hood, Francis C. 1964. *The Divine Politics of Thomas Hobbes: An Interpretation of Leviathan.* Oxford: Clarendon Press.

Horton, John. 2012. 'Political Legitimacy, Justice and Consent.' *Critical Review of International Social and Political Philosophy* 15 (2): 129–48.

Husserl, Edmund. 1988 [1931]. *Cartesian Meditations,* trans. Dorion Cairns. Dordrecht: Kluwer.

Hutchison, Abigail. 2014. 'The Whanganui River as a Legal Person.' *Alternative Law Journal* 39 (3): 179–82.

International Court of Justice. 1980. 'United States Diplomatic and Consular Staff in Tehran (United States of America v. Iran).' Judgments ICJ 1.

International Law Commission (ILC). 2001. *Articles on Responsibility of States for Internationally Wrongful Acts.* New York: United Nations.

International Monetary Fund. 2016. 'Debt Relief Under the Heavily Indebted Poor Countries (HIPC) Initiative.' Washington, DC: IMF Communications Department.

International Narcotics Control Board. 2018. 'About the International Narcotics Control Board.' https://www.incb.org/incb/en/about.html (accessed 7 June 2018).

Jackson, Patrick T. 2004. 'Hegel's House, or "People are States Too."' *Review of International Studies* 30 (2): 281–87.

Jaspers, Karl. 1961. *The Question of German Guilt,* trans. E. B. Ashton. New York: Capricorn.

Jefferson, Thomas. 1999 [1789]. 'To James Madison, Paris, September 6, 1789.' In *Jefferson: Political Writings,* eds. Joyce Appleby and Terence Ball. Cambridge: Cambridge University Press, 593–98.

Jessop, Bob. 1990. *State Theory: Putting the Capitalist State in Its Place.* University Park, PA: Pennsylvania State University Press.

Jubb, Robert. 2014. 'Participation in and Responsibility for State Injustices.' *Social Theory and Practice* 40 (1): 51–72.

Kantorowicz, Ernst H. 1957. *The King's Two Bodies: A Study in Mediaeval Political Theology.* Princeton: Princeton University Press.

Keeley, James F. 2007. 'To the Pacific? Alexander Wendt as Explorer.' *Millennium: Journal of International Studies* 35 (2): 417–30.

Kelsen, Hans. 1970 [1934]. *Pure Theory of Law.* Berkeley: University of California Press.

King, Jeff. 2016. *The Doctrine of Odious Debt in International Law: A Restatement.* Cambridge: Cambridge University Press.

Koessler, Maximilian. 1949. 'The Person in Imagination or Persona Ficta of the Corporation.' *Louisiana Law Review* 9 (4): 435–49.

Kollewe, Julia, and Sean Farrell. 2014. 'UK Bonds that Financed First World War to Be Redeemed 100 Years Later.' *The Guardian,* 31 October.

Koremenos, Barbara. 2005. 'Contracting around International Uncertainty.' *American Political Science Review* 99 (4): 549–65.

Koutsoukis, Jason, and Mark Riley. 2000. 'Penington Slams PM over Drugs Report.' *The Age,* 24 February.

Kripke, Saul. 1980. *Naming and Necessity.* Cambridge: Harvard University Press.

Kunz, Josef L. 1955. 'Identity of States Under International Law.' *American Journal of International Law* 49 (1): 68–76.

Kutz, Christopher. 2000. *Complicity: Ethics and Law for a Collective Age.* Cambridge: Cambridge University Press.

Lang, Anthony F. Jr. 2007. 'Crime and Punishment: Holding States Accountable.' *Ethics & International Affairs* 21 (2): 239–57.

———. 2008. *Punishment, Justice and International Relations: Ethics and Order after the Cold War.* New York: Routledge.

———. 2011. 'Punishing Genocide: A Critical Reading of the International Court of Justice.' In *Accountability for Collective Wrongdoing,* eds. Tracy Isaacs and Richard Vernon. Cambridge: Cambridge University Press, 92–118.

Lessay, Franck. 2009. 'Hobbes's Covenant Theology and its Political Implications.' In *The Cambridge Companion to Hobbes's Leviathan,* ed. Patricia Springborg. Cambridge: Cambridge University Press, 243–70.

Levy, Jacob T. 2015. *Rationalism, Pluralism, and Freedom.* Oxford: Oxford University Press.

Lewis, H. D. 1948. 'Collective Responsibility.' *Philosophy* 23 (84): 3–18.

Li, Victor H. 1979. 'The Law of Non-Recognition: The Case of Taiwan.' *Northwestern Journal of International Law and Business* 1 (1): 134–62.

Lind, Jennifer. 2008. *Sorry States: Apologies in International Politics.* Ithaca, NY: Cornell University Press.

List, Christian, and Philip Pettit. 2011. *Group Agency: The Possibility, Design, and Status of Corporate Agents.* New York: Oxford University Press.

Lomas, Peter. 2005. 'Anthropomorphism, Personification and Ethics: A Reply to Alexander Wendt.' *Review of International Studies* 31 (2): 349–55.

———. 2014. *Unnatural States: The International System and the Power to Change.* New Brunswick, NJ: Transaction.

Lu, Catherine. 2004. 'Agents, Structures, and Evil in World Politics.' *International Relations* 18 (4): 498–509.

Maitland, F. W. 2003. *State, Trust and Corporation,* eds. David Runciman and Magnus Ryan. Cambridge: Cambridge University Press.

Malcolm, Noel. 2002. *Aspects of Hobbes.* Oxford: Oxford University Press.

———. 2012. 'General Introduction.' In *Leviathan,* ed. Noel Malcolm. Oxford: Oxford University Press, 1–196.

Malekian, Farhad. 1985. 'International Criminal Responsibility of States: A Study on the Evolution of State Responsibility with Particular Emphasis on the Concept of Crime and Criminal Responsibility.' Doctoral dissertation, University of Stockholm.

Mälksoo, Lauri. 2000. 'Professor Uluots, the Estonian Government in Exile and the Continuity of the Republic of Estonia in International Law.' *Nordic Journal of International Law* 69 (3): 289–316.

Marek, Krystyna. 1968. *Identity and Continuity of States in Public International Law.* Geneva: Droz.

Martinich, A. P. 2016. 'Authorization and Representation in Hobbes's *Leviathan.*' In *The Oxford Handbook of Hobbes,* eds. A. P. Martinich and Kinch Hoekstra. Oxford: Oxford University Press, 315–38.

Matthias, Andreas. 2004. 'The Responsibility Gap: Ascribing Responsibility for the Actions of Learning Automata.' *Ethics and Information Technology* 6 (3): 175–83.

Matsui, Yoshiro. 1993. 'The Transformation of the Law of State Responsibility.' *Thesaurus Acroasium* 20: 5–65.

Matwyshyn, Andrea M. 2010. 'Corporate Cyborgs and Technology Risks.' *Minnesota Journal of Law, Science & Technology* 11 (2): 573–98.

May, Larry. 2012. *After War Ends: A Philosophical Perspective.* New York: Cambridge University Press.

Mill, John S. 1870. 'Treaty Obligations.' *Fortnightly Review* 14 (December), 715–20.

Miller, David. 2007. *National Responsibility and Global Justice.* Oxford: Oxford University Press.

Miller, Seumas, and Pekka Mäkelä. 2005. 'The Collectivist Approach to Collective Moral Responsibility.' *Metaphilosophy* 36 (5): 634–51.

Misiunas, Romuald J. 1991. 'Sovereignty without Government: Baltic Diplomatic and Consular Representation 1940–1991.' In *Governments-in-Exile in Contemporary World Politics,* ed. Yossi Shain. New York: Routledge.

Momtaz, Djamchid. 2010. 'Attribution of Conduct to the State: State Organs and Entities Empowered to Exercise Elements of Governmental Authority.' In *The Law of International Responsibility,* eds. James Crawford, Alain Pellett, Simon Olleson, and Kate Parlett. Oxford: Oxford University Press, 237–46.

Müllerson, Rein. 1993. 'The Continuity and Succession of States, by Reference to the Former USSR and Yugoslavia.' *The International and Comparative Law Quarterly* 42 (3): 473–93.

Murphy, Liam. 2010. 'International Responsibility.' In *The Philosophy of International Law,* eds. Samantha Besson and John Tasioulas. Oxford: Oxford University Press, 299–315.

Ndikumana, Leonce, and James K. Boyce. 1998. 'Congo's Odious Debt: External Borrowing and Capital Flight in Zaire.' *Development and Change* 29 (2): 195–217.

New York Times. 1991. 'End of the Soviet Union; Soviet U.N. Seat Taken by Russia.' 25 December.

Nobles, Melissa. 2008. *The Politics of Official Apologies.* Cambridge: Cambridge University Press.

Nollkaemper, André. 2003. 'Concurrence between Individual Responsibility and State Responsibility in International Law.' *International and Comparative Law Quarterly* 52 (3): 615–40.

Nozick, Robert. 1969. 'Coercion.' In *Philosophy, Science, and Method: Essays in Honor of Ernest Nagel,* eds. Sidney Morgenbesser, Patrick Suppes, and Morton White. New York: St. Martin's Press, 440–72.

Nuremberg International Military Tribunal. 1947 [1946]. 'Judgment.' Reproduced in the *American Journal of International Law* 41 (1): 172–333.

O'Neill, Onora. 1986. 'Who Can Endeavor Peace?' *Canadian Journal of Philosophy* 21 (supplement): 41–73.

Öktem, Emre. 2011. 'Turkey: Successor or Continuing State of the Ottoman Empire?' *Leiden Journal of International Law* 24 (3): 561–83.

Olivet, Cecilia. 2017. 'Why Did Ecuador Terminate All Its Bilateral Investment Treaties?' Transnational Institute, 25 May. https://www.tni.org/en/article/why-did-ecuador-terminate-all -its-bilateral-investment-treaties (accessed 7 June 2018).

Olleson, Simon. Forthcoming. *State Responsibility before International and Domestic Courts: The Impact and Influence of the ILC Articles.* Oxford: Oxford University Press.

Overhoff, Jürgen. 2000. *Hobbes's Theory of the Will: Ideological Reasons and Historical Circumstances.* New York: Rowman and Littlefield.

Paine, Thomas. 2012 [1791]. *Rights of Man.* Cambridge: Cambridge University Press.

Parfit, Derek. 1984. *Reasons and Persons.* Oxford: Clarendon Press.

———. 2016. 'Divided Minds and the Nature of Persons.' In *Science Fiction and Philosophy: From Time Travel to Superintelligence,* ed. Susan Schneider. Chichester: Wiley-Blackwell, 91–98.

Parrish, John M. 2009. 'Collective Responsibility and the State.' *International Theory* 1 (1): 119–54.

Pasternak, Avia. 2010. 'Sharing the Costs of Political Injustices.' *Politics, Philosophy & Economics* 10 (2): 188–210.

———. 2011. 'The Distributive Effect of Collective Punishment.' In *Accountability for Collective Wrongdoing,* eds. Tracy Isaacs and Richard Vernon. Cambridge: Cambridge University Press, 210–30.

———. 2013. 'Limiting States' Corporate Responsibility.' *The Journal of Political Philosophy* 21 (4): 361–81.

———. Forthcoming. 'Corporate Identity and Liability for Historical Wrongs.' In *The Collective Agency of States.*

Permanent Court of International Justice. 1923. *German Settlers in Poland.* Leyden: A. J. Sijthoff.

Pettit, Philip. 2008. *Made with Words: Hobbes on Language, Mind, and Politics.* Princeton: Princeton University Press.

———. 2009. 'Varieties of Public Representation.' In *Political Representation,* eds. Ian Shapiro et al. Cambridge: Cambridge University Press, 61–89.

———. 2012. *On the People's Terms: A Republican Theory and Model of Democracy.* Cambridge: Cambridge University Press.

———. 2014. 'Group Agents Are Not Expressive, Pragmatic or Theoretical Fictions.' *Erkenntnis* 79 (s9): 1641–62.

Pettit, Philip, and David Schweikard. 2006. 'Joint Actions and Group Agents.' *Philosophy of the Social Sciences* 36 (1): 18–39.

Pitkin, Hanna F. 1967. *The Concept of Representation.* Los Angeles: University of California Press.

Poljanšek, Tom. 2015. 'Choosing Appropriate Paradigmatic Examples for Understanding Collective Agency.' In *Collective Agency and Cooperation in Natural and Artificial Systems: Explanation, Implementation and Simulation,* ed. Catrin Misselhorn. Cham, Switzerland: Springer, 185–203.

Poulton, Hugh. 1997. *Top Hat, Grey Wolf, and Crescent: Turkish Nationalism and the Turkish Republic.* Washington Square, NY: New York University Press.

Pufendorf, Samuel. 1934 [1672]. *De Jure Naturae et Gentium Libri Octo,* trans. W. A. Oldfather. Oxford: Clarendon Press.

Ralph, Jason. 2007. *Defending the Society of States: Why America Opposes the International Criminal Court and Its Vision of World Society.* Oxford: Oxford University Press.

Rawls, John. 1971. *A Theory of Justice.* Cambridge, MA: Belknap.

Reid, Natalie L. 2005. 'Bridging the Conceptual Chasm: Superior Responsibility as the Missing Link between State and Individual Responsibility under International Law.' *Leiden Journal of International Law* 18 (4): 795–828.

Rojek, Wojciech. 2004. 'The Government of the Republic of Poland in Exile, 1945–92.' In *The Poles in Britain 1940–2000: From Betrayal to Assimilation,* ed. Peter D. Stachura. London: Frank Cass.

Rönnegard, David. 2015. *The Fallacy of Corporate Moral Agency.* Dordrecht: Springer.

Rossi, Enzo. 2012. 'Justice, Legitimacy and (Normative) Authority for Political Realists.' *Critical Review of International Social and Political Philosophy* 15 (2): 149–64.

Rossi, Enzo, and Matt Sleat. 2014. 'Realism in Normative Political Theory.' *Philosophy Compass* 9 (10): 689–701.

Rousseau, Jean-Jacques. 1987 [1754]. 'Discourse on the Origin of Inequality.' In *The Basic Political Writings,* trans. Donald A. Cress. Indianapolis: Hackett.

———. 2019 [1762]. *The Social Contract and Other Later Political Writings,* ed. Victor Gourevitch. Cambridge: Cambridge University Press.

Runciman, David. 1997. *Pluralism and the Personality of the State.* Cambridge: Cambridge University Press.

———. 2000a. 'Is the State a Corporation?' *Government and Opposition* 35 (1): 90–104.

———. 2000b. 'What Kind of Person is Hobbes's State? A Reply to Skinner.' *The Journal of Political Philosophy* 8 (2): 268–78.

———. 2003. 'The Concept of the State: The Sovereignty of a Fiction.' In *States and Citizens: History, Theory, Prospects,* eds. Quentin Skinner and Bo Stråth. Cambridge: Cambridge University Press, 28–38.

———. 2007. 'The Paradox of Political Representation.' *The Journal of Political Philosophy* 15 (1): 93–114.

———. 2009. 'Hobbes's Theory of Representation: Anti-Democratic or Proto-Democratic?' In *Political Representation*, eds. Ian Shapiro et al. Cambridge: Cambridge University Press, 15–34.

———. 2016. 'The Sovereign.' In *The Oxford Handbook of Hobbes*, eds. A. P. Martinich and Kinch Hoekstra. Oxford: Oxford University Press, 359–76.

Sagar, Paul. 2016. 'From Scepticism to Liberalism? Bernard Williams, the Foundations of Liberalism and Political Realism.' *Political Studies* 64 (2): 368–84.

———. 2017. 'Legitimacy and Domination.' In *Politics Recovered: Essays in Realist Political Theory*, ed. Matt Sleat. New York: Columbia University Press, 114–39.

———. 2018. 'What is the Leviathan?' *Hobbes Studies* 31 (1): 75–92.

Sager, Samuel. 1978. 'Israel's Provisional State Council and Government.' *Middle Eastern Studies* 14 (1): 91–101.

Schlemmer, Engela C. 2016. 'An Overview of South Africa's Bilateral Investment Treaties and Investment Policy.' *ICSIC Review* 31 (1): 167–93.

Schmidle, Nicholas. 2009. 'Wanted: A New Home for My Country.' *New York Times Magazine*, 8 May.

Schwenkenbecher, Anne. 2010. 'How to Punish Collective Agents: Non-Compliance with Duties by States (Response to Toni Erskine).' *Ethics & International Affairs*, Online Exclusive, 28 September. https://www.ethicsandinternationalaffairs.org/2010/online-exclusive-how-to-punish-collective-agents-non-compliance-with-moral-duties-by-states-response-to-toni-erskine/ (accessed 9 August 2017).

Schwitzgebel, Eric. 2015. 'If Materialism is True, the United States is Probably Conscious.' *Philosophical Studies* 172 (7): 1697–1721.

Sharman, Jon. 2017. 'Donald Trump Declares Flooding Disaster Day After US Withdraws from Paris Climate Change Agreement.' *The Independent*, 7 June.

Shoemaker, David. 2011. 'Attributability, Answerability, and Accountability: Toward a Wider Theory of Moral Responsibility.' *Ethics* 121 (3): 602–32.

———. 2012. 'Responsibility without Identity.' *Harvard Review of Philosophy* 18 (1): 109–32.

Shoemaker, Sidney. 1970. 'Persons and their Pasts.' *American Philosophical Quarterly* 7 (4): 269–85.

Simendić, Marko. 2012. 'Thomas Hobbes's Person as *Persona* and "Intelligent Substance."' *Intellectual History Review* 22 (2): 147–62.

Simmons, A. John. 2009. 'Political Obligation and Consent.' In *The Ethics of Consent: Theory and Practice*, eds. Franklin Miller and Alan Wertheimer. Oxford: Oxford University Press, 305–28.

Skinner, Quentin. 1978. *The Foundations of Modern Political Thought Volume Two: The Age of Reformation*. Cambridge: Cambridge University Press.

———. 1999. 'Hobbes and the Purely Artificial Person of the State.' *The Journal of Political Philosophy* 7 (1): 1–29.

———. 2002. *Visions of Politics Volume 2: Renaissance Virtues*. Cambridge: Cambridge University Press.

———. 2005. 'Hobbes on Representation.' *European Journal of Philosophy* 13 (2): 155–84.

―――. 2007. 'Hobbes on Persons, Authors and Representatives.' In *The Cambridge Companion to Hobbes's Leviathan,* ed. Patricia Springborg. Cambridge: Cambridge University Press, 157–80.

―――. 2009. 'A Genealogy of the Modern State.' *Proceedings of the British Academy* 162: 325–70.

―――. 2015. 'Hobbes and the Person of the State.' Agnes Cuming Lecture, School of Philosophy, University College Dublin, 18 November.

Sleat, Matt. 2014. 'Legitimacy in Realist Thought: Between Realism and *Realpolitik.' Political Theory* 42 (3): 314–37.

Solum, Lawrence B. 1992. 'Legal Personhood for Artificial Intelligences.' *North Carolina Law Review* 70 (4): 1231–87.

Spinedi, Marina. 1989. 'International Crimes of State: The Legislative History.' In *International Crimes of State: A Critical Analysis of the ILC's Draft Article 19 on State Responsibility,* eds. Joseph H. H. Weiler, Antonio Cassese, and Marina Spinedi. Berlin: Walter de Gruyter, 7–138.

Stilz, Anna. 2011. 'Collective Responsibility and the State.' *The Journal of Political Philosophy* 19 (2): 190–208.

Šturma, Pavel. 2017. 'First Report on Succession of States in Respect of State Responsibility.' International Law Commission, 31 May. UN Doc. A/CN.4/708.

Sullins, John P. 2011. 'When Is a Robot a Moral Agent?' In *Machine Ethics,* eds. Michael Anderson and Susan L. Anderson. Cambridge: Cambridge University Press.

Tanguay-Renaud, François. 2013. 'Criminalizing the State.' *Criminal Law and Philosophy* 7 (2): 255–84.

Tanner, Michael D. 2012. '$189,000.' *New York Post,* 29 January. http://nypost.com/2012/01/29 /189000/ (accessed 11 March 2017).

Tennent, James. 2015. 'Who Will Take Over from Sultan Qaboos, Arab World's Longest-Serving Ruler?' *International Business Times,* 28 November.

Thomas, William R. 2018. 'How and Why Corporations Became (and Remain) Persons Under the Criminal Law.' *Florida State University Law Review* 45 (2): 479–538.

Thompson, Janna. 2006. 'Collective Responsibility for Historic Injustices.' *Midwest Studies in Philosophy* 30 (1): 154–67.

―――. 2009. *Intergenerational Justice: Rights and Responsibilities in an Intergenerational Polity.* New York: Routledge.

Tollefsen, Deborah P. 2002. 'Organizations as True Believers.' *Journal of Social Philosophy* 33 (3): 395–410.

―――. 2015. *Groups as Agents.* Malden, MA: Polity.

Treaty on the Establishment of German Unity. 1991 [1990]. 31 August 1990. Reproduced in *International Legal Materials* 30 (2): 457–503.

Treaty on the Final Settlement with Respect to Germany. 1991 [1990]. 1 October 1990. Treaty Series No. 88. London: Her Majesty's Stationery Office.

Tuck, Richard. 2016. *The Sleeping Sovereign: The Invention of Modern Democracy.* Cambridge: Cambridge University Press.

Tukiainen, Arto. 1994. 'The Commonwealth as a Person in Hobbes's *Leviathan.' Hobbes Studies* 7 (1): 45–55.

Tuomela, Raimo. 2005. 'We-Intentions Revisited.' *Philosophical Studies* 125 (3): 327–69.

———. 2013. *Social Ontology: Collective Intentionality and Group Agents*. New York: Oxford University Press.

United Nations (UN). 1925. 'Affaire de la Dette publique ottoman [Ottoman Debt Arbitration].' 18 April. *Reports of International Arbitral Awards Volume I*, 529–614.

———. 1947. *First Committee. Admission of New Members. Letter from the Chairman of the Sixth Committee Addressed to the Chairman of the First Committee, Dated 8 October 1947*. UN Doc. A/C.1/212.

———. 1969. *Vienna Convention on the Law of Treaties. Treaty Series* No. 18232.

———. 1978. 'Vienna Convention on Succession of States in Respect of Treaties.' *Treaty Series* Vol. 1946, 3.

———. 1983. 'Vienna Convention on Succession of States in Respect of State Property, Archives and Debts.' *Official Records of the United Nations Conference on Succession of States in Respect of State Property, Archives and Debts* Vol. II.

———. 1991a. *Agreement Establishing the Commonwealth of Independent States*. 8 December. UN Doc. A/46/771.

———. 1991b. *Alma Ata Declaration*. 21 December. UN Doc. A/47/60.

———. 2005. General Assembly Resolution, 2005 World Summit Outcome. UN Doc. A/RES/60/1.

———. 2006. *Estate of Jean-Baptiste Caire (France) v. United Mexican States*. Reports of International Arbitral Awards, Vol. 5.

United Nations Compensation Commission. 2018. 'Summary of Awards.' https://www.uncc.ch /summary-awards (accessed 25 May 2018).

United Nations Conference on Trade and Development (UNCTAD). 2000. 'Bilateral Investment Treaties 1959–99.' UNCTAD/ITE/IIA/2. New York and Geneva: United Nations.

———. 2017. 'World Investment Report 2017: Investment and the Digital Economy.' Geneva: United Nations.

United Nations Security Council. 1999. *Report of the Second Panel Established by the President of the Security Council on 30 January 1999 (S/1999/100), Concerning the Current Humanitarian Situation in Iraq*. UN Doc. S/1999/356.

United Nations Treaty Collection. 2018. https://treaties.un.org/ (accessed 7 June 2018).

Valentini, Laura. 2011. *Justice in a Globalized World: A Normative Framework*. New York: Oxford University Press.

Van Elsuwege, Peter. 2003. 'State Continuity and its Consequences: The Case of the Baltic States.' *Leiden Journal of International Law* 16 (2): 377–88.

Van Houtte, Hans, Hans Das, and Bart Delmartino. 2006. 'The United Nations Compensation Commission.' In *The Oxford Handbook of Reparations,* ed. Pablo de Greiff. New York: Oxford University Press, 321–90.

Van Schaack, Beth, and Ron Slye. 2007. 'A Concise History of International Criminal Law.' Santa Clara University School of Law, *Legal Studies Research Papers Series* No. 07–42.

Vernon, Richard. 2011. 'Punishing Collectives: States or Nations?' In *Accountability for Collective Wrongdoing,* eds. Tracy Isaacs and Richard Vernon. Cambridge: Cambridge University Press, 287–306.

Vidmar, Jure. 2013. 'States, Governments, and Collective Recognition.' In *Chinese (Taiwan) Yearbook of International Law and Affairs* Vol. 31, ed. Ying-jeou Ma. Leiden: Brill Nijhoff, 136–59.

Vincent, Andrew. 1989. 'Can Groups Be Persons?' *Review of Metaphysics* 42 (4): 687–715.

von der Dunk, Frans G., and Peter H. Kooijmans. 1991. 'The Unification of Germany and International Law.' *Michigan Journal of International Law* 12 (3): 510–57.

Waldron, Jeremy. 2006. 'FW Guest Memorial Lecture 2005: The Half-Life of Treaties: Waitangi Rebus Sic Stantibus.' *Otago Law Review* 11 (2): 161–81.

———. 2016. *Political Political Theory.* Cambridge, MA: Harvard University Press.

Walzer, Michael. 1977. *Just and Unjust Wars: A Moral Argument with Historical Illustrations.* New York: Basic Books.

Weiss, Paul. 1939. 'The Locus of Responsibility.' *Ethics* 49 (3): 349–55.

Welch, John R. 1989. 'Corporate Agency and Reduction.' *The Philosophical Quarterly* 39 (157): 409–24.

Wendt, Alexander. 1994. 'Collective Identity Formation and the International State.' *American Political Science Review* 88 (2): 384–96.

———. 1999. *Social Theory of International Politics.* New York: Cambridge University Press.

———. 2004. 'The State as Person in International Theory.' *Review of International Studies* 30 (2): 289–316.

———. 2005. 'How Not to Argue against State Personhood: A Reply to Lomas.' *Review of International Studies* 31 (2): 357–60.

———. 2015. *Quantum Mind and Social Science: Unifying Physical and Social Ontology.* Cambridge: Cambridge University Press.

Wiggins, David. 1976. 'Locke, Butler, and the Stream of Consciousness: And Men as a Natural Kind.' In *The Identities of Persons,* ed. Amélie O. Rorty. Berkeley: University of California Press, 139–73.

Wight, Colin. 1999. 'They Shoot Dead Horses Don't They?: Locating Agency in the Agent-Structure Problematique.' *European Journal of International Relations* 5 (1): 109–42.

———. 2004. 'State Agency: Social Action without Human Activity?' *Review of International Studies* 30 (2): 269–80.

———. 2006. *Agents, Structures and International Relations: Politics as Ontology.* New York: Cambridge University Press.

Williams, Bernard. 2002. *Truth and Truthfulness: An Essay in Genealogy.* Princeton: Princeton University Press.

———. 2005. *In the Beginning Was the Deed: Realism and Moralism in Political Argument,* ed. Geoffrey Hawthorn. Princeton: Princeton University Press.

Wolin, Sheldon S. 2016 [1960]. *Politics and Vision: Continuity and Innovation in Western Political Thought.* Princeton: Princeton University Press.

Yeltsin, Boris. 1991. *Letter to the Secretary-General of the United Nations from the President of the Russian Federation.* 24 December.

Ziemele, Ineta. 2001. 'Is the Distinction between State Continuity and State Succession Reality or Fiction?: The Russian Federation, the Federal Republic of Yugoslavia and Germany.' *Baltic Yearbook of International Law* 1 (1): 191–222.

INDEX

agents: corporate, xi, 1–3, 9, 11–14, 16–34, 39, 44–47, 61–65, 67, 70, 76n2, 102, 108, 114, 172n, 176, 183–84; individual, 79–85, 100–2, 181–86; robotic, 7–8, 65, 181–86; of the state, 33–34, 72, 78, 92–94, 99, 105–6, 171 (*see also* principal-agent relationships).

analogy: in Hobbes' political thought, 2, 10, 47–48, 54–55, 58, 61, 67; between states and corporations, 4–5, 184; between states and individuals, 1–2, 17–18, 26–28, 31–32, 44–45, 110, 114, 140–42, 176–78; between states and objects, 110, 115–17; between state responsibility and vicarious liability, 1–2, 16, 33, 45–46, 65–66, 100–1, 152, 176.

Aristotle, 8, 25, 115–16.

artificial intelligence, 7–8, 181–86.

authorization: and authenticity, 80–82, 84–85; and democracy, 89–90; and the distribution of liability, 30–31, 147–48, 150, 163–66, 167n, 173; by fiction, 153–55, 158–59; in Hobbes (*see* Hobbes, Thomas: on authorization); in international law, 35–36; and state identity, 119, 120, 124; and *ultra vires* actions, 92–94.

Carr, E. H., 13–14, 104–5, 142.

China. *See* identity: of China.

Congo. *See* debt: of Zaire.

constructivism: in International Relations, 111, 142–43. *See also* Wendt, Alexander.

Czechoslovakia. *See* debt: of Czechoslovakia; identity: of Czechoslovakia.

debt: 29, 100, 106–7, 112–13, 148, 154–55, 163–64, 166, 174, 177; of Czechoslovakia,

138–39; across generations, 148, 150, 156–60, 169–73; of Greece, xi, 3–4, 6, 8, 42, 146; and inheritance, 141–42; of the Ottoman Empire, 127, 139; of the Soviet Union, 123, 141, 171; of Zaire, 37–38, 43, 106–7, 109, 171, 175.

Erskine, Toni, xii, 17–20, 24–26, 29.

Estonia. *See* identity: of the Baltic states.

Ethiopia. *See* identity: of Ethiopia.

French, Peter, 17–18.

Germany, 5, 43, 97, 102, 139, 146–47, 149. *See also* identity: of Germany.

Greece. *See* debt: of Greece.

Hobbes, Thomas: use of analogies, 2, 10, 47–48, 54–55, 58, 61, 67; on authorization, 2–3, 9, 50, 57–61, 65–67, 69–70, 77–78; on corporations, 10, 63n, 68, 72, 94–95; on representation, 48–49, 52–54, 60, 66–67, 69–70, 75–77; and representation of God, 51–52, 59n, 67, 121; on sovereignty, 59–60, 64–65, 68–69, 75–79, 85, 86n7, 90–92, 117, 119, 169.

identity: and authorization, 119, 120, 124; of the Baltic states, 111, 123, 128–29, 131; of China, 39–40, 136–37; corporate versus personal, 26–28, 32, 110, 114, 117, 142; corporate versus physical, 114–17, 142; corporate versus social, 111–12; of Czechoslovakia, 131, 134, 138–39; of Ethiopia, 130–31; of Germany, 115, 135–36; in international law, 38–41, 114–15, 128, 130n, 140n;

A NOTE ON THE TYPE

This book has been composed in Arno, an Old-style serif typeface in the classic Venetian tradition, designed by Robert Slimbach at Adobe.